"Peter Weddle is a man filled with ingenious ideas."
The Washington Post

*"Restaurant patrons looking for quality dining
have Zagat to guide their cuisine needs.
For the recruitment industry, the name is Weddle
... Peter Weddle that is."*
American Staffing Association

What People are Saying
about WEDDLE's Newsletters, Guides & Directories

"refreshingly unassuming and hype-free text…. It's all excellent stuff …."
Porter Anderson
CNN

" …loads you up with pages and pages of ideas, Internet Recruiting ideas … good ideas.
Mark Berger
The Fordyce Letter

"I think your service is great—the acknowledged leader in Internet guides for the industry!"
Tim Scheele, Chief Marketing Officer
NETSHARE. Inc.

"I picked up *WEDDLE's Guide to Employment Web-Sites* and want to recommend it to you … he lists a lot of relevant information that I figure I can use to make determinations regarding which sites to use."
Scott Firth, President
DCI Technical Services

"I have a copy of *WEDDLE's Guide to Employment Web-Sites*, which I find very useful and time saving."
Anthony Clayton-Spray
CyberCable, France

"The *WEDDLE's 2001 Job Seeker's Guide to Employment Web Sites* supplies clear, completely current information about each site's services, features and fees—helping users instantly determine which site best meets their needs. If you are looking for an objective guide to employment websites, ExecuNet recommends *WEDDLE's Guide.*
ExecuNet, The Center for Executive Careers

" … your newsletter is tremendously helpful to our recruiters. Keep up the fantastic work."
Shana Wiley
Harrahs

"Thank you for including us in WEDDLE's. We think it has made a great difference in our online traffic. For example, our number of unique visitors has doubled over the past year."
Trowby Brockman, Partner
trainingjob.com

"Peter, half an hour ago, I read another one of your columns on cnnfn.com. I truly enjoy your columns. You cover the employment scene like no other. Hats off.
Rick Myers
President, Talent Zoo

"Just read an article by Mr. Weddle and was impressed with his insight into issues in recruiting in today's new world. I have been recruiting in corporate environments for about 20 years and haven't seen these issues addressed so effectively."
Randall D. Gregory
RDG Consulting

"It's been a couple of decades since I have had a need for a resume, and found your book insightful and most helpful. Thank you for taking the time to write it."

J.H., Canada

"I've just attended [Peter Weddle's] session and it was really great. Peter is giving new information I've never heard before and has some really helpful insights. ... Please pass my compliments on to Peter for sharing his expertise. Thanks!"

Marketing Manager
DBM

"HI, I just went to your Web-site and was blown away by all the neat material. It is presented so well and is very compelling—I could hardly resist ordering ... !!!"

D.F., JobWhiz

"I found you book in the public library. Recently, I purchased my own copy from Amazon.com. It is a terrific book for breaking down the complexity of preparing resumes for the computer age. Thank you for writing this book."

R.M.

"Since the early beginnings of the Web, your site has been an inspiration to us and a 'real' source of practical advice in our business."

S. Y., JobsHawaii.com

"The program is excellent, very well thought out and the manual is extremely well done. Peter is just outstanding. I found it very useful."

President
Frank Palma Associates

"Good information for those who want to be the best of the best."

President
The RADS Group

"The information was extremely useful and can be taken back and applied to current work procedures."

Recruiting Specialist
Administaff

"Hi Peter- Just wanted you to know that ALL the participants rated today's program and presenter as excellent! You were informative, funny, and you put things into context so they could be easily understood. It was a terrific program!"

WEBS Career & Educational Counseling Service
Westchester County (NY) Library System

"Thank you for a very concise, logical and informative presentation today! I greatly appreciated your professionalism—there are enough 'screamers' out there!"

Executive Vice President
Lamay Associates

"I have perused several of your articles via CNN.com, in addition to material mailed to me by friends and colleagues, and I want to commend you on tapping into the industry and providing such a wealth of information to your readers."

T. W. thingamajob.com

WEDDLE's

Postcards
From Space

Being the Best
in Online Recruitment
and HR Management

Internet recruiting
and
Web-based Human Resource Management
are almost a decade old.
We now know what works ... and what doesn't.
More importantly, we also know what works best.
And that's the subject of this book.
It will tell you how to use the Internet
to gain a strategic advantage
in acquiring and managing top talent.

Special discounts on bulk quantities of WEDDLE's books are available
to corporations, professional associations and other organizations.
For details, please contact WEDDLE's at 203.964.1888 or visit our
Web-site at http://www.weddles.com.

FOR
Recruiters and Human Resource Professionals everywhere

Men and Women
who do a very tough job
and
deserve the best information available

WEDDLE's
2052 Shippan Avenue
Stamford, CT 06902

Table of Contents

Tactics

Introduction

The Internet and online services for recruiting and Human Resource management have had a broad and profound impact on the world of business. They have touched:

- recruiting and HR professionals at all levels and in all industries,
- the corporate HR organization itself,
- staffing firms of all sizes and with every conceivable specialization,
- executive search consultants in boutiques and in the world's largest and best known search firms,
- recruitment advertising agencies,
- local and national newspapers and, of course,
- the men and women of the workforce.

All have been influenced by this extraordinary medium, yet most are still uncertain about its appropriate role in their work and careers.

That's what this book is all about. It explores the Best Practices of online recruiting and Human Resource management. Its perspective is unique, however. The strategies and tactics, tips and techniques presented in this book are based on over seven years of research conducted by my company. WEDDLE's has been surveying recruiters and job seekers since 1996, asking them what they do online and what they don't do, what works and what doesn't, and most importantly, what works best. In short, though I'm the author, this book was actually created by your peers in the world of work. It presents, as faithfully as possible, the lessons they learned and wisdom they acquired by using the Internet on-the-job. I take full responsibility for any misanalysis, but this book is theirs and is dedicated to them.

Further, there is another characteristic of this book that sets it apart from your traditional HR tome. As its title suggests, the contents of the book are presented in short essays or postcards, rather than long chapters We live and work in a hectic, fast-paced world, and I think it's important to provide the information we need in a format that is easily accessible. So, *Postcards From Space* brings you innovative ideas, thought provoking concepts and original research findings for tapping the power of cyberspace in recruiting and HR management ... and does so in bite-sized pieces that you can read in the cracks and crevices of your work day.

These essays were originally written for my monthly newsletter (*Internet Resources for Successful Recruiting & Retention*) and my weekly column for CareerJournal.com from *The Wall Street Journal*. In each case, I've tried to provide jargon-free information that will help recruiters and HR practitioners put the Internet and online resources to work for them or, as we say at WEDDLE's: to help them maximize their ROI ... their Return on the Internet. Although they were mostly written between 2001 and 2002, all of the essays have been revised and updated for inclusion in this book.

Finally, it is important to note that—after analyzing hundreds of thousands of data elements collected in our research—I believe there is one unmistakable conclusion that can be drawn from what we have learned about the Internet to date. Despite, all of the hype surrounding it, this medium has not and will not change the fundamental principles of effective performance in the recruiting and Human Resource professions. The Internet is, indeed, a powerful new resource that must be harnessed and applied intelligently, and as such, its use is a new core competency for recruiting and Human Resource professionals. It does not, however, change or negate the core values and fundamental precepts with which they work.

All the Best,
Peter Weddle
Stamford, CT

For More Information About
WEDDLE's
Guides, Directories, Newsletters & Books
call 203.964.1888
or visit the WEDDLE's Web-site at www.weddles.com

What is WEDDLE's & Who is Peter Weddle?

What is WEDDLE's?

WEDDLE's is a research, publishing, consulting and training firm dedicated to helping people and organizations maximize their effectiveness and efficiency in using online resources for recruiting, retention, business development and job search.

- Since 1996, WEDDLE's has conducted groundbreaking surveys of:
  - recruiters and job seekers on the Internet and of
  - Web-sites providing employment-related services.

  Its findings and research have been cited in such publications as *The Wall Street Journal*, *The New York Times*, and in *Money*, *Fortune*, and *Inc.* magazines.

- WEDDLE's publishes newsletters, guides and directories that focus on the employment-related segment of the Internet. Its publications include:
  - ☛ *WEDDLE's Newsletter for About Internet Resources for Successful Recruiting & Retention*
  - ☛ *WEDDLE's Annual Guide to Employment Web Sites, The Recruiter's Edition*
  - ☛ *WEDDLE's Annual Guide to Employment Web Sites, The Job Seeker's Edition*
  - ☛ *WEDDLE's Directory of Employment-Related Internet Sites*
  - ☛ *WEDDLE's Recruiter's Guide to Association Web Sites.*
  - ☛ *WEDDLE's InfoNotes (WIN) Writing a Great Resume*

- WEDDLE's provides consultation to organizations in the areas of:
  - ☛ online recruitment strategy formulation;
  - ☛ employment brand development and positioning;
  - ☛ recruitment process re-engineering and optimization;
  - ☛ Web-site design, development and implementation; and
  - ☛ other topics central to effective staffing and retention.

- WEDDLE's delivers private seminars and workshops designed to train recruiters and recruitment managers in the Best Practices and Best Policies of Internet re-cruiting. Each session is tailored to the specific competency level of participants (be they desk recruiters or CEO's) and the mission of their organization (corporate employer, staffing firm, advertising agency or search firm).

Who is Weddle?

WEDDLE's publications and services were created by Peter Weddle, a former recruiter and business CEO turned author and speaker. He writes a weekly column about Internet recruiting for CareerJournal.com from *The Wall Street Journal* and a monthly newsletter about online resources for recruiting and HR management. Weddle has also authored or edited ten books—including *CliffsNotes Finding a Job on the Web* and *Career Fitness*—and written numerous articles for leading magazines and journals. He has been cited in *The New York Times, The Washington Post, The Boston Globe, U.S. News & World Report, The Wall Street Journal, USA Today* and numerous other publications and has spoken to trade and professional associations and corporate meetings all over the world.

More Comments about WEDDLE's & Peter Weddle

"The WEDDLE's Seminar has been held in cities around the country to rave reviews; in fact, more than 95% have said they found the seminars to both very informative and very helpful."

CareerJournal.com
from The Wall Street Journal

"I went to a seminar given by Peter Weddle on Web recruiting. Despite all my past training and seminars, it was like this time someone turned on a light. Previously, I had received 'mechanical training.' Sort of 'where to bolt the engine stuff.' But this seminar was about replacing 'horseless carriages' with 'automobiles' (really fast automobiles)."

Ken Gaffey
Staffing Consultant

"WOW!! I had the opportunity to listen to Peter Weddle speak last week at a conference and 'WOW!!' does NOT do justice to how I felt after listening to him!"

Gail Teel
American Multiline Corporation

"I would like to take this opportunity to thank you for the generosity of your time and valuable information. I'd like to briefly elaborate on my use of the word 'valuable' ... to date, your session was the most profitable investment of any 1 1/2 hour period in my life. At age 39, I'm sure that there's some pretty exciting learning experiences to come, but yesterday's session is going to take some beating! Thanks again, on behalf of myself and our organization."

Simon Pilcher
McArthur Management Services

Would You Like More Information?

For more information about WEDDLE's and its publications, consulting and training services, please visit our Web-site at www.weddles.com or call 203.964.1888.

WEDDLE's 2003 User's Choice Awards

Recruiter's & Job Seekers Pick the Best Sites on the Web

Who offers the best advice on which employment sites are most helpful to recruit-ers and job seekers? We think the answer to that question is obvious … it's you, the recruiters and job seekers who have used the sites. And that's what the **WEDDLE's User's Choice Awards** are all about. It's your chance to:

- recognize the Web-sites that provide the best level of service and value to their visitors, and
- help others make best use of the employment resources online.

For more information about the Awards and to cast your vote for the 2004 User's Choice Awards, please visit the WEDDLE's site at www.weddles.com and click on the Online Poll button on our Home Page.

**WEDDLE's 2003 User's Choice Awards
are sponsored by Bernard Hodes Group.**

☛ And the winners selected by <u>Recruiters</u> are:

🏆 Best General Purpose Job Board for Recruiters
Monster.com

🏆 Best Specialty Job Board for Recruiters
Dice.com

🏆 General Purpose Site with the Best Customer Service for Recruiters
CareerBuilder.com

🏆 Specialty Site with the Best Customer Service for Recruiters
Net-Temps.com

🏆 Most "Recruiter Friendly" General Purpose Site
HotJobs.com

🏆 Most "Recruiter Friendly" Specialty Site
ComputerJobs.com

☛ The winners selected by **Job Seekers** are:

🏆 Best General Purpose Job Board for Job Seekers
HotJobs.com

🏆 Best Specialty Job Board for Job Seekers
ComputerJobs.com

🏆 General Purpose Site with the Best Information for Job Seekers
CareerBuilder.com

🏆 Specialty Site with the Best Information for Job Seekers
CareerJournal.com

🏆 Most "Job Seeker Friendly" General Purpose Site
Monster.com

🏆 Most "Job Seeker Friendly" Specialty Site
BrassRing.com

___ Honorable Mention ___

Recruiters
AfterCollege.com
BrassRing.com
CareerJournal.com
ExecuNet.com
FlipDog.com

Job Seekers
America's Job Bank
Dice.com
FlipDog.com
Net-Temps
6FigureJobs.com
SHRM.org

■ Internet Recruiting
What Is It? Why Bother to Do It?

■ The Science Fictions of eCruiting

Vernor Vinge, a professor emeritus at San Diego State University, has devised a concept that he calls the "technological singularity." It envisions a point in time when the intelligence of machines takes a gigantic leap forward, empowering them with capabilities that exceed those of humans. Dr. Vinge has even predicted when this revolution of the nuts and bolts bunch will take place; set your alarms for sometime between 2020 and 2040.

Such forecasts of the inevitable advancement of machines are, of course, de rigor these days. After all, we live in an age that is fascinated with technology. And who cares if Dr. Vinge is best known as a science fiction writer? The fact is that we humans are doomed to evolve into second class citizens of the planet, subservient not to the apes (as Hollywood would have us believe), but to very machines we have made. Just ask any business or publication that depends on the technology crowd for its income.

This kind of collective drinking of one's own bath water has a long and distinguished ancestry. For example, back in 1950, the technology crowd breathlessly predicted that robots would, within a handful of years, change life as we know it on planet Earth. We would have robo-maids and robo-house cleaners, robo-drivers for our cars and even robo-traffic cops. Anything we humans could do, machines would do better. Well, here we are a half century later, and with the exception of assembly lines, there's nary a robot around ... except for those cute little robo-dogs your kids play with until their batteries run out.

These dire predictions of machine ascendancy would be comical if it weren't for their impact on the real world. That's especially true in the online recruiting industry. Over the past several years, a gaggle of techno-pundits have bombarded anyone who would listen with a constant stream of hype suggesting that the recruiting profession was going to change from a people business to one accomplished by machines. The Internet and computers are going to spell the doom of those who recruit the old fashioned way—by building relationships with candidates— and raise up a whole new genre of technologists who source virtual strangers at the speed of light.

Now, I would agree that technology has the potential to improve recruiting methods significantly, but not by replacing recruiters with machines. Indeed, this notion of a "technological singularity" in the recruitment industry has created a number of myths that have undermined recruiting performance online and jaundiced the view of many enterprise leaders. Let's take a look at these science fictions of eCruiting.

The Myth of Exactitude. The use of Boolean commands and search engines to probe resume databases and the World Wide Web has convinced many recruiters that finding and recruiting candidates is now an exact science. Input your criteria, hit the search button, sit back, have a pina colada, bitta bang-bitta boom and out come just the candidates you want. Unfortunately, life is not quite so simple. There are nuances among candidates and compensating factors that can turn a person who lacks all of the stated requirements into the best candidate. And as we all know, the best candidate on paper is not always the one you would ultimately want to hire. How can those judgments be made? Only with the savvy and experience of a real live human recruiter. Today's machines may have some artificial intelligence, but they are still dumb as dirt when it comes to making fine-grained distinctions among people.

The Myth of Fine Craftsmanship: A cottage industry has grown up around teaching recruiters how to do manual searches of the World Wide Web. The proponents of this school have convinced recruiters that:

(a) searching the Web by hand is effective and efficient,

(b) performing such searches involves rocket science, and

(c) only by purchasing their training programs can you acquire such knowledge.

Nothing, however, could be further from the truth. Indeed, my organization has been surveying recruiters online for over seven years, and in every annual report, respondents have fingered manual, browser-based searching of the Web as the least effective technique they use. Further, manual searches only probe the top 2 billion records online; automated agents or spiders, on the other hand, not only reach 500+ billion documents on the Web, but they do so without needing a good night's sleep or weekends off.

The Myth of Speedy Connections. From the technologist's perspective, it's all about speed. After all, recruiting is simply a transaction between buyers and sellers of labor, so those who connect with candidates first will be best positioned to close the deal. It's an appealing notion and makes imminent good sense to someone on the outside of our profession looking in. While there was a certain transaction-like quality to recruiting in the surplus labor market of years past, the most successful recruiters have always transformed their interactions with candidates into relationships. Building trust and confidence with prospective candidates was the surest and, ultimately, the fastest way to recruit them for a particular opening. It still is, even in an age infatuated with technology. People want to be informed and helped and courted by people whom they know and who know them, not by virtual strangers who blast in and out of their careers and lives.

The Myth of Small Numbers. According to this myth, the technology of online recruiting is so powerful that it can change human nature. In every other aspect of human endeavor, there is an almost infinite variation in the way things are done. But on the Web, somehow, it's different. All job seekers act like lemmings and visit the same one or two recruitment sites. And that, of course, means that recruiters can also post every job opening for every occupation at every level of skill and experience in every location at the same one or two sites. It just boggles the mind, and of course, it's absolutely wrong. Candidates online are just as idiosyncratic as they are in the real world. Maybe even more. They look for employment opportunities at a broad range of Web-sites operated by their professional associations, trade organizations, alumni and other special interest groups. All totaled, there are probably 40,000 of these sites, and the most successful recruiters consider all of them. They tailor their selection of sites to the specific demographic of their target candidate population for each opening they are trying to fill. In other words, they are inclusive, not exclusive in their use of the Web's resources.

Science fiction may be great entertainment, but it produces lousy recruiting results online. As with other technological advances, the Web and computers are likely to improve our productivity and effectiveness. They will not, however, make the recruiter less important or less central to success in the War for Talent. Quite the contrary. All that advanced technology is nothing more than a lot of expensive wafers and wires without a smart person to put it to work on-the-job. ■

■ It's Just Another Tool

Internet recruiting is just another tool for recruiters to use in the War for Talent. It's your basic virtual hammer, nothing more and nothing less. It won't disintermediate recruiters or even replace traditional tools of recruitment—you know, stuff like networking and candidate selling. In other words, Internet recruiting is simply something else you can pull out of your recruiter's toolbox to get the job done.

That non-threatening, very pedestrian view of the medium is the prevailing notion, at least among most writers, trainers and pundits in the online recruitment industry today. I've used it myself in seminars and workshops. It helps reassure those who are intimidated by technology and counters the hype that the Internet will somehow eliminate the need for human experience and savvy. While those outcomes are helpful, I've come to believe that the tool analogy for online recruiting badly misses the mark.

Viewing the Internet as a handy instrument allows us to ignore the preparation and changes necessary to use the medium effectively. It's like asking a carpenter to build a house without a blueprint. Without that vision for the finished building, there's nothing to guide the application of the tools. Lots of nails will get hammered into lots of boards, but there's no way to ensure that all of that activity will yield a product you can use.

That's precisely why Internet recruiting currently produces such modest results. Depending on whose numbers you accept, most organizations are filling just 4-8% of their openings with candidates acquired online. If you got similar results from traditional methods of recruitment, you'd be out of a job. Internet recruiting has to do better or, frankly, it's not worth the effort. And in order to do better, we will have to recognize that the medium is complex as well as capable, and hence has the potential to be misused. The only way to ensure that we actually capture its benefits, therefore, is to plan and organize its application carefully, to use it with a vision.

Without a vision, Internet recruiting has done nothing more than automate old fashioned, manual recruiting practices. In other words, job postings are simply classified ads listed in cyberspace, rather than on the printed page. Networking online is nothing more than using e-mail to make "cold calls" to strangers to see if they can be cajoled into taking a different job. And a recruiting Web-site is basically the electronic version of your standard candidate literature pinned up in cyberspace so it can be read 24 hours a day, 7 days a week.

With a vision, on the other hand, Internet recruiting becomes a methodology for re-imagining the entire recruiting process. This new process uses three elements—technology, recruiter experience and knowledge and traditional recruitment methods—to accomplish two objectives:

- to perform certain tasks better than we have ever been able to perform them
- and
- to perform other tasks that were simply beyond our capabilities prior to the Internet.

In other words, if we take off the handcuffs with which we've had to work in the past (e.g., the space and cost constraints of print advertising, the limited reach of one-on-one telephone net-working), we can redefine the scope of the recruiting process and empower it to do more for us. And getting more out of our online recruiting is the only way we're going to prevail in today's tough business environment.

What are the enhancements we should seek in this new process? As a minimum, our goal should be to:

- Reach more candidates, particularly those who are not in the job market;

- Communicate more rapidly with prospective candidates;

- Communicate more information to candidates more effectively; and

- Sell the value proposition of our openings more persuasively to the best candidates.

These upgrades are the only way online recruiting is going to have anything more than a marginal impact on our overall staffing requirement. To achieve them, however, we can't simply start hammering away with a bunch of golly-gee-whiz bang tools. Instead, we must assign the imple-mentation of each upgrade to the "entity" best able to perform it. We can count on technology to work tirelessly, manipulate huge mountains of data and make warp speed connections, and we can rely on humans to interact with other humans, make fine-grained distinctions among their various capabilities and ultimately to select the right candidate for the right opportunity. Hence, we should ask the Internet to reach more candidates and communicate with them more rapidly and ask recruiters to communicate the right information to candidates and sell them on the value proposition of available openings.

These assignments capture the strengths of both and avoid asking either to do something that is on the outer limits of their capabilities. It takes advantage of the Internet's capacity to operate 24 hours a day, 7 days a week and to access candidates all over the world in nanoseconds. And it refrains from asking that technology to empathize with candidates or to build relationships with them. This allocation also taps the experience and judgment of recruiters to help candidates ap-preciate the value of an opportunity and to overcome their inherent resistance to change. And just as appropriately, it doesn't ask them to spend days and weeks crunching through resumes hidden on the Web looking for an elusive candidate or two.

For any organization--be it a staffing firm or an employer--the resulting process can involve a wide range of different activities that are tailored to its specific culture, resources and priorities. Whatever the tact taken, however, the use of the tools must be guided by a vision that optimizes their performance, and the results that are achieved must be measured and evaluated against the real world enhancements incorporated in the vision. Otherwise, the Internet is just another tool, and a largely ineffectual one, at that. ∎

■ Web Recruiting is Dead!

The news of dot com layoffs and bankruptcies is music to the ears of some bricks and mortar recruiters. They read the reports of troubles at Jobs.com, CruelWorld, techies.com, Vault.com and other sites and conclude that Web recruiting is dead. Their gleeful summary of the situation is a short and unsympathetic: "I told you so!"

In some respects, this response is richly deserved. It is a natural reaction to the adolescent behavior and insufferable egotism displayed by some dot com recruiting company executives. The poster boy for these techno-cowboys was Jeff Hyman, who boasted in an *Inc.* magazine interview that Internet recruitment sites would make "toast" of the traditional recruiting industry. Today, Hyman's CruelWorld site is living out its name. It's been shut down, and the pieces sold off to an old school executive recruiting firm.

Over the past 3-5 years, Hyman and his buddies created an "us versus them" environment around the emergence of an industry hoping to harness a medium and technology with the potential to do great good for the recruiting profession. It made widespread acceptance of the Web's genuine advantages more contentious and difficult than it otherwise would have been.

But let's not overreact to what is essentially a relatively normal marketplace correction. The demise or diminution of a handful of job boards is a commentary on those specific enterprises, not the indictment of an entire industry. There are probably still 40,000 recruitment sites operating online, and more continue to launch every day ... despite the bum economy. Why? Because Internet usage by working men and women continues to soar. A new person comes online every 1.75 seconds, and the Net increasingly mirrors all of the workforce.

So, rather than toss out Web recruiting because of its misrepresentation by a few, I think it makes more sense to use the current shakeout to probe the lessons the past 3-4 years have taught us about how best to capture the power of this thing called the Internet. Here's my take on what we can learn:

- Internet recruiting is neither a silver bullet nor a panacea. It also does not repudiate or replace the fundamental principles of good recruiting. Instead, it is the application of those principles in a new medium. To put it another way, online recruiting can and should be integrated into the overall arsenal we deploy in the War for Talent. It works best when used in conjunction with all of the other resources we bring to bear in our recruiting efforts, not when we set sourcers and eCruiters off in the corner all by themselves.

- The Internet is not simply a place for resume sourcing or "data mining," as it's known to some Neteratti. That's a part of it, to be sure, but a more complete vision sees the medium as a resource for what I call "computer assisted recruiting." In other words, to be effective, Web-based recruiting must involve all of the activities traditionally associated with recruitment, not just some of them. Hence, it includes:

- Employment advertising (job postings)
- Research (resume and contact sourcing),

  <u>and</u>
- Networking (or what I call "digital relationship recruiting").

Leave out any one of these activities and you put yourself at a disadvantage in the competition for top quality candidates and, as a result, undercut the return on your investment online.

- The "killer app" or secret weapon in online recruiting is not oft-cited techniques of flipping, x-raying or browser-based searching with Boolean strings. It is—as it has always been in traditional recruitment—relationships. The mass 1:1 communications capability of the Net enables us to meet and interact efficiently with large numbers of prospective candidates, including those who are not actively looking for a new position. If we use those contacts to earn their confidence and trust, they will read and consider our employment opportunities while they ignore those offered by recruiters who operate as digital strangers.

- Good consumerism can make or break your online recruiting efforts. As in any other industry, there are good vendors (i.e., recruitment sites), and those that are not so good. Today's shake-out among job boards and portals underscores the importance of buying smart. Don't invest a penny before doing your homework on the capabilities, fees and, if at all possible, the financial status of any site you're considering. While admitting to some bias, I don't think there's a better source for such information than the annual *Recruiter's Guide to Employment Web Sites* that we publish at WEDDLE's.

In short, despite the wishful thinking of some, Web recruiting isn't even close to dead, but it is growing up ... and we all can be thankful for that. ■

■ Where Do You Get the Best ROI?

The Society for Human Resource Management (SHRM) has announced the results of its 2002 Recruiter Budget/Cost Survey. Among its 281 respondents, **Internet recruiting was #1 in ROI** (followed by newspaper advertising), #2 in Quality (behind employee referrals) and #2 in Volume (behind newspaper advertising). At the bottom of the heap were TV, radio and trade publications for ROI and Volume; and TV, radio and temp agencies for Quality. ■

■ Is There Still an ROI?

The dot.com bust and subsequent soul searching about all things digital has led some Recruiting Directors and staffing firm owners to question whether there really is an ROI ... a return on the time, money and effort being spent on Internet recruiting. It's a fair question and deserves something more than a knee-jerk answer.

I think that there is huge potential return on Internet recruiting **IF** two preconditions are met:

- First, the enterprise doing the online recruiting must be aware of, train its recruiters in and implement Best Practices. Online recruiting has been practiced for almost a decade now. It's time that we began to take advantage of the lessons learned by early adopters. To do so, however, we will have to cut through a lot of hype and self-aggrandizing punditry and focus, instead, on what research tells us delivers the best results.

- Second, the Internet must continue to attract prospective candidates in all professions, crafts and trades. Despite all the pronouncements from the traditional media, if more and more people continue to use the Internet more and more for information, entertainment and job search ... then, the demise of the medium as a recruitment resource will, in fact, have been greatly exaggerated.

So, what are the facts? Have people abandoned the Web in the wake of the dot.com bomb? According to a new survey by the Pew Internet and American Life Project, the answer is an emphatic "No." In fact, more than half of the poll's respondents said they are using the Internet as much as they did 6 months ago, and 29% report that they are using it more (given all of the recent layoffs, they're probably looking for a job).

Even more important, Web use is expanding in the population. Traditionally, the Web has been a resource for the best educated among us. Indeed, Pew found that 86% of college graduates in the U.S. are now online. It also found, however, that 53% of high school graduates are also using the Net. Similarly, a UCLA study entitled *Internet Report: Surveying the Digital Future* reports that 60% of adults making $15-$49,000 per year are online, as is 41% of those with incomes under $15,000.

What's this mean for recruiters?

- There are more prospective candidates than ever using the Internet, so the medium continues to have great potential for recruiting ... provided, of course, that the recruiting is accomplished with Best Practices.

- We must break out of the box that restricts our online recruitment to professional and executive level candidates. For example, iLogos has found, in its survey of Global 500 recruitment Web-sites, that 47% of all visitors to such sites do not have a 4-year degree. Yet, virtually no employer posts blue collar or even skilled trade positions online, nor do many staffing firms post light industrial or clerical positions on their sites. And that kind of "old thinking" on the Internet is precisely what hurts our ROI.

The Web has long held the promise of being a new and rich channel of sourcing for recruiters. For years, however, that promise was only partially realized because certain segments of the workforce were not online. It is ironic, therefore, that just as the Web is losing some of its aura of invincibility, its potential as a recruiting medium is finally coming true. More people than ever before are now online, and they are staying there longer than ever before. That combination is your best assurance of a great ROI. ■

■ Who's Looking for Work Online?

According to a recent report released by the Pew Internet project, 52 million Americans have used the Internet to look for a job in the past year. That's a 60% increase over 2000. Among the project's other findings:

- On any given day, 4 million people are job searching online, a 33% increase over 2000.

- On a typical day, more than twice as many men as women go online to look for a new or better job.

- 44% of executives use the Web in their job search; 49% of clerical and office workers and 55% of salespeople do. ■

■ The White Queen Principle

Most of us have, at one time or another, read the Lewis Carroll classic, *Alice in Wonderland*. Like today's Harry Potter, young Alice finds herself unexpectedly removed from her familiar surroundings and immersed in a new world that is strange and mysterious. Her trip through the looking glass introduces her to an odd, but wise cast of characters, each of whom offers a special lesson if Alice can but riddle it out. Sometimes the advice seems wacky and upside down; other times, the message is almost too simple. But always, there is the sense that true wisdom lies just beneath the surface.

Alice's adventure has always been viewed as a journey for children, but now we are learning that it might just have a lesson or two for adults, as well. Consider the White Queen Principle. Her advice seems simple enough: you have to run faster to stay in the same place. Whatever the value of that counsel to Alice, it is especially appropriate for today's hyper-velocity economy. Indeed, for recruiters competing in a labor market constricted by huge shortages of talent, speed is the only strategy that wins, and the Internet is the fastest medium available to recruiters.

It's no surprise, therefore, that this royal bit of sagacity is rapidly gaining acceptance among recruiting professionals. Unfortunately, however, the meaning beneath the surface of the Queen's dictum is almost as widely misunderstood. All too often, the quest for speed has become an effort to do the same old things more quickly. We simply use the Web to automate and accelerate the tasks we have always performed.

- We spend more time on the Web data mining for resumes. According to surveys conducted by my company and reported in my newsletter (*WEDDLE's Newsletter About Internet Resources for Successful Recruiting & Retention*), almost half of all recruiters on the Web now spend 16 or more hours per week online, and 32% actually spend 20 or more hours out there in cyberspace, cold-calling the electronic way.

- We make more use of spiders and other software applications that cruise the Web to make copies of posted resumes. Again, according to our surveys, 36% of all recruiters on the Web in 2002 rented or bought a spider in hopes that it would pull in more contacts among strangers on the Web.

- We erect stand-alone recruitment Web-sites or special recruitment areas on our organizational sites. More and more staffing firms and employers are launching such sites so that they can do more of their classified advertising out there on the Web.

There's no doubt that all of this techno-hustle accelerated the pace of recruiting, but did it improve its yield? What was the return on investment (of time, energy and, increasingly, money) for all of this speedy activity? According to our survey respondents:

- Data mining for resumes at locations other than commercial resume databases has consistently been voted among the five least effective online recruiting techniques by the respondents to our surveys.

26

- Using spiders to ferret out resumes on the Web has also been voted among the five least effective online recruiting techniques by our survey respondents.

- Kennedy Information has found, in its survey of recruiters, that employers are filling just 5% of their vacancies with candidates sourced through their recruitment Web-sites.

Why such disappointing results? Because we've misunderstood the Queen. She is not suggesting that we do old things faster. Scratching around for resumes on the Web is still scratching around for resumes. Doing it more efficiently doesn't change that fundamental premise. We're still trying to connect with people who don't know us and therefore have absolutely no reason to entrust their career to us. And launching our very own recruitment site filled with broken links and uninformative job postings is still a turnoff no matter how fast it happens. We're simply more efficient in treating candidates to a shabby experience.

So, what, then, is the Queen really saying? What is the wisdom beneath the words? I'm convinced that the message is as much about <u>what</u> we do as it is about how we do it. In other words, to move ahead, we not only have to move with dispatch, but we have to do some new things. We shouldn't harness the Web to recruiting practices that are longer effective, but instead, use it to reformulate our entire recruiting process. For example:

- From the one-on-one recruitment of strangers with the telephone, we can use the Web to move to a blended strategy of mass 1:1 communications and one-on-one follow-up by phone. By linking the information in our resume databases to the connectivity of the Web, we can build relationships with candidates through regular, personalized messages. As with traditional recruiting, those relationships will increase the information we have about each individual and their level of comfort in dealing with us. And those factors, in turn, will improve our success on the phone.

- We can drop data mining and spiders that search out strangers on the Web, and begin a regimen of eNetworking with people who share our interests, backgrounds and goals. By participating in the Web's virtual communities via e-mail, we'll be able to get to know and become known by hundreds, even thousands of prospective candidates. That familiarity will, in turn, engender a level of trust and a willingness to open our mail and consider our opportunities when we present them.

- We'll see our organizational Web-site as a recruiting process, not as an electronic bulletin board. We won't post employment information developed for the print medium or overlook the maintenance of the site's functionality (its links, job database search engine, candidate application mechanism). Instead, we'll work to create and sustain a memorable visitor experience by treating all visitors as if they were preferred customers.

Sure, we have to move quickly to win in today's frenetic business environment, but the key to winning is to channel that speed in the right direction. We mustn't simply spin up old habits, but instead devise new approaches that are as effective as they are fast and are fast because they are effective. ■

■ The Bends in the Road for Recruiters

The War on Terrorism, the Mysterious Economy and Enronism or the Plague of Leadership Crime have all conspired to make predicting the future an even more uncertain exercise than it normally is. Nevertheless, the months ahead portend to be a pivotal time in the evolution of on-line recruiting, thanks to two significant developments that will fundamentally change its character. For that reason (and with all due respect to the inherent dangers of crystal ball gazing), I've identified these new bends in the road for recruiting on the Information Superhighway and described them briefly below. I hope they'll help you move to the head of the pack in your search for top talent online.

The Era of the Niche

In retail sales, big stores provide consumers with several benefits. Their economies of scale and buying power enable them to offer both lower prices and a better inventory than their smaller competitors. On the Web, however, exactly the opposite is true. According to our surveys, niche sites that specialize by occupation, industry and/or geographic focus are both cheaper than the large, general purpose sites and, <u>in their area of specialization,</u> likely to offer a richer, deeper pool of talent.

However, big stores and large sites do share one trait in common: both are very well known and thus attract a lot of traffic. The irony is that, while customer traffic is a good thing for sales, it is a very bad thing for recruiting. Indeed, more and more recruiters are now realizing that there is no "value added" to following the herd and using the same well known sites as everyone else.

So, what will happen in the months ahead? Recruiters will discover the vast range of options that exist on the Web. There are 40,000+ employment sites online, and most are niche sites. How can you find those that will serve you best? Do what you do when shopping in the real world: ask friends and colleagues for recommendations and let your fingers do the walking (or clicking). For the latter (and while admitting to some bias), I suggest that you check out:

- the site profiles that appear in the WEDDLE's newsletter each month,
- the free Association Directory at our Web-site (www.weddles.com),
- the site profiles in our annual Recruiter's and Job Seeker's Guides, and
- the listings in our annual Directory (see the online Catalog at www.weddles.com for a complete description).

A Time for Precision

During the frenetic days of the War for Talent, approximation was the rule. There were so many openings and the talent supply was so tight that "close enough candidates" were recruited and hired fast, before the competition could lure them away. Now, of course, with a slower economy, the pace of hiring has dropped precipitously and is likely to stay there for the foreseeable future.

And in this new environment, hiring managers want a different kind of recruiting. Instead of candidates who are approximately right for an opening, they are demanding extreme precision. They want the one candidate who exactly fits their opportunity in multiple dimensions: skill, experience, temperament and commitment.

What will recruiters have to do? Adopt screening tools at every step in the recruiting process. Today, just 5% of corporate Web-sites have such tools in place. As a result, they are unable to:

(a) siphon off the tsunami of unqualified resumes generated by sites and postings today; and

(b) pick out the precisely right candidate from the approximately right one quickly, consistently and accurately.

Happily, this situation can be easily corrected with a new generation of online assessment and screening tools. These instruments are more reliable, valid and useful than earlier versions, and Web delivery makes them easy and efficient to use. They are available through such firms as:

- CareerHarmony (www.careerharmony.com),

- ComputerPsychologist.com

- ePredix (www.epredix.com), and

- Exxceed (www.exxceed.com)

A word of caution, however: the results of these tools are only as accurate as the baseline to which they are compared. In other words, the precision of the opening's profile (what's being sought) is as important as the precision of the candidate's profile (what's available). Rather than trying to measure jobs, team environments and organizational cultures, we suggest that you assess your high performers in specific fields and use those results as your baseline for screening prospective hires. ■

■ Some Final Food For Thought

Internet-based recruiting has now become an integral part of the way recruiters do their job. Whether its role is helpful or harmful, however, depends upon the wisdom with which we use it. And while we have a large and growing body of practical knowledge about online recruitment (i.e., the most efficient procedures for doing it effectively) there has been, to date, little in the way of wisdom—insights about the essential nature and purpose of the activity—that can help us apply our knowledge in an appropriate and ultimately useful way.

Wisdom is typically acquired in two ways:

- One's own experience (and certainly, as more recruiters spend more time actually doing on-line recruiting, their wisdom regarding it will increase).

- The experiences of others (in essence, we can cut down on our learning curve by borrowing the insights and understanding of others).

While Americans have traditionally been a get-it-on-your-own people, we also have a long history of learning from others. The quintessential example of that is Ben Franklin's *Poor Richard's Almanack*. Many a colonist long ago and many a schoolchild over the years has gained a bit of wisdom about life and its foibles by reading the epigrams that old Ben Franklin embedded in his annual publication.

Who hasn't read and thought about:
"A penny saved is a penny earned."
"Diligence is the Mother of good luck."
And my all-time favorite,
"A Countryman between two lawyers
is like a fish between two cats."

As you can tell, an epigram is nothing more than a short, pithy statement of wisdom. It's not meant to be overly deep or philosophical; instead, its purpose is simply to affirm some life-based learning that can be helpful to others.

Now, I don't pretend to be a Ben Franklin, but I have penned the following epigrams in the hopes that they may be helpful to you as you gain experience with online recruiting, the recruiting profession and the War for Talent.

- In the recruiting function, technology becomes transformative only when recruiters are transformed first.

- Quality always enjoys a seller's market, and the best quality is normally a reluctant seller.

- Measurement and metrics make sense only if some sense is made of the numbers.

- The key component of your recruiting process is not technology or people, but the experience they create for job seekers.

- In high performing organizations, recruiting is a line, not a staff function; its job is to increase the value of three assets: the talent database, the recruitment Web-site and the organization's employment brand.

- Victory in the War for Talent will go to those who fight the War for the Best Talent.

- Treat a resume in your talent database as a record and you have a piece of data, treat it as the start of a relationship and you have a prospective employee. ■

■ **Internet Recruiting**
What Is It? Why Bother to Do It?

■ The New Rational Labor Market

Labor markets come and labor markets go. They may not match the business cycle in terms of the public attention they receive, but shifts in the workforce population have just as great an impact on the strategies and ultimate success of an enterprise as do the rate of inflation and consumer activity.

If you find that statement hard to accept, consider the War for Talent. During the mid and late 1990's, demographic realities and the pace of business growth created a huge mismatch between labor supply and demand. The result was an irrational market. Employers adopted practices that in other times would have been considered ludicrous. Remember offering college graduates with no experience a starting salary of $75,000? Remember offering mediocre C++ programmers a BMW as a hiring incentive? And how about all those stock options? If you believed the hype about their value, we were offering anyone with a pulse the opportunity to become a paper millionaire by the age of 30.

This irrational market also produced some irrational recruiting strategies. These included:

- **Speed wins**. As long as you were the first to find and reach a prospective employee, you would be the one to hire them. Unfortunately, those who bought into that idea must have slept through high school physics. Speed doesn't win; momentum does. Momentum is mass times speed (or acceleration). And in recruiting, your mass is your recruiting process. If you have a lousy process (filled with communications gaps and duplicative actions) then speed simply increases the rate of your inefficiency. On the other hand, if you have a well designed recruiting process, then speed actually does enhance your performance and your ability to recruit world class employees.

- **Manual research techniques are more efficient than automated ones**. This notion was sold by companies that earned their living teaching recruiters how to do manual data mining on the Web. It failed to recognize or even acknowledge (in the interest of filling student seats) the fundamental differences between a computer and a human recruiter. Machines can work 24 hours a day, 7 days a week and crunch huge amounts of data. Humans, on the other hand, have limitations on the amount of time they can or will work, but can and do make fine-grained distinctions among individuals. Hence, research on the Web—which consists of sifting through over 500 billion documents to find an adequate pool of qualified candidates— is best accomplished by using automated search agents (called spiders or robots). Given their marginal value, however (Please see The White Queen Principle), an even better approach is to focus an organization's research first on identifying specific pools of candidates online (i.e., databases) that match its target demographic(s) and then on acquiring the skills necessary to mine those databases effectively. The greater precision of that strategy significantly increases the probability of <u>efficiently</u> finding qualified candidates.

But that's the past, and the irrational market created by the War for Talent (or more precisely, the War for Any Talent) has now been replaced by a rational market defined by a War for the Best

Talent. Admittedly, there is some debate about whether this new market is simply a short interval before the return to hand-to-hand combat in recruiting or a more lasting and fundamental change in the way employers will acquire workers.

- Those who believe it's just an interval point to supply and argue that there are just not enough workers to meet demand. The U.S. workforce is not growing as fast as it has historically, and the Baby Boom generation (if they act as their parents did) will shortly begin retiring in huge numbers. As a consequence, there will be a 15% drop in the 35-44 year old cohort of the workforce—which traditionally fills many of the mid-level leadership positions in corporate America—and a 33% shortfall in the technical talent needed to keep factories and service centers running.

- Those who champion the idea of a changed market point to demand and argue that it's just not as high as originally assumed and thus will not outstrip supply, except in specific fields and geographic locations. The demand-supply mis-match was based on two assumptions that are no longer true:

  (1) the rate of growth in our economy is not holding above 3% (which was the baseline for the McKinsey & Company report on *The War for Talent*) and

  (2) Baby Boomers are not retiring as early as their parents.

  Moreover, if the recovery from the current recession follows the pattern in the U.S. since the country's transition to a service-based economy, the rate of economic growth in the rebound may not exceed 2.6-2.8%.

While this debate is important, I don't think it should interfere with our efforts to understand how recruiting strategies should evolve in order to deal effectively with the labor market that exists today. In fact, I believe that recruiters can adopt a new set of rational strategies now that will prove successful not only in the near term but in the longer term, as well, regardless of which labor market theory ends up being correct. What are these rational strategies? They include:

- **Precision wins**. The key to successful recruiting in a rational market is to focus on finding the right candidate with the right skills and temperament in the right location at the right time to fill a specific position in a specific working environment in a specific company in a specific location. In other words, what recruiters must do is ensure "good fits." The more good fits an employer has—between the individual's skills and the organization's position, the individual's temperament and the organization's culture, the individual's personality and their new supervisor's personality, and so on—the higher individual performance will be. And new hire performance on-the-job is the ultimate measure of recruiting proficiency.

- **Relationship building must be systematized and automated**. The good old days of building relationships one at a time over the telephone or in face-to-face meetings are simply too inefficient and recruiter intensive for today's (and tomorrow's) competitive business climate. Recruiters must now take advantage of the mass 1:1 communications capability of the Internet to establish and nurture long term relationships with tens of thousands of prospective employees. They must transform old fashioned resume databases into powerful collections of human capital and enhance the potential value of those assets by pre-screening and pre-selling the individuals behind those resumes. Those on-going, preparatory activities are the best way to ensure that "good fits" can be:

  (1) identified accurately and

  (2) achieved quickly.

The more capable a recruiting function is in accomplishing those two tasks, the greater its impact on individual <u>and</u> organizational performance.

Labor markets come and labor markets go. For recruiters, the key to success in such a dynamic environment is a toolbox filled with the right strategies. In today's rational market, only rational approaches will prevail. And should the War for Any Talent actually morph into a War for the Best Talent—and I think it will—those same rational strategies will trump the irrational activities of the past, as well. ■

■ 2002 "Most Wanted" Tech Skills

Techies.com, an IT recruiting site based in Minneapolis, MN, announced its Tech Skills Demand Index which measures the change in the 20 skills most in demand between 2001 and 2002.

Unix remained atop the list for the second straight year, although with a twist. In greatest demand was Unix/Tornado Development, with over 15% of all jobs calling for some level of knowledge of this technology. Among Web-related skills, HTML, Visual Basic and C Language continued to see demand slip, while desktop and Internet development tools such as C++, XML and SQL held steady. ■

■ The Second Front in the War for Talent

The War for Talent is over. Although no respectable executive would say that, most are acting as if the competition for superior talent has ended. With resumes flooding into recruiter mailboxes and fewer positions to fill, they have mentally declared victory and marched off to face more pressing crises.

I find this "peace in our time" perspective ludicrously naïve. To me, it's analogous to saying, "We beat the bad guys in Afghanistan, so the War on Terror is over." Tell that to the security screeners the next time you climb on a plane. Or to the marines guarding our embassy in Indonesia. Or to the INS agents and Coast Guard personnel patrolling our borders. In point of fact, wars are fought in stages, and the current lull is simply a prelude to the next front in the War for Talent, a front I call the War for the Best Talent. Where will this new conflict be waged? The battlefields will still be in the labor market—the place where the forces of supply and demand meet head on—but the strategic scope of the War for Talent will shift.

The Second Front will move from the simplistic notion of a supply chain in human resources to a much richer and complex model of human capital formation. It will not see people as cogs in some well oiled process, but rather as cognitive beings with preferences and goals—unique attributes that must be identified and acknowledged. It will not assume that talent—at least, the best talent—is desperate for employment, but instead accepts that talented people must be convinced that an employer's value proposition delivers benefits in two directions (theirs as well as the company's) and more benefits than a paycheck. In short, the next stage in the War for Talent will take HR from a transaction-based perspective to one based on relationships, augmented by the power of technology.

This transformation has long been the Holy Grail of HR executives. Countless experiments in social accounting and human capital have been launched to push HR into the limited attention span of CEOs and Boards of Directors, and every one of them has failed. Today, as in 1955, it is the rare corporate leader who devotes as much energy to the human asset of the enterprise as they do to its capital and technology assets. So, why will the War for the Best Talent be any different? Why won't CEOs continue to spout hot air about the importance of talent and continue to manage it with strategies drawn from the Age of Steam? Because "A" level talent performs better than "C" level talent, and recruiting has finally been connected to the CEO's report card. Let's look at each of those contentions.

- **"A" level talent wins**. The First Front in the War for Talent was fought in quantitative terms. There were more openings than there were candidates, so recruiters focused on getting enough talent—any talent—to plug the gaps. Sure, every effort was made to select the best prospect for each vacancy, but the press of 40 or 50 or 60 open requirements often meant that the "best" was defined as the best that could be found right away, before the competition could hire them.

The Second Front will have a different dynamic. It will be fought in qualitative terms. The McKinsey & Company report on *The War for Talent* proved what every sports enthusiast has always known: the best talent wins. Just ask the World Series or NBA champs each year or the team that wins the Super Bowl. Differences in talent are real and have a real impact on the bottom line. McKinsey found that "A" level performers deliver a 50-100% advantage over average performers in productivity, quality and revenue. HR executives have already adjusted to that reality, and CEOs won't be far behind. Instead of chasing any worker with a pulse, the successful enterprise in the Second Front will treat every requirement as an exercise in "mass executive search." They will use new technology, Best Practices and Best Policies to perform <u>large scale precision recruiting</u>. The goal will not be to fill a position, but rather to find the one person with the right set of attributes to unlock the full potential contribution of that position in the enterprise.

- **The CEO has a report card too**. The First Front focused on process efficiency. The goal was to cut costs and improve productivity. For some organizations, this objective meant sourcing candidates with online advertisements and resume mining, while for others, the focus was on re-engineering their process with applicant tracking systems. For both, the development and maturation of the Internet meant that the Human Resource Department was finally given the communications reach and computational power to break out of an historically administrative role and focus on its one accountability that impacts the business of the enterprise: talent management. Unfortunately, however, the metrics of process efficiency— cost-per-hire and time-to-fill—do not convey the scope or magnitude of that contribution.

That's why the Second Front in the War for Talent will involve the adoption of a new language that will enable HR to measure and express its contribution in metrics that matter to CEOs. Instead of process efficiency, this language will focus on business results: return on assets and increases in shareholder value. Is that possible? A recent report by Watson Wyatt provides a resounding "Yes." In a two-year study of 400 U.S. and Canada-based companies, it found that sound human capital management practices and policies contributed to a 47% increase in a company's market value. Similarly, the return on investment in the two talent assets that the HR function manages—its candidate database and its recruitment Web-site—can be calculated and monetized. Spending money to increase the number of hires drawn from the database and Website assets and to decrease the attrition rate among those hires produces real and tangible returns that can be measured as dollars saved and, thus, higher profits for the enterprise.

Those who confuse the end of the First Front in the War for Talent with the end of the war, itself, are making a very serious strategic miscalculation. It will take time and preparation to win the looming battles for quality talent and to learn how to measure the gains achieved in terms that CEOs will appreciate. As Plato said, "Only the dead have seen the end of war," and the unprepared will be its first victims. That's true whether you're talking about the War on Terror or the Second Front in the War for Talent. ■

■ The Single Best Candidate for the Job

I recently attended a lecture where the speaker displayed the following recruitment ad clipped long-ago from a newspaper:

Help Wanted

Employee needed for a dairy farm.
Reliable and experienced--$6.00/hour.
Reliable and inexperienced--$5.00/hour
Unreliable and inexperienced--$3.00/hour
Call 357.8329 any time from 6:00 a.m. to 7 p.m.

I've changed the telephone number so that the dairy farm (which is still operating) isn't flooded with calls from proactive job seekers.

There are, of course, pluses and minuses to this ad. On the positive side, it's definitely succinct and to the point. Indeed, the reportorial style is almost Hemingwayesque. On the downside, however, the ad fails to tell us what kind of work the employee will perform, where the farm is located or any other details that might make the position appealing (or not) to specific workers. In other words, the ad fails to supply enough information for a candidate to evaluate the opportunity and make a rational decision about it. Unfortunately, when that happens, only the most desperate of candidates typically apply.

Having said all that, I think the ad is most noteworthy because of its very clear focus on quality. There's no doubt that this employer understands the substance and value of differences in candidate quality. It knows the attributes that define the best candidate for its job and the relative importance of those attributes in job performance. That's a lesson we could all take to heart as we hone our recruiting processes and practices for the next stage in the War for Talent.

The first front in the War for Talent (circa 1996-2000) was a quantitative battle. The economy was so hot that tens of thousands of positions were being created even as demographic trends were leaving us with huge workforce shortages. The resulting imbalance forced recruiters to focus their efforts on the first capable person who could be identified. There simply wasn't time either to gauge the true depth of a candidate's expertise or to look on for a better qualified person. Hiring managers were clamoring for new employees so recruiters did the best they could to find acceptable candidates fast and keep seats filled.

Then, the recession hit, and it changed (not ended) the War for Talent. In today's more cautious business environment, hiring managers will no longer accept anyone with a pulse. They want individuals whose skills and backgrounds precisely match the requirements of their openings and thus can achieve full productively quickly and make a real and sustained contribution to the work that must be accomplished. This shift has opened a new front in the War for Talent, a front where battles will be waged on quality. The winners will be those organizations with the priorities, processes and practices to find, evaluate, select and sell the most capable candidates effectively and efficiently.

What changes must organizations make to shift from recruiting the first capable candidate who is available to recruiting the single candidate who is most qualified for an opening? The following are some suggestions:

- **The acquisition of more detailed insight into the skills, personality and other factors that will define the truly outstanding candidate.** This greater level of specificity about what kinds of new employees are being sought will require (a) more and better information from hiring managers (forcing them, in turn, to be much clearer and more rational in formulating position requirements) and (b) more and better knowledge among recruiters about the specific career fields in which they recruit.

- **Better placement of online recruitment ads.** Job postings must be displayed where the best candidates for a specific requirement congregate online (which is not necessarily the most visible brand among commercial recruitment sites). In fact, identifying those locations will require continuous surveillance of the universe of alternative sites (because they can and do change) and an understanding of how those sites can be compared and evaluated.

- **More detailed job postings.** Unlike print classifieds, recruitment ads on the Internet are seldom constrained by space or time. The average job board permits postings of up to 1,400 words (the equivalent of two typed pages of information) and displays ads for 30-60 days. The resulting durable specificity of employment information signals to job seekers that the organization is looking for a very precise set of skills and experience which, in turn, motivates them to do a better job of self-selection.

- **The acquisition of detailed information about candidates.** Resumes are a start, but only active job seekers have them. Moreover, such factors as a person's work style, cultural preferences, current salary and willingness to relocate do not typically appear on a resume yet are critically important to effective candidate evaluation. Collecting this information takes time, particularly when dealing with passive job seekers, so organizations need to identify prospective candidates and begin the process of getting to know them well in advance of requirements. The longer this data collection activity goes on, the more detailed each candidate's record and the more rigorous the employer's level of pre-screening.

- **The use of online selection screens and assessment instruments.** The resume deluge continues unabated, clogging up the evaluation process and increasing the odds that highly qualified candidates will be overlooked. Online assessment instruments for both skill and behavioral evaluation provide a time and cost-effective way to redress the situation. These tools range from formal tests administered over the Net to questions embedded in an employer's auto-responder. Whatever their format, they enable recruiters to gauge a candidate's ability to per-form specified work tasks and/or their fit with the organization. A word of caution, however. All tools are not equal—some have been appropriately validated, and others have not—and every tool must assess factors that are directly relevant to on-the-job performance.

- **Better training of hiring managers in interviewing skills.** Lou Adler, the principal of PowerHiring, is fond of saying that the average hiring manager is only about 7% better than flipping a coin when it come to picking the best candidate for an opening. (Research shows that hiring managers pick the appropriate candidate about 57% of the time.) Too many hiring managers have never been trained in the skills and laws of interviewing, and thus regularly base their decisions on such irrelevant factors as a candidate's personality, clothing and/or interviewing (rather than job performance) skills. Since selecting the best employees is a fundamental precondition of effective line management, HR must ensure that the acquisition and practice of these skills becomes a standard component of leadership training and performance evaluation.

Although quantitative shortages continue, at least in certain fields and geographies, the next front in the War for Talent will be waged on quality. Victory will go to those organizations that not only keep their seats filled, but fill them with employees whose knowledge, skills, abilities and motivation make them the single best candidate for the job. ■

■ WorkLife Out of Balance

Two new surveys by TrueCareers have found that today's workers feel stressed out and determined to do something about it.

An April, 2002 survey revealed that a startling 70% of the 1,626 respondents do not think they have a healthy balance between their work and personal life. As a result, 51% said they are looking for a new job. Meanwhile, a follow-up survey in May found that 61% of respondents had decided to adopt a different course: they planned to take a vacation during the year despite the less than rosy economic climate. Of the 39% who do not plan to vacation, 68% cited lack of money as the reason. ■

■ Talent and The Tipping Point

Talent has hit the big time. It's the subject of a feature article in *The New Yorker*, a periodical that has published the ideas and arguments of some of America's most gifted thinkers. The piece runs a full six pages and even includes two of those cute, little cartoons for which the magazine is so famous. My friends, it just doesn't get any better than that.

Or does it? You see, the name of the article, which was written by Malcolm Gladwell, is "The Talent Myth" … Are smart people overrated?. In other words, talent is indeed in the spotlight, but unfortunately, the illumination is critical about both the nature and role of talented people. To summarize the author, "In the modern corporation, the system is considered only as strong as its stars, and, in the past few years, this message has been preached by consultants and management gurus all over the world. None, however, have spread the word quite so ardently as McKinsey, and, of all its clients, one firm took the talent-mind-set closest to heart … Enron."

Now, given events of the recent past, connecting talent with Enron is the moral equivalent of affixing a scarlet letter to recruitment. Recruiters, after all, are the finders and collectors of talent, and Mr. Gladwell is saying that the fruits of our labor are moral corruption, economic disaster and hardship for employees and shareholders, alike. Arthur Andersen may have helped to cook the books at Enron, but according to Gladwell, it was talent that provided the recipe. That charge makes you and me and every other recruiting professional unnamed co-conspirators in the process.

But before we accept our badge of shame and walk meekly off into the sunset, let's look at some of the author's analysis. How does he make the leap from assigning blame to the specific individuals who broke the law at Enron to describing Enron as an organization turned bad by smart people? While it is true that some of Enron's "talent" was responsible for the evil done at that firm, is it therefore logical to deduce that all talent at Enron was equally as corrupt? To me, that's like saying that all members of a Little League team are cheats because one of their pitchers lied about his age or all pilots are drunks because two were caught trying to fly while intoxicated.

The problem with such arguments is that they are based on simplistic assumptions about the concept of talent. From Gladwell's perspective, talent is all about people with high I.Q.s. Apparently, he gets that definition from his reading of McKinsey, although I'm hard pressed to find it there. In any case, he then goes on to show how "smart people" at Enron were allowed to ride roughshod over the company's policies and procedures to do whatever they wanted, whenever they felt like it. Such behavior was tolerated, even celebrated, because that's what talented people do; they shake things up. What's Gladwell's solution? A smart organization. He says, "The talent myth assumes that people make organizations smart. More often than not, it's the other way around."

That's a surprising statement from the author of *The Tipping Point*. For those of who you haven't read Gladwell's book, his premise is that much of what happens in the world today is caused by a phenomenon best described as a "social epidemic." As with real contagions, the popularity of new products or movies or music groups builds to a tipping point, at which time it achieves critical mass and becomes a self-sustaining center of momentum that propels formerly little known artists and politicians and athletes to global stardom virtually overnight. There's no organization involved, no set of policies and procedures that make it happen. It's human behavior being transmitted from one person to another.

So, Gladwell got it right, but in his book, not in his piece for *The New Yorker*. To understand what happened at Enron, you must first recognize that all talent is not equal. And second, you must acknowledge that—regardless of the kind of talent you recruit—the kind of behavior that you celebrate in an organization will eventually reach a critical mass and become its norm ... thanks to the tipping point.

- The War for (Any) Talent is over. The War for the Best Talent has begun. And determining the definition of the "best talent" is as hard as recruiting it. While one measure of talent is certainly I.Q., there are many other attributes that can be used to define qualitative distinctions among human beings. Moreover, the specific set of attributes that defines what is the best talent is idiosyncratic to each organization and to the various functions being performed within that organization. Indeed, the selection of what kind of talent an organization should access is one of the key functions of its leaders. They define the skills, characteristics, outlook, style and level of commitment that make up the desired candidate. Or, to put it another way, the problem with Enron was not that it recruited talent, but that, all too often, it recruited the wrong talent for its development as a healthy enterprise.

- Talent must be either self-directed or led. And in most organizations, it's led. The application of talent is directed and rewarded by others, typically called Chief Executive Officers, Chief Operating Officers and their direct reports. Unfortunately, however, the quality of that leadership can and does vary widely. Because leaders are talent too. If they provide strong and principled guidance for talent, the tipping point will enable them to bring the entire population of talent up to those standards. On the other hand, if they permit or encourage behaviors that are counter-productive to the mission or long term health of the organization, then talent—even great talent—will be misled. And the tipping point will transmit that malady throughout the organization. Sadly, according to press accounts and Gladwell's own article, that's exactly what happened in many of Enron's business units.

So, what does Enron really tell us about talent? Simply this: talent is a resource, but unlike energy or money or any other fungible resource, it can be acquired in a vast array of different configurations. It's our job as recruiters, therefore, to help our customers—the hiring managers for which we work—identify the best kind of talent for their requirements and to find and sell that talent on the value proposition of those requirements. It is the job of the organization's leaders to make sure that they provide the environment where that talent can thrive. Yes, the sad story of Enron can be ascribed to talent, but it was a failure of leadership talent—not the inherent maleficence of smart people—that was the culprit. ■

■ A Fairy Tale War or A Conflict for Survival?

The War for Talent was a figment of the imagination. That's right. It never existed. Near unanimity among pundits and an incessant drum-beat of media hype can't change the facts. The War for Talent—at least as it came to be popularly depicted—was a fairy tale.

Does that mean there was no labor shortage in the late 1990's? Of course not. The workforce shrank just as the dot.com bubble drove demand to historic peaks. The resulting mismatch created a real and serious conflict among employers. But this conflict was not the War for Talent we read and heard so much about. The descriptions of that war gave it the appearance of a single, homogenous event. Its characteristics were unchanging. Its essence fixed. There was a fight over talent, and it had the look and feel of mayonnaise.

Wars, however, don't unfold that way. Typically, they are fought in theatres that have their own unique circumstances. For example, the global conflict we call World War II was actually two very different, but simultaneous wars: one in Europe and the other in Asia and the Pacific. Moreover, the strategy, tactics and resources necessary to prevail on the plains of France and Germany bore absolutely no resemblance to those required for victory on the islands of the South Pacific.

The War for Talent is also a two-theatre conflict, but its constituent wars have unfolded sequentially rather than in parallel. I call the first theatre the War for Any Talent. It ran from 1996 to 2000 and was characterized by huge quantitative shortfalls in workers. The dot.com bubble created so much demand for talent that recruiters found themselves juggling 30 or 40 or 50 open requisitions at one time. While they made every effort to find and recruit top candidates, victory quickly came to be defined as getting round pegs into round holes. There simply wasn't the time or the staff resources to do any better than that.

Then, the recession hit, and some declared the War for Talent over. Sadly, however, the conflict didn't end; it morphed. Even as our recruitment Web-sites and e-mailboxes overflowed with resumes, shortages of specific kinds of talent grew more severe. As a consequence, the War for Any Talent was replaced with a new conflict that I call the War for the Best Talent. It will be the defining challenge of our profession for the coming decade or more. Why? Because in a slow growth economy—and most economists now see that scenario as the most likely—an organization's performance will turn on its ability to recruit and retain critical skills and capability. In essence, the key to victory is now the quality rather than the quantity of your employer's talent.

Quality talent, however, actually encompasses two distinct cohorts of the workforce. Although they overlap in part, they cannot be addressed as a single or uni-dimensional problem.

- The first cohort includes "A" level performers, the people who make the greatest individual contribution to corporate success. The organization that captures and retains a preponderant share of these All Stars will have a huge competitive advantage. As McKinsey & Company pointed out in their seminal work, *The War for Talent*, "A" level performers are 50-100% more productive than "C" level performers, regardless of the measure of effectiveness used.

Hence, recruiters must re-configure their strategies, tactics and resource investments to give them an edge in finding, contacting, communicating with and selling these normally passive, heavily protected (by their current employers) key players.

- The second cohort includes workers with rare skills. For example, the Information Technology Association of America (ITAA) predicts that half of the 1.1 million new IT jobs likely to be created between mid-2002 and mid-2003 will go unfilled, not because there aren't IT candidates around, but because those candidates don't have the skill sets that employers need. Similarly, a National Association of Manufacturers survey found high percentages of employers experiencing "serious shortages" in a number of other occupational fields.

Skill	Employers with "serious shortages"
Entry level production workers	16.3
Machinists	41.2
Technicians/electricians	33.9
Engineers	20.0
Scientists/R&D workers	13.6
Sales & marketing professionals	9.3

Here again, recruiters will have to change. The strategies, tactics and resource investments that worked in the War for Any Talent will simply not get the job done when it comes to recruiting those with scarce skills.

Now, it is a fair question to ask if all of this explication of the War for Talent is simply a matter of semantics or revisionist history. I don't think so. In fact, I'm convinced that understanding the real and important distinctions in the so-called War for Talent is the only way you and I can protect our own individual security and that of our employer in the months and years ahead. ■

■ The War for the Best Talent

Quantity of applicants may no longer be a problem, but attracting and recruiting quality candidates is still a huge corporate challenge. That was the key finding in a Conference Board survey of 109 corporate executives. Of the respondents, 90% said they were still struggling to get top prospects to hire on. According to Watson Wyatt, the situation is especially acute among sales people, where it's still a war for the best talent. ■

■ What Job Seekers Want

The latest results of WEDDLE's ongoing survey of job seekers (now entering its seventh year), reveal some important shifts and reinforce some long standing trends from earlier polls. Based on data collected in 2002, these new findings provide both a current profile of what individuals want from their online job search experience and a framework for turning those preferences into a competitive advantage in the labor market.

According to poll respondents, the Web is now as much an integral component of job search for seasoned workers as it is for recent entrants into the workforce. Over half (51%) of all respondents had more than 10 years experience in the workplace, and an astonishing 23% had 21 or more years on-the-job. Interestingly, just 15% said they had 0-2 years working experience, belying the conventional wisdom that the Internet is best suited for recruiting entry level and junior workers. This finding has important implications for the design and use of recruitment Web-sites.

■ To optimize your return on investment in these destinations, they should now be designed both to answer the kinds of questions normally posed by more senior and experienced workers as well as those just starting out on their careers and to advertise job openings of interest to them.

Similarly, the survey also found a shift in the career fields reported by respondents. While IT workers were still the largest single cohort, they represented fewer than one in five (19%) online job seekers. Indeed, the second largest group of responses (16%) was from those who described themselves as "Other," and specified their fields as management consulting, geology, social work, aircraft maintenance, transportation, nursing, bill collection, attorney and electrician, to name just a few.

What does that mean for recruiters?

■ Once again, it suggests that we should design our recruitment Web-sites for a wide range of visitors. These destinations now attract virtually every category of job seeker (from hourly workers and tradespeople to professionals and executives), and the most effective sites will provide the tailored content necessary to recruit the best prospects in all of the fields for which an organization recruits.

No less important, this finding points to the growing role of niche sites in Web recruiting. Some (perhaps most) of these "specialized" job seekers will not feel comfortable at large, general purpose recruitment sites (e.g., Monster.com, Career Builder.com), preferring instead to spend their time at sites designed specifically for them. That reality will necessitate a change in recruiter behavior.

■ To date, many of us have posted jobs online just as we have traditionally placed classified ads in newspapers. We advertise in a single or very limited number of publications, and we post on a single or very limited number of sites. However, while we don't have much choice in print, we have a lot of choice online. WEDDLE's estimates that there are 40,000 employment-related sites currently operating on the Internet, and the vast majority are specialty sites. To be successful in

Web recruiting, therefore, we must now be expert at finding and evaluating these niche destinations.

This survey also revealed that job seekers are using an ever-wider array of online strategies for finding a job:

- 24% are now using resume distribution services versus just 12% that did so nine months ago. While acquiring resumes is not a problem right now, it will become so again when the economy strengthens. Given the rise in popularity of the distribution services and the fact that they are typically free to recruiters, we suggest that you tap these sources, but use only those that permit you to specify the kinds of candidates you want, and send you only resumes that match.

- 43% are using commercial research sites (e.g., Hoovers Online, Vault.com) to acquire information about prospective employers. Therefore, make sure that you know what these sites are saying about your employer, and:
    - if it's correct, be consistent with that information on your Web-site; and
    - if it's wrong, get it changed.

- 56% are researching salary online. As a result, candidates are likely to be more aggressive in negotiations (particularly as the economy strengthens and demand for labor grows). To succeed in these negotiations, we must be prepared to explain any differences between publicized market rates and salary levels offered by our employers.

- 74% visit our employers' sites, first to conduct research and second to look at the job postings. To put this prospective candidate flow to best use, design your site to be an "electronic sales brochure," complete with information about your employer's culture, achievements, benefits program and other distinctive advantages as well as features that tend to enhance the visitor experience (e.g., employee testimonials and e-mail Q&A). ■

(Source: WEDDLE's, 2002)

■ **Your Organization's Employment Brand**
What Is It? How Can You Use It Effectively on the Internet?

■ Your Employment Brand

It's often said that an organization's employment brand is an essential component of its recruitment success online. Seldom, however, is there any explanation of why that is so and what you can do to put your brand to work for you. I'd like to fill those voids.

Why is brand important? An organization's employment brand—its reputation or image among passive as well as active job seekers—is established in both the real world and online. It is determined by employment policies and programs, leadership and by the experience people have when they interact with the organization's recruitment process.

As with commercial organizations, an employer or staffing firm without a strong brand among prospective "customers" has to work harder than the competition to connect with and sell them. Basically, the organization starts the recruitment process from a dead stop and thus typically takes longer and spends more to fill an open position.

Organizations with a negative brand, on the other hand, also have to work harder to connect with and sell candidates, but all that effort may well ... indeed, is likely to be for naught. They start the recruitment process two steps behind everyone else and simply may not be able to make up the disadvantage.

Organizations with a strong, positive brand, in contrast, can use their reputation as a magnet to attract job seekers and sell them on their employment opportunities. They start the recruitment process several steps ahead of everyone else, and thus recruit faster, cheaper and better (in terms of candidate quality) than their competitors.

How can the Web help power up your brand? According to Nielsen/NetRatings, the average Web user in January 2002 (among the 67.4 million people online) visited 5 sites per week and spent over 30 minutes on each site. Assuming your site is well promoted, it will see some of those visitors and thus give you a half an hour or so to build a strong and positive image for your organization. What should you do? I suggest the following:

- Make your site's careers/job posting area VERY visible on your home page. That visibility underscores the importance your organization attaches to recruitment and makes it easier for potential candidates to do their research. The average visitor spends just 56 seconds on a page, so don't make them hunt for the link to your employment opportunities. In most cases, they won't.

- Also make it easy for those visitors to return to your careers/job posting area by creating a mnemonic Web address for it. Most sites today lack this simple device for building traffic. I suggest you use either of the following because they are what most visitors expect:

    - www.yourcompany.com/**employment**

- www.yourcompany.com/**careers**

On the other hand, I urge you to avoid both of the following addresses because they are not likely to be intuitively obvious to your visitors:

- www.yourcompany.com/**about**

- www.yourcompany.com/**HR**

■ Make sure that you do more than just talk about your brand attributes. Illustrate and reinforce them with the images on your site (i.e., the graphics and pictures). Similarly, avoid the following common mistakes:

Attribute: We offer you the chance to do exciting, interesting and challenging work.

Site image: Pictures of office buildings (even if they're very cool looking).

What's better? Mini testimonials by real employees who are pictured at work. Change the articles every 3-6 months to keep them fresh for return visitors.

Attribute: We value diversity

Site image: Pictures of young white males.

What's better? Pictures of real work groups that are identified as such and illustrate the age, gender and ethnic diversity of your organization.

Attribute: We offer a nonhierarchical culture

Site image: Pictures of the CEO and other corporate executives (even if they're smiling and saying nice things).

What's better? Pictures of project meetings and inhabited workspaces to show how people work together. ■

■ What Does 9/11 Mean For Recruiters?

I would not presume to add my voice to those who have addressed the spiritual and emotional impacts that 9/11 has had on the United States and its people. These are important issues that deserve our attention. So too, however, are the workaday lessons that we can and must draw from this horrible event. For only by understanding the influence 9/11 has had on the work we do, can we ensure our continued individual success and collective prosperity

There have been numerous surveys probing the changes in American workplace values and priorities as a result of 9/11. Among their findings:

- 73% of Americans say that helping others is more important to them now than it was prior to 9/11; 67% say that serving their country is also more important after that day.
  (American Demographics/TeleNation Market Facts).

- 70% of American workers now say that tending to their families is their most important daily activity, up from 54% in 2000.
  (Randstadt North America).

Even as workers' views shift, however, so do their circumstances. For example:

- U.S. workers recently passed the Japanese in the number of hours worked per week.

- According to the Society for Human Resource Management (SHRM), mothers with preschoolers make up the fastest growing cohort of the workforce.

- A growing number of Baby Boomers—representing the largest single cohort in the workforce—are now dealing with aging parents and the prospect of not being able to retire until they are well past traditional retirement age.

- According to the U.S. Census, the number of Americans living alone surpassed the number of married couples for the first time in U.S. history in the 2002 census.

What do these shifting currents mean for those of us charged with recruiting talent for our organizations?

- First, we need to incorporate these changes in attitudes and circumstances into how we structure our organization's value proposition (or brand) as an employer. For example, one of the key issues for many workers living alone is benefits parity with workers who have children. Therefore, review the design of your benefits program and make sure that it is not—intentionally or unintentionally—biased toward any one particular group.

  Other issues that you may want to review include:

  - The opportunities provided to employees for community and other volunteer work;

  - Your employer's support for employees who serve in the National Guard and Reserve;

- Your employer's policies on telecommuting and other work-at-home options; and
- The level of support the organization provides for child care and elder care.

Obviously implementing or strengthening such programs costs money, and that means you will have to make the "business case" for doing so. However, their impact on the caliber of candidate you can recruit and on the retention of such high performers once hired is real and measurable ... and very important, even in a difficult economy.

■ Second, once we have reinforced our employment programs to address the shifts in worker attitudes post 9/11, we must then promote those advantages in our recruitment advertising. For example, the presentation of benefits and related information on your recruitment Web-site should be revised to emphasis these points. You might also set up specific areas on the site for different cohorts of the workforce and then tailor the content in those areas to each group's unique issues. Similarly, revise the information presented in job postings to empha-size these same topics, again tailoring the information you present to the issues of most import to your target candidate demographic.

What's key is that your response to their concerns becomes an integral component of the value proposition your organization presents as an employer, because that value proposition is your employment brand in their eyes. ■

■ Listening In

Job seekers are routinely advised to do research before interviewing with prospective employers. But what about recruiters? Shouldn't we know what others are saying about our employer before something comes up in an interview? Sure we should, but how can we do that? How can we get a feel for what our employer's brand is really like among prospective employees?

One way to conduct this research is to read the messages posted at the following sites:

- www.boardreader.com
- www.vault.com (its electronic watercolor)

The opinions expressed on these sites are by no means a perfect sample (either in size or in the range of views presented), but you may well learn something you didn't know about what candi-dates and others are saying about your organization as an employer. And that's important—to be forewarned is to be forearmed. ■

■ The 3 Dimensions of Diversity Recruiting

Although the "digital divide" remains a nagging problem, the online pool of diversity talent is expanding at an impressive rate. For example, according to an August 2001 Nielsen/Net Ratings survey, Internet usage among African-Americans increased by 19% over the prior year. That's five percentage points faster than the rate of growth among the overall population and means that there are now almost 8.2 million African-Americans using the Internet. In addition, the time African-Americans spend online is also increasing faster (22% year-over-year) than among the population at large (12% year-over-year).

How can online recruiters tap into this trend to enhance their diversity recruiting? I suggest that you implement a 3-dimensional online strategy that will:

■ Place your employment opportunities where your target diversity candidates are most likely to see them on the Internet;

■ Build your organization's reputation or brand among diversity populations; and

■ Create a positive, distinctive experience for the diversity candidates who interact with your organization.

Let's take a look at each of these components in more detail.

Advertise at the Right Sites

While diversity candidates do, in fact, visit all kinds of recruitment sites, from Monster.com to techies.com, they tend to spend considerable time on sites that focus on either their unique affinity (e.g., African-American, Hispanic-American, women) or diversity in general. Hence, recruiters seeking to post jobs and/or search resume databases for diversity candidates should

(a) identify the alternatives among sites that specialize in their target diversity cohort

and

(b) evaluate those alternatives to determine which are likely to provide their optimum return on investment.

Where can you find alternative diversity sites? Collectively, there are probably over a hundred now in operation. More than a dozen are normally profiled in WEDDLE's annual *Recruiter's Guide to Employment Web Sites*, and all of the sites our research team has identified are listed in our annual *Directory of Employment-Related Internet Sites*.

Given this wide range of options, it's important to distinguish between the good sites and the mediocre. How can you do that? Compare one site to another, using the following factors:

■ Traffic, reported in unique visitors per month;

■ Visitor Attention Span (page views per month divided by unique visitors per month) which indicates how long visitors stay on a site;

- Price to post a job or to search the resume database;
- Candidate Density (unique visitors per month divided by jobs posted per month) which measures the competition your posting will face from other postings on the site;
- The number of resumes in the site's database and their source;
- Top occupations among the resumes archived in the database; and
- Whether or not the site offers a job agent service for job seekers (sites that provide this service tend to attract a higher proportion of passive job seekers as it enables them to protect their confidentiality).

Build Your Employer's Reputation Online

Posting jobs and searching for resumes at the right sites will help you source top quality diversity candidates, but it will not ensure that you can recruit them. To do that, your organization must build a credible reputation as an organization that is truly committed to providing genuine career opportunities for women, persons of color and other diversity cohorts.

What steps can you take online to establish such a "diversity friendly" brand? Consider the following:

- Ensure that all of the images on your organization's recruitment Web-site—the photos of employees and views of occupied offices—reflect the true diversity of your workforce.
- Include an explicit statement about your organization's commitment to diversity on the site's home page.
- Add a similar statement about your organization's diversity commitment to every job posting on your site and include the statement in the auto-responder message you send back to all applicants.
- Encourage employee participation in newsgroups and listservs dealing with diversity topics.
- Sponsor popular content areas on selected diversity sites that cater to your target diversity demographic(s).
- Sponsor content areas and/or advertise on sites operated by the alumni organizations of historically black colleges and universities and fraternities and sororities.
- Encourage employee participation in the forums and other activities appearing on the sites of such organizations as La Raza, 100 Black Men, 100 Black Women and Big Brother/Big Sister.

Create a Distinctive and Compelling Candidate Experience

The better the candidate's experience during the recruiting process, the more likely they are to accept an offer when one is made and tell others about the (positive) way they were treated by the organization. The quality of their experience, in turn, depends upon the nature of their interactions and communications with representatives of the organization as well as the perceived usefulness of the information that is provided. In most cases, the more generic or standardized the interactions, communications and information are, the less effective they will be. Or to put it another way, the best diversity candidates want an experience that is tailored to their unique issues and concerns.

How do you create such a tailored experience? Try some of the following ideas:

- Establish a special area on your recruitment Web-site that is devoted to diversity candidates.

- Provide employee testimonials in that area that describe both the nature of the work each person has done and the challenges and opportunities they've encountered within the organization.

- Offer a "Friends" program that enables diversity candidates to submit a confidential profile and be matched with a current employee who will answer their questions and provide a "peer's" view of the organization.

- Train hiring managers and recruiters to be culturally sensitive in their interviews and other interactions with candidates.

- Get started early. Identify prospective diversity candidates during their first years of college or, for a mid-career professional, well before you have an appropriate opening. Then, use the intervening period to build a relationship with them so you can nurture their respect, interest and trust. ■

■ Make Ethics a Differentiator

Surveys show that the recent litany of corporate and executive misdeeds has pushed the subject of ethics way up on the evaluation scales of job seekers. That's especially true among the best and brightest in the workforce. The last thing an "A' level performer wants is to have their career derailed by some scandal that arrives like a bolt out of the blue and puts them out on the street looking for a job.

How should you respond to this situation? Treat the ethical concerns of the candidate population as an opportunity to differentiate your employer. That presumes, of course, that your employer—both the organization and the individuals, at all levels, who work for it—strictly adheres to ethical business practices. Assuming that's so, then the organization's commitment to such standards should now become a central part of its advertising.

Job postings. The best job postings begin with a 4-sentence summary of the position's value proposition. An integral element of this summary is a powerful, compelling statement about why the organization is a dream employer. "A" level performers care as much about the organization as they do about the job; they know that a key ingredient in their success has been and will continue to be their ability to pick and work for winners. Play to this bias by including a reference to your organization's ethics commitment in this lead-in statement and then describe it in detail in the body of the posting.

What kind of "evidence" should you offer to differentiate your organization's ethical stance? CareerJournal.com from *The Wall Street Journal* counsels job seekers to ask the following questions, so answering them in your advertising will help your organization stand out:

- Is there a formal code of ethics in the organization?

- Are workers at all levels trained in ethical decision-making?

- Do employees have formal channels available to make any concerns known privately?

- Is misconduct punished swiftly?

- Is integrity emphasized to new employees?

Recruitment Web-site. Of course, the other advertising area that should spotlight the organization's commitment to ethics is its Web-site. Here, the information that you provide can be more extensive than that which can be included in a job posting. Even more important, the site gives you the space to provide more proof. For example, while a statement from the CEO might be helpful, it's likely, particularly in today's climate, that employee testimonials will be more effective. If you think the organization can measure up, you might even want to include a Q&A hotline so prospects can speak with real employees for an "inside" opinion on the organization's ethics.

Obviously, ethics is not a matter of smoke and mirrors. But if your employer is truly an ethical organization, that's one of its key strengths. And when recruiting top talent, the trick is always to lead with your strengths. ■

■ **Your Organization's Employment Brand**
What Is It? How Can You Use It Effectively on the Internet?

■ The Big Impact of Small Differences

For the last thirty or forty years, recruiting has been based on a single, largely unspoken premise. I call it the Rule of Round Pegs. Basically, this rule posited that all round pegs were the same. In other words, for any given opening, it was the recruiter's job to weed out the square pegs and find a round peg who could do the job. Yes, of course, there was some effort to distinguish among all the round pegs out there—recruiters, after all, take a great deal of pride in the work they do. But the realities of inadequate staff levels, tight budgets and insufficient technology resources coupled with the indifferent participation of hiring managers virtually ensured that differences would be minimized ... until subsequent performance on-the-job made those differences more real and important.

This premise led to a form of mass production recruiting. Its goal was to hire lots of people as quickly and as cheaply as possible. The underlying rationale, of course, was that the longer vacancies remained unfilled, the more they hurt the organization in terms of efficiency, morale and quality of performance. But since all candidates (who fit the bill for a given position) were perceived to be the identical, most organizations set up their recruiting processes to meet production quotas while avoiding the expense and delays inherent in detailed candidate differentiation. Investments that would upgrade the ability of the process to optimize selection weren't even contemplated (except for hiring at the executive level). In effect, it was mass production circa the pre-quality improvement era.

Even when demographic trends made round pegs harder to find, most organizations continued to recruit with this mass production mentality. All the War for Talent did was raise the concept of round-peg recruiting to the Board room level. And yet, the most important message of the oft-cited McKinsey & Company report on the War for Talent was just how important the differences among people are. Indeed, the report actually calculated the monetary impact of hiring an "A" level candidate rather than an average performer. Based on surveys among employers in the sales, manufacturing and service sectors, it found that superior employees actually deliver a 50-100% advantage in terms of revenue, quality and/or productivity.

Why, then, do we persist in this out-dated approach to recruiting? Perhaps, it's the difficulty involved in changing old habits. Perhaps it's driven by the limited resources available in a slowing economy. More likely than not, however, I think it's because we haven't had another process to consider. There's been no alternative to the Rule of Round Pegs. So, at the risk of appearing presumptuous, let me propose another way to organize recruiting. I base this new approach on a principle that I call The Law of Small Differences.

This Law is based on the research being conducted by the Human Genome project. As you may know, that effort seeks to map every contour of human genetics, to identify and codify the fundamental biological and chemical elements that give each of us our individuality and make all of us different from one another. Interestingly, the project has already yielded a startling and very important finding: the real differences between one person and another amount to less than 0.0003%

of their physical and physiological makeup. That's right. Despite all of the superficial and other distinctions that we perceive between and among people, they are much more alike than they are different.

What does that finding mean for recruiting? I think it suggests that we must fundamentally re-engineer our recruiting process. The value of that process is not the speed or cost with which holes are filled, it is the nature of the people selected to fill them. In other words, the value of recruiting is determined by its ability to measure small differences, because those tiny variations are, in fact, what determine a person's contribution (or lack thereof) to their employer. Hence, sourcing is the process of identifying and contacting prospective candidates, and recruiting is the process of identifying and evaluating the differences among them. While speed and cost control are certainly important in those activities, it is the distinctions discovered among round pegs that provide the organization with the greatest advantage. In essence, recruiting moves from a mass production model to one designed for mass customization.

Historically, mass customization has been prohibitively expensive and difficult to implement. It requires both the instant acquisition of information about the key attributes of an individual and the use of that information to tailor subsequent interactions with the person. The advent of the Internet, however, and the development of powerful database management systems has now made mass customization a reality. And those organizations that have adopted the model have achieved significant bottom line benefits. WalMart, for example, has designed its inventory management system around the mass customization model. It knows exactly what products its customers are buying in each of its stores, and it tailors its replenishment strategy for each individual store with that information. As a result, this global company has more of what its local customers want to buy so they do, and that yields higher sales and profits for WalMart.

How can we build a similar process for recruiting?

- First, we must identify the small differences among candidates. We can now acquire this information cost-effectively by using automated screens, either as stand-alone assessments or in an auto-responder. These screens should be designed to build a three-dimensional portrait of each candidate that details their level of competency in required skill fields, their work preferences (e.g., the kind of environment and structure in which they are most comfortable), and their motivation. This portrait can then be archived and automatically updated with information acquired via subsequent interactions with the individual.

- Second, we must use the small differences to pre-sell candidates. We can now tailor our recruiting message to what we have learned about each candidate in their profiles, and we can communicate that message rapidly, continuously and cost-effectively using the Internet. We know what is important to each candidate and where they are likely to be most successful. Even more important, we can identify, with a much higher level of confidence than ever before, who is most likely to make the greatest contribution to our organization and devise a special program to communicate with and sell them.

This mass customization model clearly involves an investment of time, money and effort. So did WalMart's inventory management system, however. It proved that understanding the small differences among customers can make a big difference at the bottom line. And the same can be true with recruitment. ■

■ Three Strikes and You're Out

Talk to recruiters today and almost every conversation works its way around to a single issue: the deluge of resumes pouring into corporate mailrooms and e-mail boxes. According to the U.S. Bureau of Labor Statistics, about 16% of the American workforce is actively looking for a job, and most organizations feel as if all 16% are sending them a resume.

This situation undoubtedly creates a number of management and administrative challenges, but should it be viewed as a problem? Clearly, that's the status it's given in most organizations. You'll hear it referred to as the "resume tsunami" or "resume overload" or simply, "a nightmare." And yet, these resumes—for better or worse—are the *lingua franca* of our profession. They are the way candidates communicate skills and experience to us for evaluation. To see that effort to convey information to us as a problem, therefore, seems ... well, downright illogical. So where does such a view come from? I think it's based on three erroneous assumptions. Buy into those assumptions, and your organization has three strikes against it in the acquisition and management of talent.

The Assumptions

1. You'll never need these resumes in the future. Implicit in the grousing about the torrent of resumes is that they are an administrative burden that produces no value for the organization. They cascade into processes not designed to handle such a load (that, too, is a problem, but a different one), and that overflow slows down your ability to fill positions you have open right now. Moreover, many of the resumes you receive in this torrent are sent by persons clearly not qualified for your openings, making it even harder to find the candidates you want to evaluate. At the bottom line, the resume stream makes more work for you today and does nothing for you tomorrow.

Clearly "graffiti resumes" can be a pain, although we sometimes have ourselves to blame for at least some of the junk flow. After all, given a minimum of information about an open job's requirements—and that's what too many job postings provide—most active job seekers will play the odds and apply for any opening that seems even remotely connected to their background and skills.

Further, the fact that our processes for inputting and storing resumes are still rudimentary, at best, doesn't mean that the flow, itself, is bad. It simply means that we aren't equipped to handle these communications from prospective candidates. And if we were, wouldn't this excess of riches be something that could help us down the road? After all, every resume that we receive today (assuming that we process it accurately and then can find it in our resume database when we need it) is one less resume we have to look for out on the Web or in the classified ads in the future.

2. The cost of dealing with resumes now is greater than the cost of looking for them later. As with the first assumption, this view is more a function of resume processing inefficiency than it is a statement about the effectiveness of data mining online. Although resumes can be and are found by sourcing activities on the Internet, most recruiters today are still using manual techniques that are, themselves, very time consuming. Indeed, in our surveys of recruiters who use Boolean searches, flipping and x-raying to uncover resumes, over half spend 15 or more hours on the Web and 32% spend 20 or more hours online. (WEDDLE's, 2001)

Another place to look, of course, is online resume databases, but they can also take up time and effort. First, you have to locate the specific databases with the best prospects of meeting your needs—and with tens of thousands of databases available, that's hardly a trivial challenge—and then you have to familiarize yourself with the specific functions of the search engine used by the databases you select (all of which are completely different).

Finally, these searches are by no means always successful. Hence, you and your organization are making a considerable investment in time and money and, more often than not, achieving a modest return. Wouldn't it be better—at least as a first step—to conduct a low cost search of your own resume database to see if you can find the candidates that you need? That's standard practice, of course, for many organizations, yet they do not process every resume they receive (seeing those not applicable to today's openings as a waste of time), nor do they quality assure the output of that administrative process or train their recruiters to be expert searchers of their own internal databases.

3. There's nothing to be done with resumes right now because the organization is not hiring. These days, many organizations receive a constant flow of resumes even when they have no openings posted on their sites or advertised in the newspaper. With recruiting staffs downsized and budgets reduced, however, processing all of those digital and paper documents is a monumental task. And besides, they're just going to sit there until hiring picks up again, anyway, so—you ask yourself—why bother?

It's a commonly held view and not without merit, but it can also cause your organization to miss a huge opportunity. With requirements dramatically reduced, **now** is the time to invest in upgrading your database so that it's even more helpful to you when recruiting picks up.

How do you do that? By designing and implementing an internal marketing program that:

(a) pre-sells the individuals behind the resumes on your organization as an "employer of choice"

and

(b) builds relationships with them so that they will provide additional information about themselves. The former will increase your ratio of acceptances to offers, while the latter will help you to find the single best candidate with the tightest person-job fit, thus promoting better on-the-job performance and higher retention rates.

So, the next time you're hanging out with a bunch of recruiters and the conversation turns to what a pain in the neck all those resumes are, simply smile in agreement. Then, do everything you can to make sure your organization avoids the three strikes of resume collection and, instead, hits a home run. ∎

■ Pre-cruitment
The Strategic Advantage of Being Prepared

If you've been in the recruiting profession any time at all, you know that, all too often, recruiters are expected to be magicians. Hiring Managers wait around until their open positions become "mission critical" and then expect recruiters to pull top quality applicants out of the proverbial hat. When fortune smiles, you look like a hero; but far too frequently, reality occurs, and you end up getting branded as a lazy, no-account, overhead draining loser. And that can ruin even an optimist's day.

How can we avoid being set up for this kind of situation? Get ourselves out of the retro orientation of recruitment and into the proactive perspective of pre-cruitment. Here's what I mean: Traditionally, recruiters have been forced to work with a process that is reactive, inefficient, frantic, frustrating and downright ineffective or RIFFI. Other than those problems, it works just fine.

First, there is no recruiting until a requirement arrives—that's not "just-in-time recruiting," it's like yelling "iceberg" after the Titanic has already had its brush with destiny. Second and because of that reactive approach to demand forecasting, recruiters are forced to rely on the most expensive forms of sourcing—print advertising and search firms. Third, once candidates are identified, the assessment and selection process is rushed, forcing decisions to be made with a minimum of data on both the organization's and the prospects' parts. And forth, in such an overheated environment, the offer all too often goes to "the best available" candidate at that moment, rather than the individual who is the best for the job.

Unfortunately, the Internet doesn't solve these problems. Indeed, all it does is speed up their negative consequences. It's like putting RIFFI on steroids.

So, what's our alternative? Pre-cruitment. It re-imagines recruitment to address the retro orientation head-on. Its product is the radically different process that emerges from two key changes:

- A new focus
- A shift in priority.

Each of these changes corrects one of the key fallacies contributing to the no-win situation in which we find ourselves. Let's look at the changes and the new process they produce in more detail.

A new focus. This change corrects the fallacy of searching for low hanging fruit. To date, much of Internet recruiting—whether it's job posting or resume acquisition—has implicitly focused on active candidates. They are easy to reach because, unlike passive job seekers, they have a resume and the motivation to apply for openings posted online. If you have any doubt about that, check your e-mail box: 99.9% of those messages are from active job seekers. Their omnipresence means that any recruiter and all recruiters can source them. Hence, it's finding the passive job seeker that separates the winners from the also-rans on the Web.

The irony is that there are almost three times as many passive as active prospects in the job mar-ket. According to the U.S. Bureau of Labor Statistics, approximately 16% of the workforce is actively looking for a new job at any point in time, while a recent Towers Perrin survey found that 44% of the workforce is currently employed but willing to look at other opportunities—the classical definition of a passive job seeker. Hence, pre-cruitment focuses on finding that latter cohort—the top prospects in various career fields who aren't actively looking for a job—because they are a bigger target at which to aim and everyone else is aiming somewhere else.

A shift in priority. This change corrects the fallacy of assuming consistent job seeker behavior. In most cases, today's job postings, resume search strategies and recruitment Web-site designs are based on the simplistic notion that passive job seekers will act just like their active counter-parts. They will

(a) apply for a job even when there is little information provided about the opportunity (the typical "job posting as classified ad");

(b) store their resume in public databases for strangers to review and send their resume out to strangers online; and

(c) apply for employment via corporate Web-sites that do little to sell them on the organization's value proposition or to build a relationship with them.

This approach is all about sourcing. The priority is on quickly connecting with candidates and doing a deal. While that may work with active job seekers, it has no traction at all with the pas-sive population and especially with "A" level performers. They expect a different kind of experi-ence, an experience in which they are wooed. Wooing, however, takes time, because basically, it is relationship-building. Hence, pre-cruitment re-sets the priorities of the process so that recruiters spend less time looking for candidates who are available online (sourcing) and more time getting to know the best and brightest they find there (recruiting).

A different process. This new focus and shift in priorities creates a process designed to identify, contact, communicate with and ultimately sell top quality candidates before they are needed. It involves the follow activities:

- *Demand forecasting*: using historic and business plan-based forecasts to identify likely recruiting requirements by skill, skill level and location 12-24 months out;

- *Top talent targeting*: using data gathered from Hiring Managers, recruiter e-networking, employee referrals and external database mining to identify the best prospects for those forecasted positions;

- *e-Marketing*: using e-mail communications with these prospects, on the Web and eventually in your talent database, to:
  (a) build familiarity and trust with them,
  (b) acquire career information from them, and
  (c) sell them on your employer;

- *Person-job fit analysis*: using the data acquired from prospects and detailed job specifications (e.g., skill, experience, team culture, management style) acquired from Hiring Managers and HR surveys to identify the best prospects for a forecasted requirement turned current opening;

- *e-Assessment and selection*: using Web-based assessment instruments and structured inter-views with Hiring Managers (rather than their normal "whatever comes to mind" approach) to find the single best candidate for the position;

- *e-Selling*: using e-mail to influence this candidate before and after they say "Yes"
  (a) to ensure that they actually say it and
  (b) that they show up for their first day on-the-job. ■

■ The Supply Chain Fallacy

The recent arrival of Peoplesoft, SAP, Siebel Systems and other big enterprise resource planning (ERP) vendors in the recruiting area of Human Resource management has a lot of recruiters and their managers talking about something called "e-procurement." This concept has been defined as "the purchasing of talent through a systematized, supply chain management style provided on-line." It's an idea that only logisticians and logistics engineers could love.

Reduced to its simplest terms, e-procurement equates the management of talent to the distribution of cogs in a well oiled process. You can rack 'em up and run 'em through if you've got your process optimized for efficiency. There's just one little problem with this view of the world. Humans aren't cogs ... they are cognitive beings. They don't do as they're told (in most cases), but rather, make up their own minds about such things as where to submit their resumes, and which employment offers to consider. In other words, you can have the most efficient supply chain on the planet, but if you use it to try and manipulate people the way you move car bumpers and screws around, you're likely to find yourself managing vapor, as your candidates (the supply) rush off to other employers.

Now, don't get me wrong; I'm as much in favor of well designed and implemented recruiting processes as the next person. Recruiters really do deserve to work in an environment that is free of the three "Ds" of recruiting process dysfunction:

- Duplication—in which two or more recruiters perform the exact same task (e.g., call the same candidate about an open position), thereby reducing their combined productivity by 50%;

- Dumb-work—the requirement to perform a task (e.g., having each recruiter report the number of daily e-mails made to prospective candidates) that makes no meaningful contribution to the recruiting mission; and

- Disconnects—which interrupt the timely and accurate flow of information (e.g., a candidate's interview answers regarding their willingness to relocate) from one actor in the process to another, thereby adding delays and increasing the likelihood of misinformed decisions.

Far too many recruiting processes have these and a host of other problems today and introducing technology—whether its an ERP system or an application service provider (ASP) product—will not repair them. The processes, themselves, must first be redesigned to optimize recruiter performance, and then technology can be applied to those tasks in the re-engineered process where technology can best make a contribution. The key is to ask the technology to do what it does best (e.g., crunch large piles of data, make instantaneous connections between recruiters and hiring managers) so that recruiters can do what they do best (e.g., make fine-grained distinctions among candidates and sell them on the value proposition of the openings they have to fill).

It's a very big stretch, however, to go from the design and implementation of efficient recruiting processes to managing candidates as cogs in a supply chain. Consider the following:

- Once car bumpers are input into a supply chain, no other activity is required to ensure their readiness and/or ability to do the job. Their role in the supply is static and externally controlled; they remain where they are placed, at least until the decision is made to use them. Then, all you have to do is get them to the right manufacturing facility at the right time and they will dutifully let themselves be attached to the car body chosen for them. Cogs are great that way.

- People, on the other hand, come and go at will. (Indeed, they are employed at will.) Therefore, their role in the supply is dynamic and self controlled. They are not a supply, at least a supply you can count on ... unless you do something to reinforce their commitment to remain accessible for your staffing needs. That's the problem with people: they expect to be treated like rational, thinking beings. They want relationships, not transactions.

So, the whole idea of a supply chain in recruiting is misguided. It's an analogy (from logistics) that does not apply to human resources management ... which is probably why the proponents of the idea are fond of calling our field Human Capital Management (HCM). That term implies that people—like all good capital resources—can be engineered into efficient behavior. Oh, yeah? Try telling that to the best candidate supply in the talent market: all those "A" level performers who are very happily employed right where they are, thank you very much. They're the candidates you really want to recruit, and you can bet that they will expect an experience from your talent process that is more engaging and persuasive than moving them around the organization efficiently. ■

■ The Virtuous Circle in Recruiting

Most of us have heard of a virtuous circle. It occurs when one good thing leads to another. As successive events unfold, a desired outcome in the first event sets up and abets a desired outcome in the next and so on. In short, success compounds success.

Now, virtuous circles are very hard to control and even harder to create. Just ask the management of more than a few professional sports teams. They "successfully" outbid the competition and load their teams up with All Star free agents, only to see performance on the field decline into mediocrity or worse. From a recruiter's perspective, they seem to have done everything right. They have identified great talent, talked them into working for their organization, offered a deal good enough to get them in the door and repeated that process until the roster is replete with the best there is in the labor market. And still, the team fails to win.

Whether you enjoy professional sports or not, you have to wonder. These are organizations that thrive on their ability to judge and acquire talent. Their performance is visible every day in the won-loss columns of the standings. There's no finessing, and plenty of second-guessing. Yet, despite all their efforts to do one good thing that should, in turn, lead to another and another, what they often end up with is a bunch of good things that never come together to form something better. Or to put it another way, the virtuous circle becomes the losers circle.

The same kind of situation apparently exists on the Web. According to a survey by Hunt-Scanlon, fewer than 5% of the recruiters who use the Internet feel that it delivers quality candidates. They post open jobs, search for resumes, invest in corporate recruitment sites—in short, they do everything they should to create a virtual virtuous circle—and still they don't get the yield they need to win in the War for the Best Talent. It's enough to make a recruitment manager toss in the towel and pull the plug on the Net.

Doing that, however, would be a grave mistake. Why? Because the series of events described above (on the Web and in professional sports) do not actually form a virtuous circle. In fact, they don't even form a circle. They are a string of discontinuous activities. Success in one does not prepare for and encourage success in the next because each is separate and unrelated to the other. In recruiting terms, the process is disjointed and lacks the coherence necessary to create a consistent and engaging candidate experience. And when that happens, the process leaks. Instead of screening out all candidates except those with a carefully determined and very specific set of attributes, it accepts individuals with a wide range of motivations, perspectives on success, priorities and levels of commitment. What results is not a team, but a crowd (or less charitably, a mob) masquerading as one.

What do I mean? Take the following quiz to see if your recruiting process has the right stuff to act as a virtuous circle or simply as a series of disjointed events.

1. Do you know what recruiting requirements you will have next year and are you already using input from Hiring Managers, employee referrals and your own e-networking to identify key prospects for those upcoming openings?

2. Have you developed a value proposition that honestly and persuasively describes your employer's distinctive advantages for "A" level performers and passive as well as active job seekers (e.g., its culture, its commitment to individual growth and career advancement, the ethics of its leaders)?

3. Has that value proposition been presented to both the leadership of your organization and its employees and do they both buy into it?

4. Do your job postings (whether they appear on a commercial recruitment site or your own organizational Web-site) introduce and sell your value proposition?

5. Before posting on commercial sites, do you evaluate the nature of the experience they provide for job seekers to ensure it supports your value proposition?

6. Do you have an organizational recruitment Web-site and does it provide additional information that enriches the presentation of your value proposition?

7. Do you acknowledge every resume you receive and use that communication to:

(a) provide feedback to the sender on what will happen to that document during and after its evaluation; and

(b) reinforce and re-sell your value proposition?

8. Do you communicate on a regular basis with the prospects whose resumes are archived in your resume management system and do those communications sell your value proposition?

9. Do your Hiring Managers know about the organization's value proposition and:

(a) do they believe in it;

(b) can they articulate and sell it; and

(c) do they know how to interview appropriately to identify those candidates who believe in it too?

10. Do your recruiters know about the organization's value proposition and:

(a) do they believe in it;

(b) can they articulate and sell it; and

(c) do they know how to interview appropriately to identify those candidates who believe in it too?

11. Do you use online assessment instruments and other validated methods that reliably and accurately evaluate a candidate's fit with your organization's value proposition?

12. Does every other communication with prospective employees in the recruitment process include some meaningful reference to the organization's value proposition and does every other interaction with them live up to that statement?

While there are certainly other issues involved in transforming a recruiting process into a virtuous circle, those addressed above are probably the most important. They make clear that what binds staffing activities together and creates a mutually supportive relationship among them is the outlook of the organization.

Does it pull together as one in the recruiting process or does it allow things to be done by individuals who have no collective sense of what the organization stands for, as an employer? Does it nurture bonds among the actors in the process so that they see themselves working as a community or does it implicitly accept a free agent view of process participation? In other words, does the organization act, speak, believe as a ... well, as a living, corporate team that is dedicated to one mission and one vision of how it should best be accomplished? ■

■ Don't Enron Your Candidates

The unfolding saga of corporate malfeasance at Enron has been felt at many levels in many different places. From workers who have lost their entire retirement savings to the new laws being proposed for both corporate governance and financial accounting, the demise of this company has touched and will yet touch millions of Americans in ways they could not have predicted and should not have to endure. As a consequence, the name of the company, itself, has now come to have its own signature connotation in American parlance.

Around water coolers and in car pools, in cafeterias and watering holes, the greed and chicanery of Enron's leaders have coined a new verb to describe corporate behavior. To enron your employees is to keep them in the dark, disregard their right to accurate information, and ultimately, mislead them about:

- The status of the organization as a viable commercial enterprise,

- The values and goals of the organization and the principles of its leaders, and

- Other matters that will influence the course of their careers and the quality of their lives.

In short, enroning another person is to demean and diminish them.

Certainly, the vast majority of CEOs and American business people, in general, don't practice such behavior. Enron is news because it is the exception to the rule, right? Well, maybe yes, maybe no. Although individual managers and employees would never consciously perform such acts, the way they work may have the same net effect. What do I mean? Take a look at the recruiting process in most employer organizations today. Although most recruiters and Employment Managers would blanche at the thought of enroning anyone—let alone, prospective employees—the policies and activities of that process keep job seekers in the dark about:

- The organization's values and mission,

- The character of its leaders and first line supervisors, and even

- The precise nature of and expectations for the position for which they are being recruited.

Sound a little harsh? Perhaps, but then again, take a look at some of the key elements in the typical recruiting process. Job postings, for example, seem purposely designed to withhold all but the barest facts about an employment opportunity. Although the vast majority of employment Web sites permit recruiters to use up to 1,400 words (the equivalent of 2 typed pages of text) to describe their openings, most online ads are nothing more than "previously used" classified ad copy or bureaucratic position descriptions. Internet job postings have all the space necessary to provide the range and depth of information that job seekers need to make intelligent decisions about an opening, yet far too many are grossly incomplete, and therefore, potentially misleading.

And postings are not the only problem. There are other elements of the recruiting process that have the net effect of being equally as disingenuous. Consider the following:

72

- **Resume submission.** Resumes are sent to recruiters in response to job postings and through general collection points provided at employer Web sites. In other words, job seekers perceive that they are being invited (even encouraged) to send in their credentials. Despite the logic of that assumption, however, many organizations act as if the receipt of candidate resumes is an administrative nuisance that takes all of the fun out of recruiting. All too often, they build elaborate Web-based databases to hold those resumes, but never use the communications capability of that technology to acknowledge their receipt or show job seekers the simple courtesy of saying "Thank You." No wonder most applicants view resume submission as the human resource equivalent of a "black hole" in cyberspace.

- **Applicant treatment.** Even when applicants are informed about the receipt of their resume and the next steps in the process, they are normally sent a message that borders on the misleading. It often reads something like this:

  "Your resume will be reviewed against our current openings and archived in our database and reviewed against future openings for a period of six months."

  After that initial message, however, most job seekers never hear another word from the organization. Their resume gets stuffed into the vacuum of the resume database, and absolute silence descends. Despite the ease of using e-mail for mass 1:1 communications, they never receive:

  (a) more information about the organization to help them to get to know it better;

  (b) an update on its status; or

  (c) a request to update their record to reflect changes in their own status.
  The net effect is that they end up knowing as little about the organization (or maybe less) than they did when they first applied.

Recruiters are people people, so I believe that they would never consciously enron employment applicants. I also believe, however, that the process with which they work can and often does treat prospective employees as shabbily as Enron treated its own workers. And if we really believe that talent is as important as we say, we must take a stand now and force our organizations to change that process. ■

■ Asset or Sink Hole?

Each year, employers get with their recruitment advertising agencies and plot out campaigns to attract candidates and turn them into applicants. At a growing number of organizations, the resumes of those applicants are then turned into records and archived in a computer-based talent database. So far so good. Ensuring a steady stream of talent is a smart investment, even in the most difficult of economic times. It's what happens next, however, that undermines the return on that investment and on the organization's database asset.

Consider the evidence.

- According to a study by HireAbility, the average employer sources just 5% of its new hires from its talent database. That's the _net_ return after spending hundreds of thousands, even millions of dollars to fill it up.

- According to the Information Technology Association of America (ITAA), the average employer will find just 4% of its IT talent and 5% of all other talent from its own database.

- According to research conducted recently in the staffing industry, 70% of the records in agencies' talent databases have incorrect or out-of-date contact information.

However you want to measure it, at the bottom line, too many organizations have let one of their most important assets—their talent database—deteriorate into a financial sink hole.

What can be done? The key is to view your database as something other than a stack of electronic documents. Today's databases are or can easily be connected to the communications capability of the Internet. With accurate contact information (an essential precondition to achieving _any_ value from a candidate database), therefore, they can be used to interact with prospective candidates before, during, and even after they have indicated an interest in a specific position. And it is the substance and quality of that interaction—in essence, the recruiting process _after_ sourcing—that ultimately determines the usefulness of a talent database.

The best interaction resembles a marketing campaign that has three distinct elements:

- **Pre-interviewing:** the continuous acquisition of individual information. A talent database, or at least a good one, is never simply a collection of resumes. Instead, it is an archive of information that may (or may not) begin with a resume, but quickly extends beyond that document to cover such topics as salary history, willingness to re-locate and/or travel, work style and environment preferences, and career goals. Now, I know what you're thinking; the conventional wisdom is that it's difficult to get candidates—especially the best ones—to part with such information. Several recent studies, however, have found that even the most passive of prospects will part with these details IF they are assured that their confidentiality will be protected.

- **Pre-selling:** the continuous transmission of information about the organization as a business, em-ployer and corporate citizen. Initially, this information will necessarily be generic. Over time, however, these marketing messages will become more and more tailored as insights about each candidate are acquired from pre-interviewing. Just as computers and electronic databases have enabled marketers to fine tune their messages to individual buyers, recruiters must now use that technology to personalize the value proposition they offer to each candidate.

- **Pre-qualifying:** the continuous mapping of an individual's qualifications and characteristics to current and projected openings. The goal here is two-fold:

  (1) to identify the best candidate for a particular job (rather than the best available one, which is normally what you get when your database is under-stocked with talent or overstocked with out-of-date information); and

  (2) once the right candidate has been found, to re-focus the pre-selling campaign on that specific position.

All of the research shows that the tighter the person-job fit, the faster a new hire will reach full productivity, the better their performance will be over time and the more likely they are to stay with the organization. Hence, this element (in conjunction with the other two) biases the recruiting effort toward achieving more hires with good person-job fits and thus a better return on the database asset. ■

■ Just-in-Time Recruiting

The proponents of talent recruitment with supply-chain management technology often cite just-in-time recruiting as one of the potential advantages of managing people as cogs. By signing posting and/ or database search contracts in advance, they opine, recruiters can meet requirements quickly and thereby save an employer the hassle and cost of unfilled jobs. Just as Wal-Mart uses an automated inventory management system to keep its shelves stocked with just the products you and I want most, a similar system for talent can keep positions stocked with qualified workers who will make customers happy with valuable products and services.

While the metaphor is a bit strained, I think the goal makes sense. As more organizations move to the leanest possible staffing, even a single vacancy with any longevity will likely hurt morale, undermine productivity and ultimately degrade organizational performance. Yes, I think just-in-time recruiting is a key objective for any recruiting function today; it's the way that the supply-chain crowd envisions accomplishing the goal that has me troubled.

Listen carefully to what is said about the supply side of these super-duper talent management systems. In essence, the logistics crowd expects talent supply to operate the way ... well, the way an inventory of light bulbs does. Need three crates of the things? No sweat. Send an order electronically to your vendor. It will have three crates of just the kind of bulbs you want in stock, and it will ship them to you immediately. Those bulbs will then arrive back at your location just when you want them so that you can get them out on the shelves just as I come in the door to buy them. Bitta bang, bitta boom. Profits multiply.

If that all sounds a bit too mechanical for the talent with which you and I work, it is. Indeed, the very idea of a chain seems off the mark. You see, a chain implies that everything in the process is fixed and certain. Once connected, all of the links in the chain perform exactly as intended. We know that's the case with light bulbs, but what about talent? How fixed and certain is the talent chain?

The first link involves our friends, the hiring managers. Once they realize that a vacancy has occurred, they have to communicate the resulting recruiting requirement to you. To be useful, however, that notice must be accurate and complete. After all, you wouldn't tell a vendor to ship just any old light bulbs; you'd specify exactly the brand you wanted, the wattage and maybe even the packaging (e.g., 2 bulbs to a box or 4). Hiring managers, on the other hand, ... well, we all know that hiring managers are busy doing very important line management stuff so they are often times simply not able to provide us with the necessary details about the kind of talent they need. And when that happens, no matter how elegant the supply-chain design, no matter how elaborate the supply-chain technology and no matter how hard we try to make it all work, the pace of recruiting slows down.

But that's not the only disconnect. There's also the next link, our inventory vendor. That organization has to have a supply of exactly the right kind of light bulbs at exactly the time we need them, or the whole process will grind to a halt. The same is true, of course, with talent. With just one little exception. There is no single vendor or Web-site or newspaper that has an unlimited inventory of just the kind of high grade talent we need when we need it. And there's a reason for that. As I have noted previously in this column, there's a profound difference between cogs (or light bulbs) and cognitive beings, and people have this habit of doing their own thinking. They don't just sit around in some vendor's warehouse bins waiting to be told where to go.

Does that mean that just-in-time recruiting is a pipe dream? No, not at all. What it does mean is that we cannot rely on a vendor or vendors to manage our inventory. Or to put it in recruiting terms, just-in-time recruiting is not a function of how fast or smart you can acquire new candidates from external sources, but rather how well you have prepared the candidates you have previously placed into your own talent database. That's right. Your talent database. It is the only inventory you can count on. Because you own it. It sits right on your desktop where it's available for immediate access. And you decide what goes into it. You invest in filling it up. You decide whether to invest further to keep it current and to use it to pre-sell the talent whose records you've collected. In essence, you are the supply vendor, and the attention you pay to that responsibility also has an impact on your ability to achieve just-in-time recruiting.

Admittedly, talent inventory management involves activities that are out of the norm for the recruiting functions in many organizations. Basically, recruiters must become adept at both demand forecasting and top talent targeting. The only way you can ensure an adequate supply of the right kind of talent is to know, well in advance (say, 12-24 months), what the demand will be. That prior knowledge, in turn, gives you the time you'll need to identify, contact and begin acquiring information from the best talent for each of your upcoming requirements.

Trying to meet those requirements the old fashioned way—by tapping into an uncalibrated supply of active job seekers on the spur of the moment—is the functional equivalent of recruiting with dice. You may or may not roll a good match, but you will never be able to do better than the best candidate who happens to be available at that particular moment. If, however, your goal is to fill your openings with the best talent there is (and I believe it should be), then you will have to begin searching among people who are not currently looking for a job and may never be: i.e., passive prospects and "A" level performers. Filling up an inventory with that caliber of candidate, however, takes time; acquiring occupational and other information from them takes more time (they do not, in most cases, have a resume); and selling them on your organization and possible openings takes even more time. Therefore, the only way to have the necessary supply of talent for just-in-time recruiting is to acquire it continuously and in advance.

So, here's the bottom line. Talent supply management can, in fact, yield the important advantage of just-in-time recruiting. Achieving that advantage, however, requires more than the installation of a supply-chain system. Why? Because technology (supply-chain or otherwise) becomes transformative only when the people who use it are transformed first. In other words, the key to optimizing an organization's talent supply is to begin by breaking the chains of traditional practices that bind recruiters and hiring managers into unproductive and reactive practices. Start there, and you'll be well on your way to creating a recruiting function even Wal-Mart would be proud of. ∎

■ Treating Candidates As Preferred Customers

Remember the last time you went to purchase something in a store, and it wouldn't take a credit card (and you had no cash) or wouldn't accept the card you had? Most of us view such treatment as lousy customer service. If the store truly wanted our business, it would make us feel special, not left out; it would hold onto us, not push us away.

The same can be said of candidates dealing with recruitment sites (corporate and commercial) that will only accept resumes by e-mail. Yes, taking resumes by fax and mail increases our administrative burden, but let's remember what we're trying to do: attract, interest and sell the best prospects for our openings. Not the desperate job seekers. They'll apply even if you require that they send in their resume by smoke signal. By best talent, I'm talking about passive job seekers and "A" level performers, and they, on the other hand, are fickle. They see an impediment—any impediment at all—as a virtual brush-off or ... lousy service.

So, don't design your recruiting process simply to optimize efficiency; instead, design it to optimize effectiveness as efficiently as possible. That will give your prospects an experience they'll remember ... for all the right reasons. ■

■ Conducting Surveys Online

Surveys have always been an important tool for gauging performance, identifying areas requiring improvement and obtaining customer input for product or service design. Despite their value, however, they have been sparingly—at least in recruitment—used because old fashioned paper and pencil surveys are time-consuming, complicated and expensive. But what if you could put your finger on the pulse of important customer groups <u>and</u> get the information you need without a lot of hassle or cost? If you think you might use surveys more regularly, read on. Web surveying has come of age.

There are at least four groups that recruiters and HR professionals should survey regularly:

- Candidates
- Hiring managers (for in-house recruiters),
- Clients (for third party recruiters), and
- Employees.

The kinds of information that you should collect from each group is different, of course.

Candidates (including those who are selected for interviewing and those who are not—both are "customers" of the recruiting process)

1. What was their perception of customer service in your recruitment process and at your recruitment Web-site? What was the quality of their experience and how does it stack up against the level of service at the competition?

2. What content would they like to see at your Web-site? What kinds of information would keep them coming back, even if they are not looking for a job at the moment?

3. What are the attributes of your organization's employment brand that most appeal to them? What attributes are problematic? Emphasize the former in your postings and at your site and have effective counters to the latter when dealing with candidates.

4. Where did they hear about your organization and/ or its postings? (This information will tell you where to invest in recruitment advertising in the future.)

Hiring Managers

1. What was their perception of customer service during the recruitment process?

2. How helpful was the:

(a) ATS,

(b) recruitment Web-site,

(c) other technology in the process?

3. What was their perception of the quality of the output of the process (i.e., the new hire)?

Clients (for third party firms)

1. What was their perception of customer service during the recruitment process?

2. How helpful was the:

(a) ATS,

(b) recruitment Web-site,

(c) other technology in the process?

3. What was their perception of the quality of the output of the process (i.e., the new hire)?

4. What was their view of your "value added" during the process? What else could you do to enhance that value?

5. What content would they like to see at your Web-site? What kinds of information would keep them coming back, even if they do not have an assignment for you at the moment?

Employees

1. What is their perception of the internal mobility process? Does it work? Is it helpful?

2. What is their perception of the employee referral process? Is there enough incentive to participate? Is timely feedback provided on referrals?

3. What is their perception of the quality of the output of the recruitment process (i.e., their new co-worker)?

4. Based on their experience, what improvements would they suggest for the recruitment process?

5. What is their view of the recruitment Web-site? Would it attract them? Would they view it as interesting, helpful and persuasive?

What tools can you use online to conduct surveys? There are several to consider:

- **SurveyMonkey.com**
Surveys with single and multiple choice answers and drop down widows; results in real time; can be branded with your logo, look and feel.
    - Basic service (10 questions/100 responses)-<u>free</u>
    - Professional service (1,000 responses/month)-$19.95/month.

- **Zoomerang.com**
Offers custom templates or you can design the survey yourself; permits all types of questions as well as free-form comments; results in real time.
    - Basic service (20 questions/50 responses)-<u>free</u>
    - 12 month subscription plan (30 questions per survey/ 10,000 responses)-$599.

- **InstantSurvey** (at www.netreflector.com)
Offers a pay-per-response pricing model.

- **InsightExpress.com**

Market research and surveys online
  - Pricing begins at $450/survey.

- **SurveySite.com**

Online focus groups and Web surveys
  - Pricing by sales rep only. ■

■ **Your Online Recruiting Policies**
What Are They? What Should They Be?

■ Give This Column to Your Chairman of the Board

With all of the bad news circulating about corporate performance, it would seem perfectly appropriate to take a look at some depressing statistics from the world of recruitment and retention:

- According to Towers Perrin, over 50% of all employees are now looking to change companies. You can recruit all you want, but if a company's flow out the back door is equal to half its workforce, there is absolutely no way to achieve full staffing, even in a down economy.

- According to a Gallup survey, only 30% of the workforce is engaged by the work they do. Even worse, the longer workers stay at a company, the less engaged they become. Now "engagement" is admittedly a less than scientific term, but I think it serves well enough as a measure of how challenged and committed employees are. In essence, the lower the engagement, the less likely workers are to stand by and stay with their employer.

Why, you may ask, have I chosen this particular moment to point out such unpleasant facts of life? Other than the eternal pessimists among us, who can take any pleasure from these figures?

Odd as it may sound, I think they give every recruiter and HR practitioner in the United States cause to celebrate. And the reason is simple: these findings put into stark relief just how serious and untenable the staffing challenge is among employers today. Forget consumer confidence, we have **a crisis of confidence among employees**, and if it's not fixed and fixed soon, we won't need to worry about consumer spending. Even if demand drops precipitously, companies won't have the employees they need to deliver the goods and services that people are willing to buy.

And why is that realization such good news for those of us in the recruiting profession? Because with all of the debate about lapses in corporate governance, there has been nothing said about how companies should better protect their human capital asset. The discussion, to date, has focused on assuring financial integrity and safeguarding shareholders' investments. And that's clearly appropriate. But I would argue that we can do all of those things and still not fix what ails corporate America. In effect, we are repairing a "hollow enterprise," and just as we learned with our hollow military in the 1970's, an institution without adequate numbers of capable and committed people cannot accomplish its mission. Hence, the current wave of reforms is likely to do no more than ensure that we will now have more accurate reporting of the miserable financial performance of companies who lack the workers to get the job done.

It's that unpleasant scenario which leads to the following proposal:

☛ I urge that an additional step be taken in conjunction with any changes that are made (by legislation or otherwise) in Board constitution and audit performance. As Boards move to increase the number of external directors and establish independent audit committees with the knowledge to oversee financial reporting, they should also take the only action that will prevent the hollowing out of the enterprise. They should add the Vice President of Human Resources to their membership. Further, the role of this executive should be dramatically different from that played by the rare HR representative on Boards in the past. Instead of reporting on labor management issues and benefits costs, they should be charged with making the status of the organization's human capital asset visible to the Board. In other words, they are not on the Board to serve as the expert on administrative and legal matters related to HR management, but rather to report on the morale, commitment and capabilities of the organization's workforce and to lead the organization pro-actively toward strategies that will enhance them.

Such a change in portfolio for HR executives would have an immediate beneficial effect. It would, for the first time, expand the Board's visibility beyond purely financial measures when assessing organizational health. It would move Board oversight beyond post hoc metrics of organizational performance—what it has done as measured against previously established busi-ness goals—to pre hoc measures—what it will (or will not) be able to do relative to future business objectives. In effect, this shift in focus enables the Board to get out of its traditional role of reacting to problems and fixing them once they have occurred to predicting potential problems and avoiding them before they do.

To support the Vice President of Human Resources in this role, I also propose that Boards con-vene a permanent Human Capital Asset committee. This standing committee would be charged with assessing the morale, commitment and capability of the organization's human capital and reporting to the Board on its findings and their likely impact on the organization's ability to per-form its mission. In addition, this committee would be responsible for encouraging and then vet-ting proposed investments in human capital development to upgrade worker performance and commitment to the organization.

Now, I know that some organizations will dismiss this proposal as another "silly HR idea" and ir-relevant to the big issues of corporate governance now being debated among business leaders and the government. I would argue, however, that the current crisis of confidence in corporate America is driven by the very fact that financial metrics did not prevent the implosion of some of the country's largest and best known corporations and will not in the future. Despite the vaunted power of the GAAP, those Generally Accepted Accounting Principles, and all of the self-pro-claimed rigor of the accounting profession, companies can (and, given the frailties of human nature, will continue to) manipulate the numbers. That's why there needs to be another gauge of an organization's health, and the state of its human capital—the polar opposite of its financial capital—fits the bill better than any other I know. ∎

∎ Recruiter Pay Goes Up

SHRM has released the results of its 2002 Human Resource Compensation Survey. It covers 109 HR jobs from senior management to clerk. Among the 12 most common jobs, 11 saw a pay in-crease in 2002, with the largest gains going to senior compensation analyst and general recruiter —both of which increased 4.2% over 2001—bosses, please take note. Among HR managers, pay increased the most (by a wide margin) among executive compensation managers—why are we not surprised? Their median cash compensation is now $125,000. ∎

■ To Be or Not To Be
A Candidate on the Web

As resumes flood into corporate Web-sites and candidate management systems, the thorny issue of what exactly is an applicant on the Internet grows ever more important. Is it:

- Anyone who submits a resume on your site?
- Anyone who applies for a specific opening posted on your site, regardless of their qualifications for the job?
- Anyone who is deemed potentially qualified for an opening posted online?
- Anyone who visits your site and completes an online application form?
- Anyone whose resume or profile you obtain from an online database?
- All of the above or none of the above?

Given the intrusive nature of an EEOC audit and the potential liability of a negative finding, the resolution of this issue is a matter of concern for all employers. Unfortunately, it does not appear that the EEOC, itself, will make a final decision any time soon, so our only basis for proceeding is the Uniform Guidelines on Employee Selection Procedures (UGESP). Ironically, although these policies were written for the pre-Web era, they offer guidance that can be helpful today.

The Guidelines define an applicant as a person who expresses an interest in employment (e.g., by sending in a resume or completing an application form) in accordance with the employer's procedures. It is this last phrase that provides organizations with a rational roadmap for meeting the letter and the spirit of the EEO program. By inserting one word in the above statement—"...in accordance with the employer's stated procedures—it quickly becomes clear how an organization can avoid being forced to treat every resume submitter as an applicant, yet still collect EEO data on those who truly are. In essence, it should establish as policy the simple dictum that a person must follow a specific set of posted procedures in order to be considered a genuine applicant for employment by the organization.

How should this policy be implemented? I suggest the following:

① Develop a detailed, written set of procedures which all persons must follow to be considered an applicant by your organization. For example, an employer can specify that a person must:

- apply for a specific job opening;
- provide certain specified information about themselves (including that acquired by job-related assessments);
- send that information in a specified format or within a specified time; and/or
- complete a specified application form.

② Summarize these procedures in the job listing area on your Web-site. Avoid using bureau-cratic or authoritarian language; instead, explain that these procedures are designed to help the organization quickly and accurately determine the best possible candidates for an opening, and that its ability to do so is in their (the candidate's) best interest as well as the company's.

③ Add a statement to all job openings posted outside your own Web-site that only those who apply for employment in accordance with the company's stated procedures will be considered. Include a link back to the explanation page on your Web-site for their reference.

④ Collect demographic information from those who follow the procedures as early in the pro-cess as possible. For example, you might include a voluntary data submission form in the auto-responder you use to acknowledge receipt of an applicant's resume/application form.

These procedures, of course, do not obviate the need to make a good faith effort to source a di-verse pool of applicants for your employer. They do, however, hold down the administrative bur-den of collecting the data that will prove you have done so. ■

■ BuzzWord Bingo

How many times have you had to sit through a meeting or conference presentation filled with business jargon and buzzwords? It would be laughable if it weren't so boring.

Well, now there's a way for you and your friends to pass these time "productively." It's called **Buzz Word Bingo**. Just visit MeaningfulWorkplace.com/Bingo and print out as many cards as you need free of charge. "Results driven" anyone? How about "mission focused?" "Thought leadership?" "Critical Differentiator?" ■

■ A Privacy Policy & A Privacy Guarantee

Read almost any survey of Americans these days, and the issue of online privacy will register near the top on the anxiety scale. People are concerned that their personal information or resume will be mis-handled and inadvertently put them at risk with their current employer. Having your resume land on your boss's desk can turn a bad hair day into a real disaster. So too can the unauthorized sale of personal information to marketing companies. Our e-mail boxes are already clogged with solicitations, and the last thing most of us want is another three hundred breathless offers for get-rich-quick schemes.

This preference for privacy is not ironclad, however. A series of recent surveys show that most Americans are willing to release personal information in certain circumstances. Basically, they want to:

- maintain control over when, how and to whom the information will be released

   and

- receive something of value to them in exchange.

Those two elements are the basic building blocks of a permission marketing campaign.

Permission marketing can turn a recruitment Web-site into an information gathering factory. According to the Center for Social and Legal Research, almost two-thirds of Internet users are actually "privacy pragmatists." They have safely released sensitive information online in the past, and they are willing to do so again if they receive something in return which they consider to be a genuine benefit.

What will they release? According to a Greenfield Online survey, they'll happily part with:

- demographic data (including such interesting tidbits as their career field, industry, current title, willingness to travel and/or relocate, and even their salary)

   and

- contact information (including their home address and telephone number).

The quid pro quo for this information can take any of several forms. For example, Jupiter Research has found that 65% of the respondents to its survey will release personal information online if they are simply provided with a guarantee that it will not be misused. If you've ever needed a reason to establish an online Privacy Policy, now you've got it! To be effective, however, this policy should be written to inform and reassure candidates, not consumers. The language of the policy and the topics it covers must be relevant to active and passive job seekers, not to book buyers. In addition, the policy should be carefully reviewed by an attorney to ensure that it adequately protects your employer from anyone who subsequently decides that their personal information was not handled appropriately.

A good privacy policy has several other features.

- First, it is backed up with a process and set of procedures that work and a staff that is well trained in using them. It's all well and good to talk about privacy, but fail to walk the talk, and candidates will avoid your site like a company in Chapter 11.

- Second, it is believable. Have an outside, independent agency audit your policy and implementing process. There are at least three groups that perform such audits: TRUSTe, the Better Business Bureau Online and the Good Housekeeping Institute. If you pass muster, you'll be able to post their seal of approval on your homepage and differentiate your organization's commitment to privacy protection from the competition.

- Third, it is well promoted. To be effective, consumers (i.e., potential "buyers" of your value proposition as an employer) have to know about your policy. Therefore, include a privacy guarantee in the first four lines of every job posting, whether it appears on your own site or on a commercial recruitment site. This guarantee should be a short, but emphatic statement, such as "Personal Privacy Guaranteed." In addition, it should be hyper-linked to the full policy, even though few will ever take the time to read it.

Although a good privacy guarantee is one of the most effective ways to encourage site visitors to part with key information, there are others. For example, the Pew Internet and American Life Project recently polled Internet users and found that 63% would share personal information if they could personalize a site. How does that apply to recruitment? One of the best techniques is a job agent, a software application that will automatically compare a person's job objective with job postings on a site and privately inform them whenever a match occurs. Employers such as Qwest have seen a substantial increase in the number of site visitors willing to provide data to its candidate database with the introduction of a job agent feature.

Another benefit that will encourage visitors to release information is access to more or better content. If you offer visitors the opportunity to see or do something special, many will happily set aside their privacy concerns to do so. For example, in exchange for visitors completing a short registration or profile form, you might offer the results of an industry salary survey or a technical contest with a substantial prize. A Jupiter Research poll found that 39% of its respondents would accept such an offer.

But perhaps the most persuasive form of permission marketing is the offer of self-control. According to the privacy advocacy group Junkbusters, people are much more likely to give up personal information if <u>they</u> have the right to delete that information and access to an easy process for doing so at any time in the future <u>they</u> choose. Offering a simple auto-delete feature is perhaps the best guarantee you can make about your commitment to protecting individual privacy.

Permission marketing transforms do-nothing site visitors into active participants in your recruiting process. It overcomes their concern about a loss of privacy by highlighting a subtle, yet very attractive aspect of your brand as an employing organization. By offering to provide something of value to candidates in exchange for the information they release about themselves, you are recognizing their rights and stature as individuals. You are, in effect, creating an interaction between equals—the prospective candidate and the prospective employer—and there's no better way than that to get a relationship off on the right foot. ■

■ Resumes or Warez?

Have you heard of "warez?" That's the term used by Internet aficionados to describe software found online that they believe is theirs to take. "Warezing, " therefore, is the use of software or any other forms of information without the permission of the person or organization to whom it belongs. It covers everything from Adobe Photoshop and Microsoft Windows to your bank state-ment and candidate resumes. The warez gang aren't generally hackers, but if they can find some-thing on the Web—even if it has been placed there by a hacker—then, in their view, it's in the public domain and fair game. Their coda is simple: the rules of copyright protection and property ownership do not apply in cyberspace. And besides, even if they did, the crime is victimless, so what's the big deal?

Not everyone agrees with this law of the jungle approach to property on the Internet, of course. Indeed, the recent raids by Federal investigators on college campuses and in high tech companies is proof positive that there is another view. The roundup pulled in members of a group named DrinkorDie which was so brazen that it operated a Web-site to facilitate its members' unlicensed and unauthorized copying and trading of commercial software products. Before they even got the handcuffs off, however, the apologists started to rant: these software liberationists were actually striking a blow against the evil empire of corporate America.

The arguments and analogies were endless, but all had a common theme: cyberspace is different and plays by a different set of rules. We've heard that argument before, haven't we? It was the same rationale used to justify the billions of dollars invested in dot.com companies in the late 1990's. The rules of business do not apply online, the dot.com true believers argued, so profits and losses don't matter. Yeah, well tell that to the millions of Americans who have seen their 401(k) plans shrink to 201(k) plans and less, thanks to this irrational nonsense. No matter what the warez-bangers may believe, real world rules aren't suspended simply because the popular image of cyberspace is that it is someplace other than terra firma. Or to relearn a lesson from history, no matter what mapmakers may have wanted to believe in 1492, the earth simply wasn't flat.

So what does this warezing issue have to do with online recruiting? Take a look at your resume database. The Web is now awash in resumes that have been copied and recopied by companies and Web-sites that see nothing wrong with making unauthorized use of something they have "found" online. They use software agents called spiders or robots to appropriate someone else's property (a resume) and information (their work credentials) without the permission of the owner. And, in my view, that makes them no different than the DrinkorDie gang.

Now, I know that some of you will say that anyone who sends out a resume to a company or re-cruiter has the expectation that it will be copied. I don't disagree with that point. It's who is doing the copying that bothers me. When a person sends their resume to an employer, they ex-pect that employer to make copies. The recruiter needs one, the hiring manager needs one, and the other employees who will interview them need one. So, every job seeker expects, indeed encourages the employer to make as many copies as it needs.

That implicit permission granted to the employer, however, is a far cry from authorizing anyone and everyone to make whatever copies they want. And that's just what spiders and the organizations that use them do. They assume that a resume is a public document and, therefore, may be copied endlessly. But is that assumption correct? Does the use of a resume to inform prospective employers mean that the information it contains about a person's occupational abilities is in the public domain? Absolutely not. That's like saying that your drivers license, which is the document you use to convey information about your driving ability, may be copied and used by others at their discretion.

Moreover, resume warezing is not victimless. Making endless copies of a person's resume, without even their explicit approval, is an invasion of personal privacy. Even if a person places their resume in a public database, making unauthorized copies is still an assault on the person. Why? Because the individual puts their resume in the database with the expectation that it will be viewed by prospective employers, not that it will be copied and recopied and then sold as a commodity. Indeed, such commercial cloning dehumanizes them and forces them into interactions they did not seek or authorize others to promote. In short, warezing resumes turns people into chattel.

So, what do I think we should do?

- First, if you're an employer or staffing firm and using a spider to scrape resumes from online databases, stop it. Shut down the operation or cancel the service if it's provided by an outside vendor and get rid of the resumes.

- Second if you're a commercial recruitment site offering free or for-fee access to a database of resumes and some or all of those resumes were acquired by unauthorized copying, stop it. Build a value proposition that will encourage job seekers and prospective candidates to submit their resumes to you directly or get out of the business.

- Third, change your Privacy Policy to include a statement confirming your organization's commitment to using only candidate resumes submitted to it by the candidate. Make that principle a part of your brand.

The War for Any Talent encouraged behaviors that sometimes fell below the standards of our profession. The unauthorized copying of resumes was one such misstep. Now, however, the competition for talent has eased, and we have the time to reflect on which behaviors we will accept going forward. I urge that we stand up for the property rights of job seekers (and, perhaps, ourselves one day) and stop the practice of warezing resumes. ■

■ The Business Case for Recruiting

Watson Wyatt researchers Ira Kay and Bruce Pfau have released a book entitled *The Human Capital Edge: 21 People Management Practices Your Company Must Implement (or Avoid) to Maximize Shareholder Value* (McGraw Hill). It documents human resource strategies and activities which, if implemented effectively, can increase shareholder value by up to 47%. Among the companies studied, those with lower scores averaged a 21% five year return, while those with high scores returned 64% to shareholders over five years. No less important, the study also shows that superior human capital management practices lead, not follow, future financial results.

When this study was first completed in 2001, Kay & Pfau found that recruiting and retention excellence was the single greatest contributor to shareholder value among HR practices. Oddly, when the 2002 results were published, recruiting and retention had dropped to third place, behind total rewards & accountability and a collegial, flexible workplace. An examination of the data, however, finds that four of the elements that contributed to the higher score for total rewards & accountability actually belong in recruiting and retention. When that change is made, recruiting and retention is, once again, the single set of practices with the greatest impact on shareholder value.

According to our calculations the final rankings and percentage contribution are as follows:

Practice	Impact on Shareholder Value
Recruiting and retention excellence	13.7%
Total rewards & accountability	10.7%
Collegial, flexible workplace	9.0%
Communications integrity	7.1%
Focused HR service technologies	6.5%

■

■ **Your Online Recruiting Procedures**
What Are They? Do They Help or Hurt You?

■ Moore's Law Redux

Even if you're not a technology aficionado, you've probably heard of Moore's Law. Derived in 1965 by Gordon Moore, one of the founders of Intel, it held that technological development had begun to advance so rapidly that the number of transistors on an integrated circuit would double every 18 months. It was an engineer's way of saying that the capability of chip-based systems was going to increase exponentially. That's why we now have laptops and personal digital assistants with the processing power of computers that filled entire buildings less than a decade ago.

What's that have to do with recruiting? I've derived a corollary of Moore's Law that addresses the reality of skill and talent shortages in the workforce. Although partially masked by current economic conditions, it is still extraordinarily difficult to find and recruit "A" level talent in any field and even more difficult than that in a growing number of specific fields (e.g., certain IT and engineering specialties, nursing, machinists).

To grapple with this situation, a growing number of organizations are investing in candidate management systems. Whether these resources are Web-based (and called Application Service Providers-ASPs) or located on your own internal computers, the idea is to use technology to store candidate information so that it is easily accessible when needed. Recruiter efficiency goes up, and sourcing costs and cycle times go down. It's a great idea, but fundamentally flawed. Why? Because it views the system as a static database of resumes rather than as a platform for dynamic interactions with prospective employees. All of which leads us to **Weddle's Law**. It states that

The power of an organization's candidate database doubles with every 18 months of effective communication between the organization and the candidates whose resumes are archived in the database.

Weddle's Law sees candidate management systems as organizational assets composed of two separate elements:

- a database for candidate records and
- an e-mail hub for continuous candidate communications.

These systems store information so that it can be efficiently revisited, <u>and</u> they send and receive messages so that relationships can be built with prospective employees. Utilizing one of these functions but not the other dramatically reduces the value of the asset. In most cases, that value is the number of candidates an organization is able to transform into new hires from its own database (thereby avoiding additional sourcing time and/or investment whenever a new requirement arises). And according to Weddle's Law, the number of hires hired from your candidate management system will double every 18 months <u>if</u> the organization pursues a carefully planned and executed campaign of information collection (thereby getting to know more about prospects than what's on their resume) and marketing (thereby pre-selling the prospects on the value proposition of employment with the organization) during that period.

What is the key characteristics of this communications campaign? They should include the following:

The messages should be personal. Candidate management systems should not be used for mass communications, but for mass <u>one-to-one</u> messages that are tailored to each recipient's career field, experience level and principal motivations (which should also be identified through system-based messages).

The messages should be helpful in <u>two</u> directions. Like networking, the best messages "give as well as get." Hence, they should be designed to provide value to recipients (in managing their careers, expanding their professional knowledge) as well as to acquire information for the organization or sell it as an employer of choice.

The messages should respect the recipient's privacy. Always give recipients a way to "opt-out" of receiving future messages and make sure that the opt-out function actually works when used. The percentage of those electing to opt-out will also tell you how well you're doing in providing messages that are perceived to be helpful in two directions.

Why are such communications important? Because it's the rare "A" level performer or passive candidate who does not want to be courted, who will make a major career change without a lot of information and who is willing to be recruited by a stranger. That's why most organizations fill just 5% of their openings with candidates sourced from their own databases. If you want to do better than that, make database communications a part of your standard operating procedures. ■

■ Weddle's Law Redux

The previous postcard introduced Weddle's Law, an extrapolation from the time-proven prediction of computing power's exponential growth enunciated by Intel founder, Gordon Moore. Weddle's Law holds that the number of high quality candidates who have records in your resume database <u>and</u> are willing to consider your organization's employment opportunities will double with every 18 months of <u>effective communications</u> between your organization and those candidates. With most employers now acquiring just 5% of their new hires from their candidate database (accord-ing to a study by HireAbility), the law offers a reasonable and viable strategy for upgrading this important corporate asset.

But what are these "effective communications?" I've received a number of calls and e-mails asking for more information about the design and operation of a database communications cam-paign. Here are some suggestions to get you started:

■ Every campaign must be tailored to the organization and the talent it recruits. Perhaps one of the most effective ways to design your message content is to ask recipients what kinds of in-formation they would find most interesting and/or useful. This approach will ensure that your messages are welcomed and give candidates a sense of involvement in the company—a taste of what it will "feel like" as an employee even before they are.

■ Treat every message as an exercise in permission marketing. In other words, each message should both give the recipient information they will consider valuable (identified in #1 above) and ask for information the organization considers valuable (in evaluating them).

■ Send a new message to candidates every 6-8 weeks. Begin every message with a standard prefix in the Subject line so that they will come to recognize it as a communication from your organization and pay attention to it (assuming you have done #1 well). Just as online advertisements often begin their Subject lines with ADV:, begin yours with your company's name (e.g., INTEL: Latest News on Chip Industry Prospects in 2003).

■ There are any number of subjects that you might suggest to your candidates (in the first bullet above) and thus cover in your messages. These include:

   ▪ News about the company's major announcements and successes. Do not, however, send marketing or promotional messages about your products and services.

   ▪ Updates on your organization's industry. This information should address the state of the industry and major developments, but not lobby for support of legislation or regulatory change.

   ▪ Updates in key occupational fields for which you are always recruiting. This information should not get into personalities or controversy, but instead focus on topics that will contribute to a person's professional development.

- Invitations to chats and other presentations conducted by your organization's employees and addressing topics of interest to specific occupational fields and/or to everyone in the industry.

■ Every message should also include:

  - a Privacy Protection Warranty for all information requested of candidates, and

  - the opportunity to opt-out of receiving future messages. ■

■ Screening
A Key Weapon in the War for the Best Talent

The War for Talent has morphed from a War for Any Talent (back in the go-go days of the dot. com bubble) to a War for the Best Talent (in today's hyper competitive marketplace). As a result, the recruiter's challenge is now qualitative, not quantitative; it is not to find the first qualified candidate who is available, but rather, to identify the single best candidate there is for an opening.

Traditionally, recruiters have used screening to help them sort through the applicants for a given position. In many organizations, the approach has been simply to review resumes and conduct interviews. Resumes, however, provide a notoriously incomplete portrait of a person's motivation, preferences, skill levels and competency, while interviewers are barely 7% better than flipping a coin in their ability to pick the best prospect for a job (that according to Lou Adler who, in turn, cites a University of Michigan study).

So, what's the bottom line? While screening the old fashioned way may have been adequate for selecting "any talent," it is clearly not up to the task of selecting the "best talent." Equally as important, according to the Small Business Administration, employers save from $5 to $16 in reduced absenteeism, lower turnover, improved productivity and decreased employer liability for every $1 they invest in screening.

How should screening evolve to meet today's qualitative challenge in recruiting? It must become a much more robust and multi-faceted strategy. Here's what I think it should look like:

Longer Time Line and a Bigger Net

Right now, screening is often a rushed process that occurs only after candidates are quickly sourced for an opening that appears without warning from some hiring manager. Worse, this reactive approach all but ensures that only those who are actively in the job market (and not the more passive "A" level performers) will be identified. Hence, the current process must be replaced with one based on both demand forecasting and the continuous acquisition of talent prior to the time when it is needed. This extra lead time enables recruiters to identify top prospects (including those who aren't looking for a job and, therefore, don't have a resume) and to acquire more information (than that typically found on a resume) about them. The best tools for collecting these data are a talent database that can accept both resumes and non-resume data and a carefully constructed, on-going permission marketing campaign.

Multiple Screens at Different Points in the Process

- **Point 1:** an input data screen, using one of two filters—either the judgment of a recruiter who has sourced a top prospect or the auto-responder in an e-mail system (which returns a message that both acknowledges receipt of an applicant's resume and includes a brief skill test which the applicant must complete to be considered a genuine candidate)—to determine who will be accepted into and who will be excluded from an employer's talent database.

- **Point 2:** a talent record screen implemented by the recruiter's search of the employer's applicant, internal mobility, alumni and employee referral databases. Of course, this screen is only as good as the Boolean search competency of recruiters.

- **Point 3:** assessment and testing, using online instruments wherever possible. These tools can address a prospect's skill level, work preferences (e.g., culture, management style—both of which research has shown to have a significant impact on performance and retention), personality and motivators. There are a number of vendors offering these tests, including:
  - ComputerPsychologist.com
  - Development Dimensions International (www.ddiworld.com)
  - ePredix.com
  - SHRM Assessment Center (www.shrm.org/assessment)
  - SkillSurvey.com

- **Point 4:** interviewing, using carefully prepared interview guides, recruiters, and hiring managers who have been trained in interviewing principles.

- **Point 5:** reference and background checking. First, check your applicable state laws governing the acquisition and use of reference information. Then, obtain written authorization from the applicant to check references and background information and acquire that information in writing wherever possible. Background information can also be collected by third party organizations, including the following:
  - PublicData.com to check criminal background, driver's license, sex offenses and other matters via databases built with public records.
  - Employment Solutions (www.empl-solutions.com/referencechecking.html) to check a person's education, credit, work performance and other matters.

Capture of Collected Data in the Talent Database

With the appropriate release form (see Point 5 above), the collected data can and should be retained in the applicant's talent record. These data will support further screening of the candidate if they are not selected for a current opening and thereby improve the efficiency of that effort in the future. In addition, the data will support an analysis over time of which attributes and factors are the best predictors of performance and retention in the organization, and thus enable it to select the best talent for its needs the first time every time. ■

■ Graffiti Applicants

Unfortunately, the recruiting space on the Web is increasingly being overwhelmed with *graffiti applicants*. These are the individuals who spray their resume at just about any job posting they see, regardless of their qualifications for the position or even their interest in it.

The behavior of these individuals dramatically increases both your workload and your risk. Here's how it works:

- First, you post an opening, let's say for an engineering position. These days, that will undoubtedly yield a deluge of resumes. Some will come from highly qualified candidates, but many others will have been sent by graffiti candidates—sushi chefs and sportscasters who lack any knowledge of or background in engineering.

- Next, you have to decide who is qualified and who is not. That means you have to read and evaluate every resume. Your workload goes up, as a result, and so does the risk that you will overlook someone who is qualified or include for further evaluation someone who is not.

But wait a minute. This manual approach to evaluation is certainly time-tested—for years, it's been the way we recruiters have sorted through the resume deluge generated by newspaper ads—but is it the best we can do today? Hasn't the state-of-the-art gotten any better?

Of course, it has. The Internet gives us a way to automate our screening, so that we can quickly eliminate the graffiti applicants and focus our time and effort on recruiting top talent. To take advantage of this capability, I suggest that you use a 3-screen strategy. It provides a progressively tighter focus on a candidate's qualifications so that you can efficiently evaluate their fit with your opening and compare them to the other candidates you are evaluating.

Now, I know what you're thinking, so before we go any further, let's deal with the old saw that the best candidates will not sit through even one screen administered on the Internet. According to several recent surveys, that's simply not true. Even top performers will respond to a screen if:

(a) it is used after they have made the decision to apply for a position (i.e., not as an impediment to actually applying);

(b) it is well constructed and meaningful (i.e., it is not overly long and is clearly relevant to the job); and

(c) they are assured that the results will remain confidential and be properly protected.

So, what does my screening strategy entail? While there are a growing number of commercial sites that offer online screens for skill assessment, I prefer the following "in-house" approach:

- **Screen 1: A well written and detailed job posting.**

According to WEDDLE's surveys over the past 6+ years, recruitment sites, on average, permit you to include up to 1,400 words in a posting. The more information you provide on the skills, knowledge, experience and background a person must have to be successful in a position, the higher the number of graffiti applicants who will se-lect themselves out. Why? Because the more detail you provide, the more certain the message that you have a very clear and precise definition of it means to be a qualified candidate.

- **Screen 2: A virtual pre-screening interview.**

Replace the traditional, but time-consuming pre-screen telephone interview with an auto-responder, an application that automatically acknowledges the receipt of an applicant's resume received over the Web. Expand the text of the response to include:

(a) a thank-you for their submission;

(b) a request for their current salary, availability date and, if applicable, confirmation of their willingness to travel as required; and

(c) a strongly worded privacy guarantee. Just as when it is collected by telephone, this information will help ensure that you focus on those candidates who are appropriate for your opening and ready to go.

- **Screen 3: A virtual talent & experience assessment.**

For those candidates who "pass through" the salary and availability screen, use a second auto-responder message to ask the following question:

"This job involves [cite a critical task or key function]. Please briefly describe a similar aspect of your background and how you dealt with it. Or, if you haven't had such an experience, please briefly describe how you would handle it in the future."

All candidates, but especially "A" level performers, like to recite their accomplishments (at least briefly), and comparable accomplishments in the past make very good predictors of future performance.

Though based on technology, this screening strategy isn't designed to replace recruiters' assessments of candidates. It provides, instead, an unobtrusive, yet fast and effective way to acquire the data that recruiters need to identify and eliminate graffiti applicants and other unqualified respondents to their ads. ■

■ Improving Candidate Interviews With the Web

Lou Adler is well known as a trainer and consultant in the recruiting field. Recently, I attended one of his POWERHiring seminars and was mightily impressed with his counsel for recruiters. One of the most startling insights he provided had to do with the effectiveness of our interviewing efforts. He cited a study that came to a sobering conclusion. It found that the typical interview is just 7% more accurate in picking the best candidate for an opening than flipping a coin. In other words, no matter how good we are at sourcing candidates or how skilled we are in evaluating their resumes or how carefully we assess their references, our ability to hire smart is undermined because we make the right choice in an interview just 57% of the time.

Now, there are many possible reasons for such mediocre performance, but two, it seems to me, hold the key to a potential solution:

- First, recruiters and hiring managers often ask the wrong questions, probe the wrong issues and base their decisions on the wrong factors when interviewing. As Lou points out in his program, if you focus your interviews on who can best get the job (i.e., on the people who interview best) and not on who can best do the job (i.e., those who have the skills and the personality to fit in and perform well), then in many cases, your decision will be off the mark.

- Second, recruiters and hiring managers typically receive precious little training in conducting effective interviews. Some of that is the organization's fault, and some of it is the result of hiring managers who view interviewing as an activity just slightly more skill-based than reading the comics in the morning newspaper. The organization blithely assumes that interviewing is an innate skill—that anyone who has achieved the status of recruiter or hiring manager should be able to ask a couple of questions and figure out from the answers who should be hired. That's what gut instinct is all about, right? And hiring managers? Well, they think interviews are something to be squeezed into the chinks and crevasses of a schedule that's already crammed full with all of the really important stuff they have to do each day.

Add modest skills to nonexistent training and sub-basement priority, and we're lucky to be doing as well as 57% in our interview selections.

However, organizations that accept such mediocre levels of interviewing competence, implicitly accept that 4 out of every 10 of their hires will fail. While .600 may be a good winning percentage in professional sports, in the world of business, it's a disaster! The cost of having to replace individuals who do not work out as well as the cost of the work that doesn't get done while the recruiting process is underway quickly erode an organization's ability to compete in the marketplace. Even worse, those ill advised interviews and incorrect hiring decisions release 4 candidates who could be working for your organization, but instead are now probably happily employed with the competition. At the bottom line, accepting the current quality of interviews in most organizations is equivalent to fighting the War for Talent with one arm tied behind your back.

So what's to be done? Some organizations are turning to sophisticated Applicant Management Systems to automate and streamline all functions in their recruiting process. While these systems are a step in the right direction, however, they do no solve the skills problem among interviewers. Indeed, installing advanced technology systems that ease the logistical burdens of scheduling interviews and coordinating comments and feedback can actually lead organizations into a false sense of security. The acquisition of such systems without the installation of a complementary training program in interviewing skills simply improves the efficiency of a faulty process. Acquiring the system <u>and</u> the skills, on the other hand, is a sure-fire way to gain a real and sustainable competitive advantage in recruitment.

The Internet, of course, offers an efficient and effective way for us to achieve this advantage. It enables us to deliver training content to the desktops of interviewers so that they can access it whenever and wherever it is convenient for them.

- This content can teach recruiters and hiring managers, alike, how to make an objective and thorough evaluation of a candidate's capabilities, how to assess their ability to fit into the organization and make a contribution, and how to avoid the pitfalls that undermine getting the right information for good selection.

- This same content can also be used to organize the interviewing process and provide a common focal point and vocabulary among recruiters and hiring managers in their efforts to identify the best candidate. It can provide a way to coordinate which areas of a candidate's background will be evaluated by whom in a series of interviews and ensure that everybody understands and probes those aspects of a candidate's credentials that are essential to their success on-the-job.

- No less important, when all of the representatives of an organization participate in such a clearly well prepared and coordinated approach to interviewing, candidates get a powerful and very appealing message. They see an organization that values the time and effort both candidates and employees spend in the interviewing process and has organized the process to deliver a superior experience for all. Treat candidates (and employees) with that kind of attention and respect, and they'll sell themselves on working for your organization.

While this approach makes eminent good sense, there is, I must·acknowledge, a downside to Web-delivered training for interviewing skills. It can improve an organization's performance above that norm of 57%, but <u>only if priorities change</u>. In other words, the leadership of an organization must convey to all interviewers, but especially to hiring managers, that interviewing competency <u>is a part of their job description</u>. Indeed, to achieve a sustainable culture of effective interviewing, an organization should deny hiring privileges to anyone who fails to self-certify that he/she has taken the training program, understands its purpose and content, and agrees to use the skills it provides on-their-job. Without that level of commitment, they may as well pick new hires by flipping a coin and save the time and hassle of interviewing. ∎

■ Recruiting Safety

CareerBuilder.com recently surveyed over 1,000 full time workers and found that 82% now identify **safety** as a significant component of job satisfaction. To put it another way, after 9/11, your employees' sense of security on-the-job will play a key role in their retention.

Obviously, there are a number of factors that influence workplace safety. One of the most important, of course, is the "character" of new hires. Traditionally, background checks have been used to ensure that candidates are who they say they are and that they have been complete and completely honest in their description of their capabilities and record. According to Paul, Hastings of Janofsky & Walker LLP, a law firm specializing in labor issues, background checks should now cover:

- Education degrees and credentials,

- Prior addresses,

- Former employers,

- Criminal record (convictions, not arrests),

- Licenses and certificates required for the job,

- Credit, and

- Work authorization.

Many employers have chosen to outsource these checks as they can be time-consuming and do require some specialized knowledge. You will find any number of vendors offering such background checking services over the Web. In just the last 60 days, for example, we have been contacted by:

- ADREM profiles (www.adpro.com)

- CIAdvantage.com

- Rapsheets.com

Thanks to the Internet, however, and the growing accessibility of government databases, it is now possible to do at least some of your background checking in-house. That not only saves money, but it also ensures that the work gets done up to your standards.

There are three steps in the background checking process:

- **Step 1: Obtain the necessary forms.**

  - I-9 Forms required by the Immigration & Naturalization Service. You'll find printer friendly versions of forms at www.ins.usdoj.gov/graphics/formsfee/ forms/index.htm.

- General Release Form for checking an applicant's credit report, criminal record, motor vehicle record and references. See the sample form at www.backgroundcheckgateway. com/ authorization.html. Review any form with your attorney prior to using.

- Fair Credit Reporting Act release forms can be obtained from your corporate attorney.

- **Step 2: Acquire information from the applicant.**

Use the applicant interview to determine whether there is a sufficient possibility of employment to warrant a background check. If so, use the forms to acquire all necessary information from the candidate.

- **Step 3: Verify the information provided.**

(a) To confirm name address and telephone number: start with your local telephone directory; then, use an online crisscross directory (e.g., www.whowhere.com or BigFoot.com). Enter the phone number to verify the address; enter the address to verify the name.

(b) To check criminal records: use www.backgroundcheckgateway.com/statelist.html. It provides a tutorial on record checking and a directory of online county and Federal courthouse addresses.

(c) To check motor vehicle records: use backgroundcheckgateway.com/dmv.html. ■

■ Sophistication With a Blind Spot

WEDDLE's has just concluded its fifth annual survey of Best Practices in online recruiting. (To cast your ballot for the best techniques and the top recruitment sites, please visit the Online Poll at www.weddles.com). The results reaffirm lessons we have learned in earlier polls and uncover a potentially crippling blind spot among many recruiters.

In line with our earlier surveys, the poll shows usage of the Web growing among recruiters. This year, 61% of recruiters said they went online 11 or more times per month, up from 51% last year. It's what they're doing when they get there that's the potential problem. Over half of the respondents (51%) said they visited just 3-4 recruitment sites, and 20% said they visited only 1-2 sites. Despite having over 40,000 options from which to choose, recruiters seem to wearing ruts in the Information Superhighway by visiting the same few sites over and over again.

Does that mean they're satisfied with the sites they're using? Maybe, but even if that's true, I think the level of their satisfaction would move up even further if they shopped a little smarter on the Internet. Using a wide array of sites tailored to your hiring needs has several advantages:

- No one site or handful of sites has so much of the market that they can charge outrageous fees for their services;

- Since job seekers roam all over the Net, using additional sites to cover more of this population is likely to improve your candidate quality; and

- Since recruiters tend not to roam all over the Net, using additional sites to tap more of the applicant pool will likely to reduce the competition you face at any one site.

This tendency to "recruit in a rut" aside, recruiters showed increased sophistication in their use of the Web. As in previous years, they used a full robust toolkit of sourcing methods online. Their favorites changed a bit, however, as shown in the Table below

Top Five Best Practices in Online Recruiting

Method	2000	2001	2002
Posting jobs on for-fee sites	1	1	1
Searching for-fee resume databases	4	3	2
Posting jobs on your own corporate site	3	2	3
Posting jobs on free sites	5	4	4
Searching free resume databases	2	-	5

- = did not make top 5

What lessons can we learn from these rankings?

- Those who shop exclusively at free sites are probably sub-optimizing their yield.

- Despite all the brouhaha about corporate sites (and they are important), using commercial sites and those sponsored by professional and technical associations continue to be an important part of any successful online recruiting strategy.

- Although it's not apparent from the Table, the percentage of respondents selecting each of the five tools above was about the same, indicating that no one tool, by itself, is adequate. Instead, the best results occur when a range of tools is used in an integrated strategy.

Also noteworthy was the fact that 57% of those recruiters who cited posting jobs on their own site as a highly effective tool also said that their organization used a special, dedicated site—rather than a section of the corporate site—for recruitment.

What techniques garnered the fewest votes as effective online recruiting tools?

- Using a resume distribution system to acquire resumes

- Searching for resumes and posting jobs in Usenet newsgroups

- Using a spider to acquire resumes

  and

- Using datamining to acquire resumes

Of all the tools, using spiders experienced the greatest change, falling from among the Top Five Best Practices (5th place in 2001) to a distant 11th place this year.

Finally, nine in ten of our respondents also felt that the Web was more effective for recruiting in some fields and industries than others. Their votes for the best appear in the following Table.

In Which Fields Does eRecruiting Work Best

Field	2001	2002
Information Technology	1	1
Sales & Marketing	2	2
Engineering	3*	3
Finance & Accounting	3*	4*
Management	7	4*
Administration	6	5
Human Resources	3*	-

* = tie - = did not make top 5

Our poll respondents were a relatively seasoned group. Over a fifth (21%) had 11 or more years of experience and 13% had 21 or more years of experience in recruiting. ■

■ Recruiter Skills for Online Recruiting
What Are They? How Can You Acquire Them?

■ The Core Competencies of High Tech Recruiting-I

There's been much written about the growing importance of fighting the War for Talent with high tech weapons. The theme of these articles is tediously consistent: those recruiters who ignore the Internet and computers in a tight labor market are setting themselves up for an ignominious defeat and unconditional surrender. Technology, the authors opine, is a pre-condition for victory; there are other factors, to be sure, but they are simply inadequate to the task without the reach and power of advanced hardware and software.

While I would agree that technology is a powerful and important weapon for recruiters, I think that point, at least as it is typically expressed, is incomplete, at best, and all too often misleading. The truth of the matter is that computers and the Internet are nothing more than a lot of expensive wafers of sand and tiny wires if the people who operate the technology lack the knowledge and skills required to use it effectively. To put it a bit more emphatically, computers are as dumb as dirt without the involvement of a smart recruiter.

All too often, however, the skills that a recruiter needs to use advanced technology effectively on-the-job are ignored. Companies and staffing firms race out to acquire Candidate Management Systems, T-1 lines for high-speed Internet access and the latest training in Internet sourcing techniques, but they forget to give their recruiters the core competencies of high tech recruiting. To carry on with the martial theme of the War for Talent, they arm their soldiers with the best weapons available and teach them how to aim and fire them. They don't, unfortunately, teach recruiters the individual tactics and organizational strategy of applying those weapons on the battlefield. As a consequence, many organizations have lost most of the capability inherent in the expensive high tech weaponry they now own.

I believe these tactics and strategies are the true pre-conditions for success in today's competitive labor market. They spell the difference between the recruiting organization that uses the Internet and computers to save money and time and acquire higher caliber candidates than ever before and those that have all the machines but still source most of their candidates the old fashioned manual way. What are these skills? This and the following article will focus on some of the most important.

- **Establishing rapport with hiring managers.** In the past, this skill was exercised in face-to-face meetings that were often delayed and/or squeezed into the tiniest sliver of time on a hiring manager's schedule. Today, the use of ASP- (Application Service Provider) or Web-based candidate management systems enable these managers to initiate recruiting for a vacancy with a keystroke or two. In order to source the best possible candidates, however, recruiters still need to understand fully the hiring manager's goals and preferences, but now, that insight must be acquired, more often than not, in writing. In other words, recruiters must be able to communicate clearly and build trust with hiring managers by e-mail. While face-to-face meetings are obviously still important, recruiters will increasingly have to use electronic messages to create and strengthen their relationships with hiring mangers.

- **Communicating the hiring manager's requirements effectively to prospective candidates.** The prohibitive cost and limited space of print publications forced traditional recruitment advertising into the truncated and artificial language of classified ads. These messages didn't sell prospective candidates, they simply notified them of an opening—good enough for a labor surplus market, maybe, but definitely lacking for one with an acute shortage. The Internet, thankfully, lacks these constraints and thus offers a way to connect more powerfully with the best and brightest in the workforce. To capitalize on that capability, however, recruiters must be able to develop detailed and compelling advertisements that effectively communicate the value proposition of their opportunities. They must know how to write with the right words and how to format that information for online reading so that the ad touches even the most passive candidates and influences them to action.

- **Making judgments about which sourcing channels to use for which openings.** Back in the good old days, there was only one newspaper in town so there was no choice involved in recruitment advertising; candidates in all career fields and at almost all levels of experience read the newspaper to find employment opportunities, and that's where recruiters put their ads. Today, however, there are 40,000+ employment-related sites on the Internet; there are sites that specialize in candidates by career field, industry, and/or geography and sites that try to serve as national newspapers and attract virtually all candidates. To tap these resources effectively, recruiters must know which sites focus on which segment of the workforce and how to "comparison shop" among the available options for any specific candidate cohort. In effect, they must tailor the sites they use for sourcing to the unique requirements of each opening.

- **Providing great customer service to all candidates.** Although recruiters always knew it was important, they have seldom had the time or the resources to acknowledge every resume and thank every applicant for their submission. Such lapses in customer service probably didn't matter much in a surplus labor market, but with today's shortages, they can undermine an organization's employment brand and turn off all but the most desperate candidates. Hence, recruiters must learn to use the auto-response and communications capabilities of advanced technology to craft and convey timely and powerful messages that will make every applicant feel like a "preferred customer." Indeed, even those applicants deemed unqualified for current and future openings should be treated to the best possible customer service so that they will participate in a "friend referral program" for the organization and thus increase its reach into the candidate population.

What gets left out in all of the paeans to recruitment technology is the role of the humans who use it. That oversight is particularly harmful as the competitive advantage inherent in the technology can only be unlocked by a well trained recruiter. It takes special skills and knowledge to put technology to work effectively on-the-job, and sadly, many organizations fail to arm their recruiters with such fundamental preparation. ■

■ The Core Competencies of
High Tech Recruiting-II

Recruiting organizations have gone high tech. Whether they work for staffing firms or direct employers, today's recruiter has enough technology to run a Mars mission. It represents a sizable investment, and sadly, it's likely to be wasted. Why? Because in too many organizations, buying hardware and software is the only investment that's made. In relative terms, at least, next to nothing is spent on preparing the people who will actually use all this golly-gee-whiz-bang technology on-the-job.

Oh sure, employers and staffing firms have sent some (maybe even all) of their recruiters to training programs in online recruitment and the use of their candidate management system. Unfortunately, however, most of these programs focus on teaching manual resume sourcing and the mechanics of logging in a new requisition. Those that go beyond that typically teach a bit about how to write an effective job posting and how to find the best commercial site on which to post it. Now, these skills are definitely important, but they are only a part of the knowledge required to recruit effectively online. In effect, we've taught recruiters how to run the machines, but not how to devise and use the tactics and strategy for integrating those machines and their own activities into a total recruitment campaign online.

I believe these process skills are the true core competencies of Web recruiting for staffing firms and direct employers. My previous article introduced four of them. What follows are four additional competencies that underpin an organization's effective use of technology in recruitment.

■ **Building trust and interest among candidates.** The War for Talent has brought a new dynamic to recruiting—candidates, particularly "A" level performers, will no longer entrust their career and employment plans to "digital strangers." If the hallmark of a surplus labor market was transactions between buyers and sellers who knew very little about one another, the baseline for today's tight labor market is relationships built on long term involvement and mutual knowledge. Recruiters, therefore, must acquire the skills of written as well as oral communications and of partnership building so that they can use the Internet and their candidate management system (as well as traditional media) to establish preferential connections with the people they want to hire, today and tomorrow.

■ **Communicating judgments about candidates to hiring mangers.** One of the most important areas of a recruiter's expertise is their ability to assess a prospective hire's fit with both an open job and their organization's culture. In today's warp speed recruitment process, however, recruiters must be able to convey their judgments about a candidate quickly, accurately and persuasively, and more often than not, do so in writing via the Internet or a candidate management system. They must be economical in their e-mail, but also timely and clear in providing their evaluation and insights so that their internal customers will use them to make smart hiring decisions.

- **Selling the best candidate on their opening and their employer.** Top contributors—those individuals who can make extraordinary personal contributions and raise the performance of their peers—are always being recruited, even in an economic downturn. To prevail in this competition, recruiters must be able to differentiate and sell the unique value proposition offered by their organization. They must know how to use every interaction online as an opportunity for building interest, overcoming objections and getting to "yes." And if, for some reason, a key prospect doesn't "buy" a particular opportunity, recruiters must then also be able to keep on selling that person on the organization and the opportunities it will have in the future.

- **Re-recruiting new hires until they actually report.** Top talent is vulnerable, even after they've said "yes." Between the time they give notice and their first day at a new job, they can experience "buyer's remorse," receive an enticing counter-offer from their current employer, and/or be approached by another recruiter with a different opportunity. To protect their organization from such dangers, recruiters must now know how to continue selling candidates until they actually walk in the door. They must learn how to extend their own dialogue with the new hire as well as marshal online interactions and communications from across the organization (e.g., the appropriate supervisor and team, the HR Department, the CEO) to keep the enthusiasm and commitment of soon-to-be-employees intact.

Experience has proven that effectively implementing technology in any organization requires two sets of skills: operational and process. The former enables individual performance, while the latter integrates that activity into successful organizational outcomes. For staffing firms and direct employers, therefore, it's not enough to train recruiters in job posting and resume sourcing skills. They must also be prepared with the tactics and strategies of recruiting together as a unit online. Those capabilities are the core competencies of organizations seeking <u>to put the power of the Internet to work for the corporation.</u> ■

■ The Baseline Skill of Online Recruiting

Ask recruiters about the key competencies of their profession, and you're likely to get a long list that includes research or sourcing, interviewing, assessment and selection, negotiation, selling and closing, and written and oral communications,. All of these are clearly important to the practice of recruiting, and all are very traditional. They are skills that have been essential to success in our field for the last fifty years or more.

There is, however, one skill that is missing from this list, and it may be the only competency requirement that is new and directly related to the advent of recruiting on the Internet. Prior to the arrival of the Web, recruitment advertising was largely a local endeavor. For all but the most senior and hard-to-fill positions, the search was confined to the reading audience of the nearest city newspaper. And, since there were few cities with more than one daily newspaper, there was no evaluation involved. You simply called up the only option you had, paid the per-line rate for a daily or weekend insertion, and that was that.

The newspaper was obliged to provide an audited circulation number so that you knew how many people were likely to see your ad, but it didn't make much difference. Even if you took note of that number and subsequently measured the number and quality of applicants the ad produced, there was no other place for you to go. You couldn't shop for better pricing or for another source that might produce better results (unless you wanted to forego advertising altogether and use staffing or executive search firms, instead). Economists have a word for this kind of situation; it's called a monopoly, and for decades, newspapers enjoyed monopolistic power in recruitment advertising.

The arrival of the Web brought competition to this environment, of course, but not as much as might have been first envisioned. Clearly, there was now an alternative to the print classifieds, but for many recruiters, that option was limited to a single site: Monster.com. In fact, 48 cents of every online recruiting dollar was (and continues to be) spent on that one site alone, creating, as a consequence, a de facto monopoly. The site was able to charge virtually any price it wanted because we recruiters acted as if there were no other viable recruitment sites available to us on the Internet. In effect, we left ourselves open to the worse of both worlds: a monopoly in print advertising—the local newspaper—and a monopoly on the Web—Monster.com.

That depressing situation brings to the fore the baseline skill—the skill that is the precondition for using all other skills effectively—in online recruitment. It is derived from the reality of choice that exists on the Internet. Rather than a single source for hiring, the Web offers over 40,000 sites that provide some combination of a job board, resume databank and job agent. These sites fall into a bi-modal distribution: on one side, there are the general purpose department stores that stock talent across all or most professions crafts and trades. These sites probably number no more than 1000 and range from mega-stores, such as Monster.com and HotJobs.com, to smaller operations such as BestJobsUSA.com and NationJob.com. On the other side of the distribution, there are literally thousands of recruiting boutiques that specialize in providing a narrow, but deep inventory of talent in a specific career field, industry, location or combination of those factors. They range from BrokerHunter.com and EngineeringJobs.com to IMDiversity.com and ScienceJobs.com.

Equally as important, this array of sourcing options changes all of the time. Each year, new sites launch, extant sites morph, and old sites "retire." Here at WEDDLE's, we publish our recruitment site guides and directories on an annual basis just to stay on top of this constant churning. (Indeed, our print newsletter profiles ten new sites every month.) It is a beneficial development because it creates a vast, dynamic and extraordinarily rich universe of talent that is always being refreshed and redefined.

The range and variability of that universe, however, mean that recruiters must now know how to be smart consumers online. This baseline skill is a distinctive competency that encompasses two constituent sets of knowledge:

- The knowledge of what sites exist that might provide access to a specific pool of talent on the Internet. As with any other consumer activity—from dining in restaurants to patronizing dress shops—the universe of online recruitment options is ever changing, so recruiters must both acquire this knowledge and keep it perpetually up-to-date.

- The knowledge of how to evaluate those sites so as to select the best options for a specific requirement. Recruiters must know what data to collect about the sites and where and how to collect it. No less important, they must also know how to use that information to compare one site to another and determine which offer the best combination of services, features and fees.

Why is this new skill important? Because it is the only way to maximize your return on investment in online recruiting. That investment includes time and effort as well as money, and all three are scarce. The return, on the other hand, has both a quantitative and a qualitative dimension. It involves both finding adequate numbers of new hires <u>and</u> new hires with the right set of skills, experience and motivation to make a real contribution on-the-job. Hence, the most effective recruiters will be those who apply this baseline skill and, as a result, acquire the best talent for their organizations at the lowest cost-per-hire and shortest time-to-fill. ∎

■ **Buying, Implementing & Using Technology & Systems**
   Why Bother? What's the Best Way to Do It?

■ The Technology Losers Club

The go-go days of buying technology may be about to end. There's a sobering new report out from Morgan Stanley that is giving corporate executives pause. It estimates that U.S. companies wasted $130 billion on dysfunctional software and other technology in just the past two years. Worldwide, companies are throwing away 20% of the $2.7 trillion they spend each year on technology, according to the Gartner Group. Despite the hype in the press about the power of new golly-gee-whiz-bang bytes and bits, when companies actually get the stuff in-house and try to make it work on-the-job, they are simply not seeing the advertised improvements in productivity, efficiency and capability.

Now, don't get me wrong. I'm not focusing on this issue because I think technology is not helpful or that technology purchases are a waste of money. Quite the contrary; I have long advocated for the rational application of technology in government and industry. My emphasis, however, has always been on the word, rational. And it's not rational to buy such technology as candidate management systems, vendor management systems, applicant tracking systems, resume processing systems, candidate assessment applications and Internet recruiting platforms, when:

- the processes into which this technology is going to be embedded are poorly designed or designed for an era of manual work and face-to-face interactions;

- there is not a clear understanding of what level of change the on-board staff can assimilate and what new skills they can reasonably be expected to acquire and use;

- the senior leaders in the enterprise do not have a realistic understanding of the time, financial and support commitments required to implement the technology effectively and, instead, rely on the rosy projections of the vendor;

- the Human Resource executives responsible for implementation and use of the technology do not spend the time and energy necessary to educate themselves on what that means for their organization and, instead, turn it all over to the IT Department;

- and so on.

You get the picture. The problem is not with the technology (although there are plenty of crummy systems for sale out there), but with the way technology is introduced into the enterprise.

It's the dirty little secret of all those technology vendors out there. Despite Herculean efforts on their part, most recruiters and hiring managers are using but a fraction of the capability built into the systems their companies have bought, and most are not seeing anywhere near the projected improvements in recruiting performance. Vendors provide weeks of up-front training for staff and years of on-call support, yet most surveys continue to show that the majority of positions are filled the old fashioned way: by low tech telephone and face-to-face networking.

Does that mean that the recruiting function should avoid buying new technology and pitch out the stuff they already have? Of course not. I'm simply suggesting that the acquisition of technology should now proceed in a far more ... well, rational way than it has in the past. What do I mean by rational? Consider the following guidelines:

1. NO technology will be purchased until there is a detailed, written statement about what the purpose of the acquisition is and what the technology will be expected to accomplish. This plan must articulate what the system will be expected to do (thereby eliminating the acquisition of un-necessary functionality and vendor created bells and whistles) and what staff (recruiters, recruiting managers, hiring managers, and HR managers) will be expected to do when working with the system. This plan must be reviewed and revised, as necessary, by a team composed of representatives from every group that will use the system and the Vice President of Human Resources.

2. NO technology will be purchased until the CEO, CFO and CIO have been completely briefed on and agreed to the anticipated requirements of acquisition and implementation. This briefing must take the vendor's projection of time required for implementation and pay back and triple it. It must budget as much for training, cultural change, organizational development and support as it does for system acquisition. And it must call for periodic reviews with these senior leaders so that they stay abreast of its implementation and provide timely guidance for mid-course adjustments.

3. NO technology will be purchased until the organizational process in which it will be embedded is completely reengineered. This reengineering must identify practices and procedures that will be made obsolete by the technology and eliminate them. It must identify new activities that will be required of staff and make sure that they have a logical and useful purpose. It must also ensure that appropriate staff (i.e., staff that is well trained and motivated to perform all of those activities) will be available before the system is introduced so that they can help guide its implementation.

These and other similar measures are the only way we can ensure that our enthusiasm for technology does not outrun our ability to manage its acquisition and implementation effectively. The business world is littered with organizations that failed to take this tough skinned approach, and they paid dearly for their mistakes. Indeed, Gartner estimates that U.S. companies threw away more than $1 billion on Web-based technology between 1998 and 2000. They are the accidental, but fully vested members of the Technology Losers Club. ■

■ It's the People, Stupid.

Companies and staffing firms everywhere are rushing to climb on board the technology band-wagon. No respectable recruiting manager, today, would admit to any reluctance at all about using the Internet, intranets, Application Service Providers, organizational recruitment Web-sites and online resources for interviewing, reference checking and employee referral programs. No one wants to be viewed as a latter day Luddite, so millions and millions of dollars are being invested in high technology solutions to the War for Talent. These investments may have slowed with the economy, but there's probably not an organization anywhere that doesn't have its high tech wish list ready to go, once things get better.

This impulse to acquire and use high technology for recruiting and retaining talent is definitely long over due. The HR Department has been at the end of the corporate investment food chain for far too long. I'm worried, however, that in our head-long rush to catch up with the technological sophistication of our counterparts in other functional areas of the enterprise, we will forget a fundamental fact: we are in a people business. As intellectually appealing as the metaphor may seem, hiring and managing people is simply not the same as managing a supply chain of widgets.

Widgets can be carefully ordered and organized with straight forward formulas. Do this, and widgets will do that. They don't have minds of their own. The outcome is mathematically precise and predictable. People, on the other hand, don't behave according to rational rules of inventory management. They can and do think on their own and, thus, make self-serving and often mathematically nonsensical decisions. As a consequence, the acquisition of technology for candidate and employee management must be based on a different formula.

What's that formula? How about something as simple as $1 + 1 = 2$. Sure, it's grade school-level math, but understanding the elements of that equation can make a huge difference in the degree of success you achieve with your investments in technology. Moreover, the rules that govern the operation of this equation are fundamentally different from the guiding principles of old fashioned arithmetic. Call them the "new math of recruiting technology." Here's how they work.

Each of the 1's represents a category of people in the recruiting equation. The first 1 is the recruiter; the second 1 is the candidate. The plus sign is technology. And the 2, of course, represents the addition of a new hire to an organization. In a highly competitive market, however, achieving that addition is no trivial feat, especially if the candidate being recruited is a star performer. So, technology is the "operator," the "power factor," that ensures the equation works. It brings the talent of the recruiter to bear on the candidate so that a successful outcome is achieved.

Really simple stuff, right? Well if you look at the way most organizations are buying technology, apparently not. Many organizations are now spending huge sums on the hardware and software of new systems, but failing altogether to invest in the people who will use it. They ignore their training and the key collateral issues of organizational redesign, cultural change and altered management responsibilities. They stick a whirring, humming piece of high tech machinery in the middle of their organizations and expect a miracle to occur.

And that's where the new math comes in. You see, failing to invest in people when you buy technology changes the equation to $0 + 1 = 0$. In other words, no matter how good the technology and how qualified the candidate, if the individual using the technology lacks the appropriate and necessary knowledge, skills, motivation, support and leadership, then the hire cannot be made. Technology cannot compensate for a "missing" element, and failing to invest in recruiters is the same thing as eliminating them from the equation.

How can that oversight be corrected? How can recruiters be reinstated in the equation so that the new math works? Obviously, organizations must do a much better job of understanding and managing the impact of technology. It is cultural change, process redesign and organizational development all rolled into one. Instead of being handed the results after management has made up its mind, recruiters must be an integral part of the vendor evaluation and selection team, a co-developer of the organizational recruitment Web-site and the project leader for any new system's installation. They alone can avoid the following pitfalls:

- **The VCR effect.** Studies show that most families use only 20% of the functionality built into their VCR. All of the other knobs and dials are just too complicated to understand, or worse, simply irrelevant to their everyday lives. Most recruiting technology has the same fatal flaw. It has been designed by engineers, not by the people who are supposed to use it on-the-job. Unfortunately, however, your organization pays for all that wasted capability and, all too often, pays again when it breaks.

- **The Web-site as IT playground effect.** Despite countless horror stories, many corporate Web-sites are still designed and managed by the IT Department. These groups seem to think the purpose of the site is to strut their programming and design skills. They create overly complicated sites that require a T-1 line to download and open. Such designs may give them goose bumps, but they turn off and turn away the real customer for whom the site was developed—the "A" level candidate.

- **The dumb is dumber effect.** Too many organizations invest tens, even hundreds of thousands of dollars on a new technology system, yet are loath even to assign a project manager or a team of recruiters and hiring managers to the task of overseeing its implementation. As a consequence, communications about the new system are limited, leaving objectives, priorities and expectations unclear. In addition, after a vendor's quick training program on their system, there is seldom any additional instruction or other support to help recruiters and hiring managers put it to work on-the-job. It should not be surprising, therefore, that these unfamiliar and/or misunderstood systems become nothing more than marginal adjuncts to the conduct of business as usual.

The new math of acquiring recruiting technology is, on its face, childishly simple. The logic on which it's founded, however, introduces a fundamental shift in focus. It requires that the enterprise consider not what the technology can do, but rather what its recruiters can do with the technology. As earth shaking as that may seem, the successful use of high technology for recruiting depends upon the engagement, support, trust and talent of recruiters. Or, to put it another way, it's all about the people, stupid. ■

■ The Real Lessons of SCM

Long time readers know that I am not a big fan of the ongoing infatuation with logistics meta-phors in recruitment. While there are definitely lessons we can learn from certain logistics con-cepts, the dynamics of that discipline are fundamentally different from those with which we work. Logistics is the science of moving cogs from point A to point B and supporting them adequately so that they work as designed. We, on the other hand, work with people, and as we all know, people aren't cogs; they are—thank goodness—cognitive beings. Hence, they don't (necessarily) move when and where directed, nor will they perform as designed with the simple addition of a little grease or oil.

So, what are the lessons we can draw from such logistics concepts as Supply Chain Management (SCM)? A recent report by AMR Research, Inc. entitled "Supply Chain Software Yields ROI – But It Takes Time" offers some food for thought. Although it was intended for the cogs and widgets crowd, the report identifies at least three lessons that we in recruitment should consider:

- It takes time to implement the systems and software of automated supply management, whether that supply is made up of nuts and bolts or people.

- It takes a significant investment of money to acquire and implement systems with enough capability to deliver genuine improvements.

- The most important functionalities of effective supply management are those which are often the least developed and/or used in today's candidate management and applicant tracking systems.

Let's take a look at each of these lessons-learned in a bit more detail.

Time. The report found that, despite vendors' claims to the contrary, it takes considerable time to:

(a) implement supply management systems and

(b) to see real and measurable results from their operation.

Some vendors claim that products can be implemented within six weeks. The study, on the other hand, found that only 16% of SCM projects are fully operational within six <u>months,</u> and most projects take more than a year to complete. Indeed, 20% of such projects actually take more than two years to get up and running effectively.

So, what's the lesson we can learn? Manage the expectations of both the executives who must approve the funding for a new system and the staff who will use it on the job. Take the timeline estimate provided by the vendor and <u>triple it</u>. If you get it done sooner, you'll look like a hero; if you don't, you'll still look like you were on top of the project and have the time to do it right.

Budget. The study found that 39% of companies spend more than $10 million annually on sup-ply chain projects. And while that's clearly a lot of money, 69% of all companies surveyed actually have plans to make such investments in the coming year. What about the other 31%? Of that group, 68% said they intended to make a supply chain management investment within the next three years.

What's the lesson to be learned here? Think big. Being good corporate citizens, HR managers normally try to buy recruitment management systems with the least outlay of corporate funds. While such attention to budget is a virtue, underestimating the scale of an investment is more akin to the old Ben Franklin axiom: "A penny wise is a pound foolish." Systems with the scale and capability necessary to deliver real results cost real money, so make the business case for a mean-ingful investment or don't make the investment. You simply can't buy improved management capability—whether its for cogs or cognitive beings—on the cheap.

Functionality. The AMR Study reported that the supply chain modules that had the largest posi-tive impact on critical operating metrics were demand planning and forecasting, supply chain planning and order management. In other words, what happens in advance of actual supply man-agement is as much or even more important as what happens during it.

What should that tell those of us in HR? No matter how effective our systems for moving candi-dates through the recruitment process (which is where 99% of most candidate management system functionality is now focused), we will sub-optimize our performance if we don't:

(a) proactively identify our workforce requirements (by skill, skill level and location) and

(b) create adequate supply streams (internal and external) in advance to meet those requirements when they arrive.

So what's the bottom line? The way to take advantage of logistics concepts is not to follow them slavishly, but rather, to learn from the mistakes and acquired wisdom of our colleagues in the logistics field. ■

■ Assessing ASPs

There has been an overwhelming proliferation of products in the marketplace as more and more organizations look to Web-based technology for resume management, candidate management, recruitment process management and Web-site implementation. The value proposition of these solutions is very appealing: they provide a way for you to capture the efficiency and robust capability of the Internet without the cost, headaches and maintenance hassles of traditional client server products (i.e., those that reside on your own mainframe computers).

At least that's the PR from the companies that offer these products. Called Application Service Providers (ASPs), they all claim to be a heaven-sent solution. But as with every other product category, there is a wide range of variations on the theme. To help you compare apples-to-apples and sort out the differences between various ASP products, I've assembled the list of "vendor assessment" questions below:

1. Was the product built from the ground up for Web delivery?
Client server-based systems that have a Web front end bolted on as an afterthought tend not to perform as well as solutions born on the Web.

2. Does the ASP have core expertise in the field of recruitment?
Products that are built by technologists or specialists in another field often lack needed functionality or design it incorrectly.

3. Does the ASP have core expertise in your kind of recruiting (i.e., in-house, staffing firm, executive recruitment)?
Without that background, products are often mis-designed (with too little or too much capability) and, as a consequence, do not deliver the advertised advantages.

4. Was the software developed by the ASP or by an independent software producer?
Products that are not developed by the ASP in-house often do not receive the continuous improvement that ASPs claim to offer.

5. Can the product be <u>customized</u> and <u>integrated</u> with your other systems?
These two issues are the keys to successful <u>function-specific</u> and <u>enterprise-wide</u> implementation, and ASPs must be able to deal with them at little or no cost or their advantage disappears. ■

■ Why Applicant Tracking Systems Don't Work

Fundamentally, an Applicant Tracking System (ATS) is an investment in quality improvement. The technology is designed to upgrade recruiting productivity and performance. The purpose of acquiring such technology, therefore, should be to achieve specific operating improvements, defined by such metrics as a shorter time-to-fill openings, a lower cost-to-recruit and an increase in applicant quality. In other words, it is the recruiting organization's quantified, measurable quality improvement objectives that are the value proposition of an ATS, not its database capacity, data transmission speed or calculating power. And, by those standards at least, today's ATS solutions don't work.

Now, before my friends in ATS companies rise up in righteous indignation, let me acknowledge that their products have, in fact, produced positive outcomes among recruiting organizations. So, what's my problem? Simple. I think an ATS solution should do better than the modest level of improvements achieved to date. Among the public domain case studies and research that I've seen , ATS-related improvements in cost-per-hire and time-to-fill have been in the 10-30% range. Is that respectable? Yes. Is it good enough for an organization that strives to be a world class employer? Absolutely not.

To be an industry leader in recruitment, an organization must achieve truly significant and continuous improvements in the metrics that define operational quality. And, to accomplish those objectives, it must devise an ATS acquisition strategy with both of the following two elements:

- **First, the technology must work as advertised.** It must archive files accurately, provide an easy means of finding specific files when they're needed, and support efficient communication with the individuals described by those selected files as well as the organization's recruiters and hiring managers. And although there are clear differences in capabilities among individual Applicant Tracking Systems, most perform these tasks reasonably well.

- **Second, the application of the technology by the organization must have a sufficient impact on its operations to influence recruiter productivity and performance significantly.** And there's the rub. In far too many recruiting organizations, today, the ATS has been bolted on as an afterthought and thus changes very little in the way business is done. When that happens, the return on investment in an ATS is eroded or eliminated altogether.

This application issue is particularly important in the corporate setting. Why? Because in many companies, the in-house recruiter is consumed by in-house concerns. As one recruiter recently noted on an Internet discussion forum:

> *"... the corporate position is one focused on*
> *'process.' Process being scheduling, inter-*
> *viewing, hand holding and consulting to*
> *managers, basically facilitating the flow.*
> *There is little time actually spent on 'recruiting."*

If that's true and my observations suggest that it often is, then an ATS can only improve recruiter performance if the process with which recruiters must work is optimized. Indeed, optimizing the process might even enable recruiters to spend less time on in-house "hand-holding and consulting" and more time on outside-the-house tasks ... you know, such allegedly important activities as finding, evaluating and recruiting "A" level performers.

But, what does "recruiting process optimization" mean? Basically, it involves re-engineering the tasks and procedures performed by an organization's recruiters, hiring managers and other process actors so as to:

- Eliminate unnecessary or outdated activities

- Eliminate redundant activities

- Assign those activities best performed by machines to machines and those activities best performed by recruiters to recruiters

- Improve access to information when and where it is needed for timely action and decision-making, and

- Improve communications fidelity and speed to ensure coordination, common purpose and superior customer (i.e., candidate) service.

In short, optimization serves to redesign the recruiting process end-to-end so as to achieve an organization's specified operating improvement objectives.

For this process change to "stick," however, it must be buttressed with a change in culture. The quality improvement efforts initiated during the 1980's proved that point beyond all doubt. At that time, America's production line and service delivery quality was less than lousy, and corporate competitiveness at home and in world markets was suffering, as a result. Initial programs to upgrade manufacturing performance made very little difference, so companies looked to the competition for a solution. That's when they discovered that Japan was using a set of quality improvement principles espoused by an American, W. Edward Deming. Of his 14 points for operational excellence, #1 was "Create constancy of purpose for improvement of product and service." In essence, the cultural parameters—an organization's priorities, values, leadership and rewards—must all be in place first, before any other action can be taken to achieve performance improvements.

That's as true for recruiting organizations as it is for a manufacturing plant. The acquisition of an ATS is not the goal. It is the means, or more precisely, one subset of the means by which an organization implements performance improvement. The framework for that implementation effort is the recruiting process. The better its design, the better both the technology and the human players in the process—hiring managers as well as recruiters—will work. And, of course, the better their performance, the higher the productivity and quality of output (i.e. the new hires) of the organization.

In-house recruiters may, in fact, be fixated on process, but the substance of that process is not fixed in stone. It is "hand holding and consulting" only if we let it be. If we want to spend our days working on different kinds of activities—those that focus on sourcing and recruiting high caliber candidates—then, we have to redefine our process to do so. To achieve that transformation, however, the organization will need committed leadership and an imaginative, no-holds-barred approach to organizational development. Those requirements are admittedly not trivial, but their omission—not the technology or the recruiters on staff—is the real cause of the less than spectacular performance improvements achieved to date with Applicant Tracking Systems. ■

■ Guarding the Work Environment in the Electronic Era

The proliferation of electronic communication devices has, unfortunately, made it all too easy to broadcast potentially offensive statements to our employee populations. Individuals can disseminate inappropriate jokes and play pranks on others, purposefully or inadvertently creating a hostile work environment.

Because computers keep detailed records of all communications, the potential for damaging litigation from such situations is significant. To protect your organization, I suggest that you:

- Train and retrain your employees on the appropriate uses of electronic communications and on the potential dangers of inappropriate use.

- Develop and post a written policy forbidding employees from making threatening, harassing or offensive comments via e-mail or voicemail.

- Enforce the policy without exception and in a speedy fashion.

- Make supervisors and managers responsible for their staff's adherence to the policy and evaluate how well they (supervisors and managers) do so in their performance appraisal. ■

■ The Definition of a "Company Computer"

A recent court case has helped to define just what is meant by the term "company computer."

In this case, an employer provided two computers to an employee; one was for home use and the other was for use in the office. The individual then signed the employer's "electronic and telephone equipment policy statement" which stipulated that the computers could be monitored by the employer.

Subsequent monitoring revealed that the employee had broken the organization's policy by accessing sexually explicit sites with the home computer, and the person was terminated. When the company asked for its computer back, however, the ex-employee refused and sued for wrongful termination, arguing that what was done on the computer at home was not subject to the employer's policy.

The trial court held in favor of the employee, citing his right to privacy. The appeal court, on the other hand, overturned the lower court, explaining that the computer was company equipment and the employer's policy clearly voided any expectation of privacy by the employee. The termination was permitted, and the ex-employee was ordered to return the computer.

What lessons can we learn from this situation?

- Make sure you have a clearly written policy for the use of your organization's computers and require all employees to sign it.

- Although Shakespeare said, "A rose by any other name is still a rose," avoid terms such as "a computer for home use" or designations such as a "home computer" versus a "work computer." Such distinctions are inappropriate and potentially problematic as a company's computers are work computers wherever they are used. ■

■ A Warning Note

Technology has taken the HR world by storm. After spending years at the bottom of the food chain, the Human Resource function is finally seeing a larger share of the high tech investment pie. While that's good news, the headlong rush to install technology in a wide range of HR activities does have a dark side. Ironically, it can cause a degradation in service and thus impact negatively on customer satisfaction.

Take the case of Workforce Self-Service (WSS) technology. These tools make information about vacation time, healthcare benefits, pay, training, and 401(k) pension plan services available to employees. There's less human interaction, so information is more accurate and administrative costs are reduced. Indeed, according to one survey, such technology can cut HR transaction costs by up to 75%, enabling companies to recoup their investment in under two years.

That kind of data is enough to make any CFO smile, so it comes as no surprise that the survey found that 57% of North American respondents had bought the technology and were delivering HR services through a corporate portal. Moreover, use is also accelerating—the 57% figure was up from 40% in 2000.

The momentum is clearly on the side of doing more with technology. And that's what makes a recent survey by CIGNA Corporation so troubling. It found that, while employers think WSS is definitely the wave of the future, employees aren't so sure. Among those polled, 57% of the companies think workers can perform benefits transactions online satisfactorily, but only 20% of employees agree.

Why the disconnect? According to CIGNA, the use of technology is fine for processing data, but that represents only a part—and the least important part, at that—of what employees seek from the HR Department. The support that employees most need and WSS can't deliver involves help with the day-to-day issues of benefits delivery, claims reimbursements and service questions.

Therefore, employers that buy into WSS (or any other technology) thinking that they can use it to off-load all of the benefits management work onto employees, make a grave mistake. That kind of thinking reflects a fundamental misunderstanding of how technology can be used in a human enterprise. The trick to doing it right is to avoid asking technology to do two things:

- Those tasks that it cannot do well, and
- Those tasks that humans do best.

When it comes to empathizing with colleagues, helping them understand benefits rules, and sorting out their benefits problems, even state-of-the-art technology is no match for the well trained and compassionate HR professional. ■

■ **Recruiting Metrics**
Are They Useful? How Do You Use Them?

■ The Way of the Mop

According to the American's Use of Time project at the University of Maryland, you and I are spending less and less time keeping our homes up to the standards of the Good Housekeeping Institute. On average, we now spend 12 fewer hours per week cleaning the baseboards and curtains than we did in 1960.

Certainly, for some of us, that's an irrelevant benchmark: after all, 12 less than 0 is still 0. But for most Americans, the decline in housekeeping performance is real and the inevitable outcome of increasingly overloaded and frenetic days. It also seems to fly in the face of another reality: the past year or so has seen the introduction of more new models of mops than at any other time in the history of humankind.

A visit to any grocery or hardware store quickly brings this mop mania into focus. You'll find dry mops and wet towel mops and mops with built-in reservoirs for cleaning fluids. You'll see disposable mops and mops that are designed to withstand repetitive use even in a teenager's bedroom. Sure, the old fashioned string mop is still available, but now it shares shelf space with sleek decorator models fit for the tastes of Martha Stewart.

It just makes you wonder. If we Americans are increasingly disengaged from our housework, why are we so fascinated with tools designed specifically for that purpose? Although I'm sure some Ph.D. candidate somewhere will see this dichotomy as the perfect subject for their dissertation, I think the answer is really rather simple. Americans will do the work, if it can be done with minimal discomfort. We'll even mop the floors as long as we don't have to get our hands dirty.

Now, I'm not saying that's a bad thing. I mean, who wants to stick their hands into a bucket of grimy, foul smelling water? And besides, in many cases, the actual performance of these new fangled mops does, in fact, appear to be better than that of the more traditional variety. In other words, they deliver both a better user experience and better results.

What does all of that have to do with recruiting? I think it's an interesting metaphor for today's growing fascination with metrics among Human Resource recruiters. For years, legions of recruiters and HR professionals avoided metrics like housecleaning. They didn't have time to fiddle with quantified measures and besides the metrics they did have—stuff like cost-per-hire and time-to-fill—were labor intensive to use and not all that helpful (at least when it came to describing the work of the recruiting function to the CEO).

But now, we're seeing a whole new generation of shiny, new metrics, and we in the recruiting profession are lining up like lemmings before a late night infomercial to order up one or two or twelve of those things for our organization. Everyone wants to be measuring performance as long as it can be done with one of these super advanced, Twenty-first Century mathematical marvels.

And that's great, <u>if</u> the metrics we use actually get the job done and done efficiently. Kinda' like a mop.

What do I mean? The rush to metrics has two hidden dangers that must be addressed if they are to deliver true value to the recruiting function:

- **Paralysis by analysis**—the overuse of metrics, resulting in so much information that it's impossible to tell what is actually going on.

- **Misguided metrics**—the collection of information that is not relevant or important to the clients of the recruiting process.

When either of these situations occur, your use of metrics fails to help you identify problems and evaluate alternative solutions to them—which is the cleaning that metrics should do.

Having visited many employers and staffing firms and looked at their recruiting processes, I can understand their pressing interest in metrics. Many of the activities and information flows, policies and procedures of their on-the-job "household" haven't been given a good cleaning in years (if ever). Moreover, the hype about all these new approaches to metrics would make even mop manufacturers proud. Measurement has definitely caught the eye of the HR consumer, and the queue of paying customers is quickly lengthening for this metrics model or that. All we need to remember is that metrics—like mops—are only worth buying if they deliver a better user experience for your customer and help them (and you) get better results. ■

■ Prying Open Wallets

A survey by McKinsey & Company last year found corporate officers seemingly alert to the shortcomings of their organizations' efforts at talent management. Among respondents:

- 75% said that their companies are either "chronically talent-short across the board" or "suffer from insufficient talent sometimes."

- Only 33% thought that their companies attract highly talented people.

- Even fewer—just 10%—believed that their companies were good at retaining high performers.

- And sadly, just 3% thought that their employers "actually develop people effectively" or "move low performers out quickly."

Now, some in our profession would say that such self awareness, especially among corporate officers, is a good thing. Self awareness, after all, is the first and necessary step to self improvement. You can't begin to get better until you know that you have a problem. And, of course, that's true; but I also believe that such a rosy reading of these findings misses the mark. Indeed, it makes a classical surveying mistake.

Take market surveys. For years, our friends in the Marketing Department have surveyed consumer behavior to figure out what features and capabilities consumers really want. The long (and lengthening) list of new product failures, however, attests to the less than perfect track record of surveys as predictors of human action (or inaction). Why is that so? Because the fact that a consumer says he or she wants a product does not mean that they will open their wallets and pay for it once it's available. In other words, in the mind of the consumer, wanting something and buying it are two different states, and one doesn't necessarily lead to the other. And why is that so? Because every consumer has more than one "want" and a limited budget. Hence, they must compare the perceived benefit of each new product to the benefits of all other competing products and decide where they will get the greatest return on their investment.

Which brings us back to our seemingly self-aware corporate officers. They clearly recognize that they have a talent problem in their companies, but that recognition doesn't necessarily mean that they will dip into their budgets to pay for its correction. They, too, have competing wants—they want the talent problem fixed, but they also want to see a key product upgraded or a new marketing strategy launched or a new financial management system installed—and their limited budgets will require that they make choices among those competing priorities. It is at this "choice point" that HR has historically lost out. The acquisition and retention of talent is important, but not important enough to make the cut.

So, how can we convince corporate officers to open their wallets? Increasingly, HR Departments recognize that the best leverage comes from metrics. Numbers are the *lingua franca* of the business world, and metrics translate HR activities into numbers. They quantify the potential benefit of an investment in HR so that executives can understand and appreciate it. That's the upside to metrics. There is also a downside, however.

Metrics can easily be miscast and misused. Just as a poorly crafted question on a consumer survey can provide false or misleading information, the wrong metrics can actually work against the case that HR is trying to make. How do we pick the right metrics? We have to remember the audience we are trying to reach. Just as good advertising copy is written for the target consumer, the best metrics in HR are designed for those corporate officers who will evaluate its performance. They convey information that is meaningful to them, information that is important enough to influence their behavior. And open their wallets.

And there's the rub. All too often, HR uses metrics that measure what HR wants to know. Take cost-per-hire and time-to-fill. These metrics gauge process efficiency, and in today's tight budget environment, being efficient is a fundamental component of good management. It enhances the performance of the HR Department, which, in turn, also pays a dividend to the enterprise. The perceived value of that efficiency, however, is felt most keenly closest to its point of impact. In other words, the metrics of efficiency convey information that is most meaningful to HR. They measure _its_ success. They give the Vice President of Human Resources goose bumps, but mean little or nothing to other corporate officers because they have no impact on _their_ success.

To influence the behavior of other corporate officers, therefore, HR must use metrics that have a proximate impact on those officers. It must adopt metrics that can meaningfully convey what HR is doing to ensure _their_ success. What are such metrics? There are any number of possibilities, but I suggest you begin with just four: Two that quantify the direct contribution HR is making to line departments and other operating units, and two that quantify the contribution HR is making to the enterprise as a whole.

- The first two are _quality of hire_ and _retention rates among high performers_. If only 33% of corporate officers think their companies attract highly talented people and just 10% think they retain them, then these measures will have meaning and be important to corporate decision-makers. They are proof positive of what HR is doing to help them get and hold on to good talent.

- The second two are _return on investment_ and _return on assets_. These measures will resonate with the 75% of corporate officers who say that their companies are chronically talent short and the 3% who think that their companies are ineffective at managing and developing people. In most cases, they recognize that solving such problems will require an investment, but they want to know that the investment will yield tangible results that are clearly helpful to them. These measures provide the proof.

Not every corporate officer will be swayed by such measures, of course. Even the best advertising sells only a percentage of prospective consumers. These indicators do represent a powerful step in the right direction, however. They shift the focus of measurement from the Human Resource Department to its customers, from information that is helpful primarily to recruiters and HR managers to information that gauges how HR is helping other corporate officers be successful. And in the competition for corporate resources, there is no better way to pry open wallets. ■

■ What Metrics Matter?

It can make you dizzy. All of the conversations, I mean, and conference presentations about metrics going on of late. It seems as if everyone has an opinion, and every opinion is different. So, how do you know what metrics matter most?

In my view, there are two issues that cloud our ability to implement metrics in the recruiting function.

The first I call the **Wannabe Factor**. Having been chastened more than once by the abstruse calculations of the CFO and his/her hench-people in Finance, many HR professionals are convinced that their metrics must produce calculations that are accurate to the 15th decimal point. In other words, they believe that HR metrics have to be just like financial measures in order to have validity and usefulness. What they don't realize (and current news reports are now making clear) is that, for all their seeming rigor, financial measures—like any other metrics—are based on human assumptions. In other words, we need to stop wringing our hands about having metrics that are accurate enough to land people on the moon, and instead devise those that provide meaningful information based on our best business judgment.

The second issue standing in the way of metrics implementation is a misunderstanding about the difference between an organization's strategy of measurement (its ends) and the selection of the specific metrics it will use (its means). I call this the **Means and Ends Mix-up**. Unfortunately, most of the time and effort devoted to the installation of metrics puts the cart before the horse. It focuses on numbers before the purpose of those numbers is clearly defined and understood. In essence, we begin arguing about whether to use cost-per-hire or time-to-fill before we understand what activity we want to measure and what we'll do with the data we collect (i.e., our strategy).

An organization's strategy of measurement can be uni-dimensional or multi-dimensional. It can focus on one aspect of the recruiting function or on several. What deter-mines the correct approach? The organization's readiness for measurement, its understanding of and commitment to the use of quantified measures for performance evaluation and improvement. The greater the organization's readiness, the more complex the strategy can be.

What is the optimum strategy? A 3-dimensional assessment that measures:

- **Efficiency:** how well are the function's resources (money, time, people) used during the accomplishment of its activities?

- **Output:** what is the quantity and quality of the candidates who are:

(a) attracted to the organization and

(b) willing to pass through all of the recruiting function's activities to an offer?

- **Contribution to the enterprise:** what value does the function create in the operation of the business and/or the accomplishment of its mission?

There are, of course, a wide range of specific metrics that can be used to measure performance in each of these 3 dimensions. For example:

(a) efficiency can be measured with cost-per-hire or time to fill;

(b) output can be measured with post-hire performance appraisal scores or the percentage match between the skills of new hires and stated requirements; and

(c) contribution can gauged with return on assets (the percentage fill achieved with the talent data-base or the recruitment Web-site.)

There is no universally accepted "best" metric in any of these areas, so the key is to pick a metric that fits your culture and to define it based on your best business judgment. ■

■ Measure, Measure on the Wall

Even before the "official" recession began in March 2001, company CEOs were feeling the pinch at the bottom line and reverting to old behaviors. Despite countless magazine interviews and statements on business talk shows to the contrary, corporate leaders still weren't convinced that workers were a resource too critical to lose. Hence, the second that business turned soft, they turned to talent-diminishing, but traditional strategies for enterprise preservation: they laid people off and cut the budget of the Human Resource Department.

Now, the cynic in me says that this situation is simply one more example of the prevailing "leadership lapse" in corporate America. Most CEOs have learned all the glib phrases about the importance of people, but barely a handful really understand (or believe) what they are saying. And what do you expect when virtually every corporate chieftain on the planet has come up through the ranks of Finance or Marketing. The only time they ever spent in the HR Department was when they were first hired and that was to set up their benefits selections.

This Human Resource illiteracy among CEOs is clearly a problem, but it's by no means the sole culprit in the talent mismanagement during the late (we hope), unlamented recession. Indeed, just as big a problem is the "leadership lapse" in the Human Resource Department, itself. What am I talking about? A recent study by Watson Wyatt says it best. The study—*eHR: Getting Results Along the Journey*—found that four out of ten companies do not develop a business case for their investments in HR technology. In other words, a significant percentage of HR Departments in corporate America do not believe that they should justify the company's investment in talent management systems or that they should link those investments to the success of the enterprise. Talk about abdicating leadership!

Moreover, among the 61% of companies that did make a formal business case for investments in new HR technology, most focused on measures of operating efficiency within the HR Department. In other words, they sold the investment on the basis of improvements in cost-per-hire and time-to-fill. Now, these are clearly important measures, but they do nothing for the one person who must be sold on the value of the investment: the CEO. In fact, when I talk to CEOs, they tell me that they _expect_ efficiency in the processes of HR, just as they do in the processes of accounting or manufacturing. To them, efficiency is (or should be) a given. And when it's not, their inclination is to get rid of the Vice President of Human Resources and find a manager who delivers it and more.

So, what will catch the attention of CEOs? A return on investment that accrues value to _their_ report cards. In other words, CEOs, being rational economic actors, will allocate corporate monies where they will do the most good: at the bottom line of the enterprise. Why? Because that's how they—CEOs—get evaluated. By the stock market, by shareholders and by the Board of Directors. Absolutely, HR executives must make a business case for their proposed investments in technology, but that business case must articulate its results in such measures as:

■ Return on investment

138

- Return on asset
- Increase in shareholder value.

You can bet that the competition—the Vice Presidents of Sales and Marketing and Business Unit Executives—will be making their case that way, and HR must too. These and similar metrics are the *lingua franca* of enterprise (or C-level) decision-making; everything else is a foreign language and communicates nothing.

Now, I know what you're thinking. Unlike those other functional areas, the assets that HR manages are intangible and thus can't be measured. We focus on process because people don't behave like buildings and research and other capital resources. That's been the cry of the HR profession since the invention of the time clock. And I wouldn't disagree. People are a fundamentally different kind of asset, and it's about time CEOs figured that out. But that fact doesn't excuse us from having to prove the economic contribution derived from our management of that asset.

How can we do that? Here are a couple of suggestions:

- **Treat your resume database as a talent asset.** Invest in technology as a recruiting as well as a sourcing tool. In other words, use it both for database management (requiring efficient data input, storage and search) and for communications ... for building relationships with and selling candidates on your employment opportunities. Then measure the return on that combined strategy, using as your metric the improvement in the percentage of hires derived from the database. Right now, HireAbility reports that the average employer finds just 5% of its new hires in its resume database, so any gain in that performance is definitely a return on asset. It sends savings (in sourcing costs and better productivity) right to the bottom line.

- **Treat your workforce as an asset.** Invest in retention-building programs (e.g., an Employee Worklife Support Center or Career Development Center on the Web), and then measure the return on those investments. For example, calculate reductions in attrition rates and monetize that result as savings in sourcing costs and output shortfalls; similarly, determine improvements in performance (e.g., fewer product defects or better service quality) and monetize those results as reductions in customer returns or more repeat visits by customers.

Granted many of these measures are based on relationships that have not been blessed by the keepers of Generally Accepted Accounting Principles. Given the performance of the GAAP at Enron and other firms, however, I wouldn't worry too much about being a purist for the green eye shade crowd. The important issue is that these examples present a logic that is sensible to CEOs and calculations that can be evaluated on their own merits. As a consequence, they do what the GAAP has too often failed to do for the rest of the enterprise: make visible the role and the performance of those charged with managing the HR function. ■

■ Using Metrics to Avoid the Post Shopping Blahs
(written for the Holiday Season every month of the year)

Holiday shopping is well underway, and merriment is in the air. As we roam the malls and specialty shops, however, many of us are conflicted. Not about the gifts we want to give—we know the kids' wish lists by heart and have a pretty good idea of what we want to get for the rest of the family. No, this tension comes from another source: we are torn between our desire to find a great bargain and our trepidation about what happens, if the gift flops.

In one way or another, we've all calculated the costs of "a bad gift":

- For recipients over the age of 21, it's the brave but artificial smile when they first open the present.

- For recipients under the age of 21, it's the frown, tears and even tantrums when the gift isn't what was expected.

- It's also the guilt you feel for making such a bad decision.

- If you return the gift, there's also the time you devote to standing in line at the Return Desk.

- And the unpleasantness of enduring the sullen attitude of the hassled return clerk.

- And the time you spend to find something to replace that "bad gift."

- And the irritation you feel at having to invest the time to get it right the second time.

- If your recipient returns the gift, it's the embarrassment you feel when they discover how little you paid for it.

- And the sadness that weighs on you for making them shop for the gift they really wanted.

- And the frustration you feel when they come back with something that wasn't on their list or even remotely similar to anything they ever asked for.

- And finally, it's the vow you make never, ever to repeat this experience again.

Add it all up and the emotional, psychological and, occasionally, financial cost of "a bad gift" is significant indeed. Therefore, the smart shoppers among us do whatever is necessary (e.g., re-engineer their shopping list development process, improve their sourcing of bargain opportunities, invest in new gift idea screening tools) to make sure that they don't have to pay such a steep price ever again.

This cost avoidance/self improvement dynamic makes eminent good sense, and you would think that it would naturally lap over into recruiting, as well. After all, most recruiters are also holiday shoppers, so we should be equally as aggressive at avoiding the cost of "a bad hire." If you look at the data, however, there's still better than a 50% chance that an organization will select the wrong candidate for employment. Year after year, through boom times and recessions, we head

140

out to the recruitment malls and specialty stores online and select the one person our employer won't like.

Why do you think that is? I suppose there are any number of contributing factors—ranging from below market salary offers to inept interviews by hiring managers—but the most important, I think, is that the cost of "a bad hire" is not as readily apparent as the cost of "a bad gift." While some of the consequences clearly impact on the recruiting function, many others are felt else-where in the enterprise, and that makes it hard to get a full sense of the management, productivity, performance, financial and other costs of a poor selection decision. So, in the hopes that this will be one of your good gifts, I offer the following list of cost elements that will enable you to calculate just how expensive it is to make "a bad hire."

Post Hoc Costs (unlike with bad gifts, you can't return the bad hire for a refund)

1. The cost of advertising used in sourcing the bad hire.

2. Agency fees incurred in sourcing the bad hire.

3. Internal labor fees associated with interviewing, evaluating, selling and negotiating with the bad hire (i.e. salary and benefits for recruiters, hiring managers, associates, administrative support personnel).

4. The cost of travel to bring the bad hire in for interviews (i.e., transportation, hotel, per diem).

5. Relocation costs for the bad hire (the one cost element that can be partially or completely recouped if the bad hire leaves quickly enough).

6. Training costs to introduce the bad hire to the organization's processes, procedures and standards (i.e., the preparation and delivery time spent by formal trainers, supervisors and associates).

7. The decline in customer satisfaction and repeat business as a result of poor performance by the bad hire.

8. The decline in associate productivity as they compensate for the poor performance of the bad hire.

9. The decline in morale among associates as they have to pick up the slack for the poor hire.

10. The degradation in unit performance as projects are not completed and sales are not closed as a result of the bad hire's work.

11. The cost of the time and energy devoted by supervisors and managers to counsel the bad hire and improve their performance.

12. The cost of the time and effort devoted by the Human Resource function to prepare for and implement a legally defensible exit strategy for the bad hire.

13. Any severance or other payments made to the bad hire in conjunction with their departure.

Current Costs

1. The decline in customer satisfaction and repeat business as a result of poor performance due to inadequate staffing (the vacancy resulting from the bad hire's departure).

2. The decline in associate productivity due to inadequate staffing.

3. The decline in morale among associates due to inadequate staffing.

4. The degradation in unit performance as projects are not completed and sales not closed due to inadequate staffing.

5. The cost of the time and energy devoted by supervisors and managers to deal with the problems in 1-4 above.

6. The opportunity costs incurred by having to do every recruiting activity twice in order to get it right (i.e., assignments and responsibilities that are not completed).

7. The loss of internal capital (i.e., esteem, stature, internal customer satisfaction) result-ing from HR and recruiters being blamed for the "bad hire" (no matter how complicit hir-ing managers and others are, HR and recruiters almost always take the fall).

The costs of "a bad gift" are high, but they pale in comparison to the costs of "a bad hire." As the lists above clearly indicate, even one bad decision can impose a heavy toll on the organization, its employees and its managers. The avoidance of those costs, therefore, makes good business sense, and that single fact provides all the rationale that's needed to support improvements in HR and re-cruiting, even when hiring activity is low and resume flow is heavy. Moreover, it takes time (as well as money) to implement process re-designs, technology upgrades, staff training and proce-dural adjustments. So, don't wait 'til the last minute to begin preparations for your talent shop-ping. There's only a limited number of days until the recovery really takes off. ■

■ Asset Managers or Paper Pushers

In today's competitive business environment, everyone wants to perform at peak levels. In the recruiting world, that impulse typically translates into a discussion of process efficiency. How do we do more with less? How can we cut our cost-per-hire or our time-to-fill? In short, how can we take what we have now and use it to perform at optimum levels?

While those measures of merit are helpful, it's important to recognize that they are not the metrics that get Chief Executives Officers worked up. Cutting cost contributes to survival; it does not contribute to growth. Or to increased market share. And on the CEO's report card, an "A" (and its accompanying financial reward) can only be earned by building the organization up, not enabling it to hang on.

So, where do CEOs focus most of their attention? On such measures as shareholder value and the return on assets. To put it another way, the CEO is most interested in knowing how the organization can maximize its return on investment in certain assets so that shareholders realize the greatest possible gain from their stock holdings. Now, for most CEOs, the assets that spring first to mind are facilities, capital, real estate and technology. These assets are tangible, they depreciate according to Generally Accepted Accounting Principles and the benefit that they provide to the organization can be measured quantitatively. In short, they are everything that talent is not. And that's the reason that most Human Resource Departments and their staffing functions focus on process improvements; it is one of the few areas in which their performance can be measured with numbers—the *lingua franca* of CEOs.

The irony, however, is that staffing does invest in and manage an old fashioned, kick the tires asset. It's called the resume database. Whether it's described as talent, human capital or just plain old resumes, that asset is tangible, its value does depreciate (although the accounting profession has as much competence in measuring that depreciation as it does in managing finances at Enron) and the benefit it provides to the organization can be measured with numbers. So, what kind of return are we recruiters earning on our asset? Let's go through the numbers.

First, we need to measure the investment. The sunk cost, of course, is the cost of the organization's applicant tracking system, the technology that processes both digital and paper resumes and stores them in a database resident on a computer somewhere. The variable costs are the time and wages of recruiters and the posting and search fees necessary to acquire the resumes. And if you really wanted to be complete, you could also throw in the cost of the facility that houses the database and the recruiters and the cost of benefits and training provided to recruiters. Add all of that up, and it quickly becomes clear that the organization's total investment in its database is far from trivial.

Next, let's measure the return on that asset. According to a study by HireAbility, on average, most employers fill just 5% of their vacancies with candidates sourced from their own resume database. We can monetize that percentage fill by calculating what it would have cost if that 5%

had been sourced from the employee referral program or through traditional advertising. Whatever the methodology used, I don't think there is any doubt that this level of performance is hardly something the CEO would brag about to his or her boss, the Board of Directors. Indeed, with any visibility into such a poor ROI, it's more likely that the CEO would:

(a) write the database asset off as non-performing,

(b) fire the manager who is supposed to be overseeing its development, or

(c) both.

How can recruiters get themselves out of this bind? The key, it seems to me, is to see the database differently. We need to throw out the notion that it's an electronic stack of documents and see it, instead, as a platform for relationships with talent. In other words, if a resume is good enough to be archived in our database (because the candidate it describes is a potential hire at some point in the future), then that candidate is important enough to invest in.

That investment involves a range of activities all designed to transform the digital stranger represented by the document in the computer's database into an individual who has a genuine association with your employer. Its goal is to build rapport and trust, to pre-sell the candidate on the organization, and to get to know him or her better so that there is the tightest possible fit between the candidate and any position they are offered in the future.

How do you measure the return on that investment? There are several measures that can be used, including the two below:

- **Rate of Success.** For most hiring managers, success in recruiting is defined as the organization's ability to hire their preferred candidate. Therefore, rate of success is the percentage of selected candidates (i.e., those who are rated #1 on the hiring manager's list) who accept the organization's employment offer. It is directly affected by the amount and quality of pre-selling done with the candidate prior to the commencement of recruiting for a specific requirement. Why is that important? That pre-selling delivers process efficiency (i.e., lower cost- and time-to-fill), but just as important, it upgrades the quality of talent accessed by the organization. And that quality enhancement is a genuine return on investment.

- **New Hire Performance**. If your organization hires a significant percentage of new employees from its own candidate database and you have invested in getting to know those candidates better, then the person-job fit will also be better. Research clearly shows that the better suited a person is for a particular position, the faster they are able to achieve full productivity, the higher their level of performance over time, and the better their morale. All of those factors can be monetized so that the return can then be expressed in numbers.

What's the bottom line? Basically, if recruiting wants to be seen as a strategic function (and I believe that it deserves to be), then we will have to think the way the CEO thinks. That means we must prioritize our activities so as to make money for the organization, not simply to save it. We must allocate our investments of corporate dollars so as to achieve the highest possible return on the asset we manage, not simply to improve process efficiency. In short, we must re-imagine ourselves as managers of a talent asset, not as pushers of digital paper. ■

■ **Picking the Right Recruitment Web-Sites**
Why Is It Important? How Do You Do It?

■ Herdball

Ever watch little kids when they join their first organized soccer league? The two opposing teams face off, the ball is put into play, and then every kid on the field begins to chase after it en masse. From the sidelines, this *ballet de sport* looks like a huge herd of indistinguishable arms and legs wheeling around the field behind a bouncing black and white ball.

For little kids learning to play soccer, such a "do what everyone else does" approach to competition is probably all that we can expect. For recruiters, however, people who are responsible for winning the best talent for their organizations, "herdball" is a sure fire strategy for losing.

Who's playing herdball on recruitment's "friendly fields of strife?" Lots of us. According to a recent survey by Wetfeet.com, $0.52 of every dollar spent on the Web goes to just 1 site: yep, you guessed it ... Monster.com. And $0.80 of every dollar spent online goes to just four sites: Monster.com, HotJobs.com, CareerBuilder.com, and HeadHunter.net. Now, that's herdball!

Clearly, there's absolutely nothing wrong with using these sites. They have all very real and significant capabilities as recruiting resources. They cannot, however, support every kind of recruiting requirement in every industry in every location. As with any vendor, they have their strengths and their areas where they aren't so strong. Equally as important, with over 40,000 employment-related sites now operating on the Web, recruiters have plenty of options from which to choose. Making those choices is what spells the difference between a successful online recruiter and one who isn't. Indeed, according to the Wetfeet survey, over half of the respondents reported that they sourced fewer than 10% of their new hires from a job board. That kind of lousy return on investment is about the best you can expect when you follow the herd.

What causes this kind of noncompetitive behavior among otherwise rational recruiters? There are several possible explanations:

- **Dumb policies.** This situation occurs when an organization negotiates an annual contract with Monster or one of the other big sites. These contracts are expensive, and organizations are loath to see any of their money wasted. So what happens? The CFO or (sadly) an HR executive dictates that recruiters use that one site for every single recruiting requirement no matter how unique its specifications.

- **Low risk.** Everyone has heard of the four big sites, even the CEO. Hence, there's very little risk in using them. On the other hand, when you pay to post a job or search the resume database at a site that's not very well known, you leave yourself open to second guessing and criticism. In short, following the herd will probably keep you out of trouble, even if the results are less than what your organization needs to meet its business goals.

- **Don't know your options**. There are more than 40,000 options out there for you to consider when selecting a recruitment Web-site, but it's not always easy to find them or the information you need to evaluate and compare them. Even worse, these sites are like restaurants: many come and go so rapidly that it's hard even to keep track of those that you have uncovered. (If you're facing this dilemma, all is not lost, at least according to the American Staffing Association. It called *WEDDLE's Guides* the "Zagat" of the online recruitment industry.)

- **Not enough time to do research**. It takes time to make smart site selections, and with downsizing and budget cuts, time is a resource most recruiters don't have. That's why I created the SmartSelect™ process; it's a 5-step methodology for picking the right site the first time so that you save time <u>and</u> maximize your return on investment. The process is described in our annual *Recruiter's Guide to Employment Web Sites* and in the next Postcard.

Recruiting, like soccer, is often called a contact sport. So, following the herd may be a useful way to learn the game. It is not, however, the way you win when the stakes are high and the competition is tough. If your goal is to hire the best talent, don't play herdball ... play like a pro. ■

■ Buying Smart Online

A Proven Process for Web-Site Selection

Let's face it; finding the right Web-site for each of your recruiting requirements is no easy task. In essence, you have two choices:

■ You can follow the herd and post your jobs and search for resumes at the same old sites that everyone else is using, or

■ You can shop for recruitment sites with the same consumer savvy you use when shopping for any other important service or product.

And if you' re determined to be a smart consumer, the **WEDDLE's SmartSelect**™ process is just what you need to get the job done!

The SmartSelect™ process is based on a very simple premise: You can be an expert in all of the best techniques for online recruiting and still not connect with high caliber candidates **if** you do not use those techniques on the right Web-site(s) for your specific recruiting requirement. Indeed, selecting the best site(s) for a given assignment is a prerequisite for effective recruiting on the Internet.

SmartSelect™ is a 5-step "recruiter friendly" process for making smart Web-site selections from among the more than 40,000 options you have available to you. It draws on the experience and lessons-learned of successful online recruiters and the rich array of site information found in the annual *WEDDLE's Guide to Employment Web Sites*.

Step 1: Determine Your Options.

Use the *Guide*'s Cross-Reference Index to identify those recruitment Web-sites that serve the occupational field and/or industry for which you are recruiting. For example, if you are recruiting for a position in Finance, the Index will identify 14 sites worth considering. You should also check with your colleagues for their recommendations and, perhaps, tap the views of others at recruiter listservs (online discussion groups), such as recruitersnetwork.com or erexchange.com. The goal of this step is to narrow the number of sites at which you are looking down to about a dozen.

Step 2: Evaluate Your Options.

Use the *Guide*'s Site Profiles to evaluate each of your site options. The profiles provide a wide range of descriptive information about each site that can be used to:

■ Assess each site on its own merits, and

■ Compare each site to all other site options.

First, evaluate each site on its own merits. While admitting to some bias, I think the following criteria from our *Guide* will provide the best insights into a Web-site's capabilities and the extent to which those capabilities match your service needs and expectations:

If posting a job:

> The kinds of jobs the site posts (e.g., full time, part time, contract, consulting)
> The most prevalent types of jobs it posts (e.g., entry level, senior level)
> The primary geographic distribution of the jobs it posts
> Whether or not your posting can be linked to your own Web-site

If searching the resume database:

> The kind of database service offered (e.g., resumes, profiles, public private)
> The source of the resumes/profiles in its database
> The top occupations among the resumes/profiles in the database
> The length of time the resumes/profiles are posted
> If there are any restrictions on who can post a resume/profile

---

Second, take each of the sites you found acceptable on their own merits and compare them to one another. I suggest that you use the following criteria from our Guide for this exercise in "comparison shopping:"

If you are posting a job:

The Site's	Metric or Definition
Traffic	Unique visitors per month
Visitor Attention Span	Pages views per month divided by unique visitors per month
Price	For a single job posting
Posting Period	In days
Candidate Density	Unique visitors per month divided by the number of jobs posted

---

If you are searching the resume database:

The Site's	Metric or Definition
Traffic	Unique visitors per month
Visitor Attention Span	Pages views per month divided by unique visitors per month
Price	Per month
Database size	Number of resumes or profiles in the database
Candidate focus	Top 5 occupational fields among the resumes/profiles in the database
Database quality	Source of resumes/profiles Direct from candidates (best), Resume distribution cos. (O.K.), Resume spiders or automated collectors (poor)

Use these evaluations to select the 3-5 options that (a) best match your recruiting requirement and (b) provide the best value.

Step 3: Visit the Sites Online.

The best way to narrow your options further is to pay each of the 3-5 sites a visit online. In fact, I strongly recommend that you never use a site until you have "test driven" it from a job seeker's perspective. If you don't enjoy the experience, chances are the candidates won't, as well. And when that happens, your return on investment in a job posting or resume search will be far less than optimal and, just as bad, it's possible that your organization's image will be tarnished by its use of the site.

What factors should you consider when "test driving" a site? I suggest that you look at the following:

- **How easy is it to open the door?** Job seekers, in general, but passive job seekers, in particular, are busy people and move around the Web quickly. Therefore, it's important to check how long it takes to download the site's Home Page. Research has shown that if it takes more than 14 seconds for the site's content to present itself (that's about two sips of coffee), job seekers are unlikely to hang around.

- **How easy is it to figure out what's there?** Ask yourself these questions:
  - Is the layout of the site's Home Page intuitively obvious to the first-time visitor?
  - Does it clearly identify the different sections or areas of the site and provide easy access to them?
  - Does it provide a Table of Contents or a "site map" so that visitors can quickly determine what's available on the site (for first-time visitors) and what has recently changed there (for repeat visitors)?

- **How easy is it to get where you want to go?** Is the site designed for easy navigation? For example, if you click on a word or image to go to one area of the site, there should be a clearly identified way to return to your original location. A good Web-site design will make it easy to go "forth AND back." It will also provide a way:

  (a) to return to the Home Page, so that you can start all over again if you lose your bearings while roaming around and

  (b) to move from one major content area (e.g., the database of job openings) to another (e.g., the database of resumes).

- **How "job seeker" friendly is the site?** Does the site require visitors to register before they can use any of its services? Does it provide information and insights that job seekers would find helpful? Is the site well maintained (e.g., are there grammatical errors and misspellings in the content, do pages not open or do hypertext links not work)? If the site provides a question and answer feature (which is a good sign), does it answer questions promptly? And are the images on the site inclusive or do they show a lack of sensitivity to cultural, age or gender diversity?

Step 4: Make Your Selection and Track Your Results.

Just as you would with traditional recruiting methods, the best way to recruit online is to select and use several venues or sites simultaneously. Each will provide you with a different channel into your target candidate population, and it's impossible to know, in advance, which will work best for any given recruiting requirement. To avoid this uncertainty in the future, keep track of each site's performance, using such metrics as the number of candidates they generate, the cost-per-candidate and their quality.

Step 5: Continually Reassess and Fine Tune Your Selections.

It's easy to become creatures of habit and return to the same site(s) over and over again when recruiting online. The Internet, however, is an extraordinarily dynamic medium, and successful online recruiting depends upon a continuous reassessment and updating of your strategy. To conduct your evaluation, use both the lessons you've learned from previous recruiting efforts (see Step 4 above) and your annual WEDDLE's *Guide*. Based on your assessment, fine tune your selection of recruitment Web-sites for each and every new requirement. ■

■ The Recruiter's "Value Add"

Lately, two disturbing trends have appeared that should give recruiters cause for serious concern. A growing number of hiring managers and clients of staffing firms are now saying that:

- they can find the same candidates online that recruiters do, and
- the caliber of candidates sourced online is sub-par or even unacceptable.

In a down economy (or a recovering one), when any unhappiness among customers can lead to layoffs or contract cancellations, such views must be quickly and aggressively countered.

How can you do that ? I suggest you develop (and tout) a "value add" capability that hiring managers and clients cannot duplicate or are unwilling to take the time and/or make the effort to do so. What is this extraordinary capability? The knowledge and skills of smart consumerism in online recruiting. Why is that expertise a value-add? Because despite today's economic angst, our customers still need to hire top talent. According to a survey by the Bureau of National Affairs, taken in late 2001, 40% of respondents still report having trouble filling vacancies. That's down just 10% from a year ago and far ahead of the early/mid-1990's.

Ironically, "finding" candidates is increasingly downplayed as a key recruiter skill. It's as if we recruiters have bought into the notion that the Web has leveled the playing field when it comes to sourcing. Nothing, however, could be further from the truth. As I have often noted, there are some 40,000 employment-related sites on the Internet, so there are plenty of places to look for special candidates (i.e. "A" level performers and those with scarce skills). If you limit your efforts at "finding" candidates to Monster.com, CareerBuilder.com or HotJobs.com, then yes, you will have plenty of company, including, more likely than not, your customers. On the other hand, if you learn how to locate, evaluate and select the best sites (niche and general) for finding your target candidates, you'll have a capability that will ensure you add real value to your customers, no matter how proficient they are online.

What does good consumerism entail on the Web? Basically it involves just two competencies:

- Tracking
- Comparison Shopping.

Tracking. First, you have to identify and locate those sites that could potentially provide the kind of candidates you seek for a particular opening. These include:

- niche sites that specialize in a specific candidate cohort (e.g., ChemJobs.net for chemists, GasJobs.com for anesthesiologists, Secsinthecity.com for secretaries in London)

and

- general purpose sites where the candidate cohort is among the largest in the site's resume database or its visitor traffic (e.g., in *WEDDLE's 2003 Guide*, Hotjobs.com lists Finance and Accounting professionals among the top 5 cohorts in its resume database).

Tracking these sites down takes effort and research and networking skills; hence, this competency is one that distinguishes the "expert candidate sourcer" from the "occasional sourcer" online. Where can you hone your Tracking knowledge? The following resources will get you started:

- The site profiles that appear in the WEDDLE's newsletter each month (*The Newsletter About Online Resources for Successful Recruiting & Retention*);

- The Green Book or *WEDDLE's* annual *Recruiter's Guide to Employment Web Sites*; and

- A recruiter listserv or online discussion forum (e.g., www.recruitersnetwork.com for corporate recruiters and erexchange.com for third party recruiters).

Comparison Shopping. Once you've identified a number of potential sourcing sites, you're ready to compare their value propositions and select the best. You can perform a quick evaluation using the formula TAP:

- **T = Traffic** This metric measures the number of people who visit a site in a given month. I think the most useful metric for traffic is Unique Visitors per month. It is important because the higher a site's traffic, the greater the number of people who might see your posting. It can include Target Visitors (i.e., those in the specific field/industry for which you are recruiting) or General Visitors (i.e., undifferentiated candidate traffic).

- **A = Attention Span** This metric measures how long people stay on a site. It's a ratio of the site's Page Views per month divided by its traffic or Unique Visitors per month. The metric is important because the longer people stay on a site, the higher the probability they will see your job posting or decide to put their resume into the site's resume database.

- **P= Price** This metric indicates the site's fee for posting one job for 30 days or more.

You can find this data in a *WEDDLE's Guide* or obtain it by asking the site. Then, build yourself a table and compare the sites one to another. I think the following rules will yield the best choices:

Your BEST Bets:
1. More Target Visitors + Highest Attention Span + Acceptable Price.
2. More General Visitors + Highest Attention Span + Acceptable Price.

ACCEPTABLE Buys:
1. More General Visitors + Higher Attention Span + Acceptable Price.
2. Fewer Target Visitors + Higher Attention Span + Acceptable Price.

DON'T Bother:
1. More General Visitors + Lower Attention Span + Acceptable Price.
2. Fewer Target Visitors + Lower Attention Span + Acceptable Price.
3. Fewer Target or General Visitors + Lower Attention Span + Free.

Anybody can shop at the biggest and best known recruiting sites, but only discriminating shoppers know how to find, evaluate and select those sites that will yield the uncommon candidate. And that ability is the hallmark of recruiters who add value to their customers through online recruiting. ■

■ Nothing But the Facts

"Just the facts, Ma'am; nothing but the facts" That was the signature line from *Dragnet*, a popular television program in the 1950's. Delivered by the laconic detective, Sergeant Joe Friday, it was the terse admonition that, in the real world, only empirical evidence counts. Not wishful thinking and not Clintonesque fudging. If you want to know the truth about a situation—or about a service or product—you need the facts.

That's the rationale behind my annual guidebook to employment-related sites on the Internet. Each year, I select 350 sites out of the 40,000+ in operation and publish the facts that recruiters need to know about them. Unlike other guides, however, I don't anoint these sites as the best of their breed because, in my view, what's "best" is relative. Each recruiter's needs are unique because they are based on their particular requirements at a given point in time. Or to put it another way, depending on the opening, one recruiter's gem of a site is another recruiter's zirconia. For that reason, I choose sites that, I believe, represent the range of resources currently available to recruiters on the Internet, so that they can make their own buying decisions.

Each of the sites in the Guide is described with a full-page profile of its features, services and fees. The data for these profiles are acquired directly from each site and attested to by a representative of the organization that owns it. I ask them to provide only the information that would help a recruiter make smart site selections. And guess what? Based on the data collected for my *2002 Guide to Employment Web Sites*—the 2003 edition is now available at your local Borders or Barnes & Noble or by calling WEDDLE's at 203.964.1888—it appears that a significant percentage of recruitment sites don't think you should have the facts. Evidently, they want you to make your consumer decisions in the dark.

What follows are two of the kinds of questions I asked the sites and their all-too-frequent responses:

Question #1
"How many unique visitors come to your site in a given month?"

The Response of Some Sites
"Confidential" or worse, the customer service equivalent "We're too lazy to look it up."

The number of unique visitors to a site is similar to a newspaper's circulation figure. It tells you how many people come to a site and thus have some chance of seeing the information posted there. The information you care about, of course, is your job posting, and the more people who visit a site, the more likely it is that your target candidate will be among them. You never buy a classified ad from a newspaper without knowing how many people read it each day (its audited circulation figure), so why would you patronize a site without knowing its traffic? The short answer is ... you wouldn't (or shouldn't).

For example, if you're recruiting to fill an engineering position, which of the sites below provides the facts you need to make a smart buying decision:

Site	Traffic
National Society of Professional Engineers	39,500 unique visitors/month
EngineeringJobs.com	No information provided

(Source: WEDDLE's 2002 Recruiter's Guide)

The traffic figure for the National Society of Profession-al Engineers can be compared to the traffic figures at other engineering sites to assess one aspect of each site's potential return on your advertising investment. By refusing to divulge such information, however, EngineeringJobs.com undermines your ability to conduct such basic consumer analysis and, as a result, increases the likelihood that you'll make a mistake.

And traffic is only one of many facts you can (and should) use. Add the number of job postings, for example, and you can extend your analysis even further. Divide the site's traffic (measured in unique visitors per month) by its number of job postings, and you get a factor that I call Candidate Density. It indicates how much competition your job ad will have from the other ads posted on a site. In other words, the higher the number of visitors per job posting, the lower the level of competition your ad will face. In the engineering search we began above:

Site	Candidate Density
National Society of Professional Engineers	557 visitors/job posting
EngineeringJobs.com	Cannot be determined

(Source: WEDDLE's 2002 Recruiter's Guide)

As with traffic volume, Candidate Density can also be used to compare one site's performance to that at other sites and thereby enhance the rigor of your site selection decisions.

Question #2
"How many pages of information do your site visitors view each month?"

The Response of Some Sites
"Confidential" or worse, the customer service equivalent "We're too lazy to look it up."

Page views are one way to indicate how long the visitors to a site hang around. And the longer they hang around, the higher the probability that they will actually see the job opening you have posted there. Although the total number of page views can be helpful in this regard, I prefer to use a factor that I call Visitor Attention Span. It's calculated by dividing the total number of pages opened on a site each month by the site's total number of monthly unique visitors. The result is the average number of pages *each* individual visitor opens each month. That metric gives you a pretty good indication of a site's "stickiness" or its ability to hold the attention of the prospective candidates it attracts. For example:

Site	Attention Span
National Society of Professional Engineers	15.5 page views/unique visitor
EngineeringJobs.com	No information provided

(Source: WEDDLE's 2002 Recruiter's Guide)

As with the other measures discussed above, Visitor Attention Span can be used to compare sites and thereby identify the "best" specific sites for your specific requirement. Without the facts, however, such analytical consumerism is inevitably replaced by decisions based on anecdotal evidence, if your lucky, and on the slickest sales pitch, if you're not.

So, what's my take on the sites that won't provide the facts about their capabilities and performance? Simply this: either they see you as a particularly dumb consumer (who is willing to spend their organization's money on a whim) or they have something to hide (such as a lack of traffic or an inability to hold onto the traffic they do attract). Whichever is the case, I don't think they deserve your patronage. Or to reprise the wise words of Joe Friday, when it comes to selecting a site for job posting or resume search, it's the facts or nothing. ■

■ Site Insight

WEDDLE's recently surveyed a sample of 350 recruiting sites selected for inclusion in our *2002 Recruiter's Guide to Employment Web Sites*. (The 2003 edition is now available at your local Borders or Barnes & Noble or by calling WEDDLE's at 203.964.1888.) We looked at four cohorts of this population:

- **Large, general purpose sites** (e.g., Monster.com, CareerBuilder.com, HotJobs.com)

- **Small, general purpose sites** (e.g., EmploymentGuide.com—formerly CareerWeb.com, JobBankUSA.com, NationJob Network)

- **Commercial specialty sites** (e.g., EngineerJobs.com, Hcareers.com, CareerJournal.com)

- **Not-for-profit specialty sites** (e.g., typically operated by professional associations and trade groups such as AMA.org, ISAjobs.org, SHRM.org, and NAPM.org)

Our goal was to determine how to invest among these options so as to optimize yield while minimizing cost. Here's what we found:

Median job posting prices do not follow conventional wisdom. For years, the rule of thumb has been that not-for-profit sites are the cheapest for posting. After all, most are operated by professional associations and societies, so the employment service is normally viewed as a benefit of membership, not a money-making activity. Or is it? As the Table below indicates, we found that not-for-profits are actually the most expensive of the four groups.

Category	Price/Posting
Large, general purpose sites	$100-150/posting
Small, general purpose sites	$100 or less/posting
Commercial, specialty sites	$101-150/posting
Not-for-profit, specialty sites	$151-200/posting

☛ What's the lesson we should draw from this finding? Posting jobs at large and small general purpose sites (and commercial specialty sites) can be a smart move IF you select the right sites. How do you do that? Only post positions that play to a site's demographic strength. For example, in our 2002 *Guide*, it notes that BestJobsUSA (a small, general purpose site) is strongest in engineering, management, IT and sales/marketing (as indicated by the fact that those are the largest candidate groups in its resume database). Hence, post there for any openings you have in those fields, but not for your openings in finance.

Does this finding mean you should never post at specialty sites? Absolutely not. But there is a way to determine where you are most likely to maximize your ROI. It's called candidate density, or the number of candidates per job posted on the site. It measures the competition your posting will have from other postings. The higher the density, the lower the competition. Think of it as a way of:

(a) making sure that you're posting where the candidates are and the competition isn't or

(b) not following the herd.

Take a look at the Table below; density is measured in unique visitors/posting.

Category	Candidate Density
Large, general purpose sites	Most achieve 16-25; others only reach 6-15
Small, general purpose sites	Most achieve 6-15; others reach 25-50
Commercial, specialty sites	Almost all achieve 50+
Not-for-profit, specialty sites	Almost all achieve 50+

☞ What's the lesson for recruiters? Compare candidate densities among the specialty sites you are considering (it's calculated by dividing unique visitors by job postings on a site) and use those sites with the highest density. (Candidate densities are calculated for the 350 sites WEDDLE's profiles in its annual *Recruiter's Guide.*)

O.K., but what about resume databases? Here, we did find a price advantage with not-for-profit sites.

- The majority of **large, general purpose sites** charged more than $500 per month or more than $4,000/year to search their resume databases.

- The **small, general purpose sites** charged less than $500/month or less than $2,000/year and many included resume searching in the cost of posting.

- Similarly, **commercial specialty sites** charged less than $500 per month with a few including resume search in the posting fee.

- Most **not-for-profit sites**, on the other hand, offered access to their resume databases for free, and those that did charge were under $500 per month.

Before you leap to what seems to be the obvious conclusion, however, there are qualitative differences among resume databases. As shown in the following Table, the size of these resources at some not-for-profit sites may be too small to support effective recruiting.

Category	Resumes in Database
Large, general purpose sites	Most have 2-4 million; several over 4 million
Small, general purpose sites	Most have 1-500,000; others have 10-100,000
Commercial, specialty sites	Most have 10-100,000; others less than 1,000
Not-for-profit, specialty sites	Most have under 1,000; others have 1-10,000

What does that mean for recruiters? While price is important, making smart site selections also has a qualitative dimension, at least when using the resume databases at not-for-profits. If the occupational field the not-for-profit serves is narrowly defined, (e.g., interior decorators), then a small database may be just fine. On the other hand, if the field is large and has many sub-specialties (e.g., engineering), a larger database is likely to be a precondition for success. ∎

■ Are Job Boards Toast?

(Part 1 of 2)

A recent editorial opined that job boards are history. Finished. Toast. Made obsolete by the arrival of DirectEmployers.com, a site launched by a consortium of major employers, and the spreading use of corporate recruitment sites by employers in general. The author's argument was as old as capitalism: employers are going to stop paying the middleman—that would be job boards—because they can now obtain the same results at less cost by advertising on their own sites.

It's a familiar piece of logic, but in this case, it's dead wrong. Whether they're owned and operated by commercial companies, professional associations, trade organizations or other affinity groups, job boards (and their cousins, the resume databank and career portal) are not only far from obsolete, they're becoming increasingly important to employers searching for top talent. Why is that? The following points make the case.

1. Anger and angst wear off. Although the folks behind DirectEmployers.com are careful to say that their venture is not an attack on Monster.com, many of its members will tell you privately that they are fed up with what they view as that site's poor customer service and rich prices. For many other employers, however, Monster.com works just fine. Indeed, in our 2002 User's Choice Awards, Monster.com won Best General Purpose site for recruiters and was a strong second or third in the other categories of Best Customer Service and Most "Recruiter Friendly." (To cast your ballot for the best sites on the Web, visit WEDDLE's Polling Station at www.weddles.com.) Now, don't misunderstand; I'm not shilling for Monster.com. I'm simply saying that the angst that has driven many employers to a greater reliance on their own Web-sites will eventually wear off and when it does, they will likely return to using Monster.com (and other sites) to supplement the yield from their own sites, especially as the economy picks up steam and labor shortages reappear.

2. The idea that employer sites completely replace job boards fundamentally misunderstands job seeker behavior. Whether they're "passive" or active in the job market, most people want a choice. While they probably do focus on those organizations that are viewed as "employers of choice," they also believe that no one employer can offer all of the best opportunities for their personal development and career growth. To put it another way, today's job seekers have accepted full responsibility for managing their own careers, and implicit in that notion is that they—not employers—are the best judge of what jobs will serve their career and employment objectives. Hence, they will continue to visit job boards because those sites offer openings from an array of different organizations and thus enable them to get a sense of the larger job market and of those specific openings that represent genuine opportunities for them. Given that behavior by job seekers, employers have no choice but to follow their lead and advertise on those sites.

3. "A" level performers and most passive prospects, on the other hand, do not act like active job seekers. They aren't looking for a job, so they seldom venture out to employer sites and search through the openings that are posted there. Instead, they hang out with their peers at places they know and trust, and on the Internet, those are usually the sites managed by their professional association, trade organization and/or affinity group. Only there can they comfortably network with others in their field, learn something from discussion forums that cover topics in which they're interested and, in the course of doing all that, stop by the job postings to see if there's anything available that might further their career. Hence, if an employer hopes to hire "A" level performers and passive prospects—and what employer doesn't—they will have to use those same job boards.

4. For every good employer site, there are three or four that could have been used as models for Dante's circles of hell. In fact, according to our surveys of job seekers, corporate recruitment sites dropped from first to fourth place in terms of their perceived helpfulness in 2002. While virtually every employer site is attracting a torrent of resumes at the moment, once the economy picks up steam, those sites that are poorly designed and/or managed will see the best and brightest job seekers head for other destinations fast. Where are they likely to go? According to our 2003 User's Choice Awards, they'll head off to such job boards as HotJobs.com, Monster.com, ComputerJobs.com, Dice.com and BrassRing.com.

5. Employers often turn to their own recruitment sites because they view job boards as expensive. While prices do vary among boards, most charge less than the fees newspapers have traditionally imposed for print advertising. In fact, the high fee rap against job boards is due mostly to poor shopping habits. There are over 40,000 employment-related sites now operating on the Internet, yet 52 cents of every dollar spent on job postings is spent on Monster.com, and 80 cents of every dollar is spent on advertising at just four (now three) sites: Monster.com, HotJobs. com, CareerBuilder.com and HeadHunter.net. This addiction to a single site or small set of sites has, in effect, created a monopolistic situation, and some sites have taken advantage of that de facto lack of competition to charge high fees. Now, however, recruiters are becoming better consumers and using more of the choices available to them. As a result, niche sites have become increasingly popular. Not only do they often offer a more competitive fee structure, but they also eliminate one of the key problems faced by the better known general purpose boards: when you post an opening for a nurse on the big name sites, you're as likely to get resumes from sushi chefs and truckers as you are from nurses. When you post a nursing position at a site that specializes in nurses, however, the only resumes you'll receive are those from nurses.

That's five reasons why job boards are here to stay. Obviously, a well designed and managed corporate recruitment site (or gateway site to a group of employer sites viz DirectEmployers.com) can enhance an organization's online recruiting performance. As the evidence above makes clear, however, it cannot replace the role of job boards in a comprehensive, integrated strategy for hiring top talent. Moreover, these five points are just part of the case for job boards. In my next postcard, I'll cover five more. ■

■ Are Job Boards Toast?
(Part 2 of 2)

Recently, there's been a spate of op-ed pieces forecasting the demise of job boards. These articles base their predictions on the growing use of self-operated recruitment sites by employers, the arrival of the employer-sponsored site, DirectEmployers. com, and the precarious position of the middleman in capitalist economies. While these are all important factors in the maturation of on-line recruiting, I think that Mark Twain's oft-cited description of the premature announcement of his own death applies here, as well: reports of job boards' passing are greatly exaggerated. In fact, the future of these retail recruitment sites—whether they're managed by commercial companies, professional associations or trade organizations and other affinity groups—has never been brighter. In my last postcard, I listed five reasons why that is so. What follows are five more reasons to be optimistic about the future of job boards.

6. Historically, employers have never used a single method of recruitment. Instead, they tailored their approach to position levels, past difficulties encountered (or not) in filling various openings, the cost of certain methods and the impact of a position on the company's performance. To put it another way, they typically used classified advertising or staffing firms to fill hourly jobs, display advertising in newspapers and select journals or staffing firms to fill low-to-mid range professional openings, and search firms to fill senior professional and managerial positions. Often, they also supplemented those tactics with networking and employee referral programs, job fairs and campus visits. In short, they employed a comprehensive, multi-faceted strategy that tailored methods to requirements. And that will not change with the advent of employer-operated recruitment sites. Recruiters will use whatever source they can find that will yield the highest caliber candidate at the lowest cost and in the shortest time. If that source happens to be a job board—and for many types of position openings that just may be the case—then recruiters will happily use it, even as they continue to rely on their own recruitment sites for other openings.

7. Job boards are getting better. While their core value proposition remains unchanged—they offer the job seeker and the employer a convenient, neutral meeting place—much of what surrounds that proposition has undergone a remarkable transformation. In fact, the irony is that many of the best job boards now resemble newspapers. Their employment sections are surrounded by content and activities that are designed to inform, entertain and even uplift those who use them. As a consequence, the experience of visiting a job board has been dramatically enhanced (at least at many of the better sites), and that change has lead to increased traffic to these destinations among all cohorts of the workforce. Now, some will say that this bump up in popularity is simply an artifact of the sputtering economy, and that's undoubtedly true ... in part. Some of it, however, is also due to what visitors find when they get there. At least, that's what they told us in WEDDLE's latest survey (April, 2002). For the first time since we began conducting these polls in 1996, job seekers ranked commercial job boards ahead of employer sites in terms of their usefulness.

8. Brands count. Despite all of the dot.com hype about the power of technology, attracting visitors to a Web-site is essentially an exercise in traditional marketing. Success depends upon the visibility and perceived value of what an organization stands for. And that's where all too many employer sites fall short. While there are undoubtedly exceptions, far too many companies are more than willing to invest millions of dollars in building the brand of their commercial products or services (including elaborate ads on their site's Home Page), but will niggle over pennies when it comes to promoting their employment brand—their reputation as a place to work and grow. This kind of thinking is an artifact of the good, old labor surplus days circa 1952, yet it is still alive and well between the ears of many a corporate CFO and CEO. Meanwhile, the job boards, whose core service is the provision of employment services, are spending millions of dollars building their brands as places to advance one's career. Indeed, according to one estimate in the late 1990's, just three of these sites—Monster.com, HotJobs.com and HeadHunter.net— collectively spent over a half a billion dollars building their brands with Super Bowl ads, airport billboards, magazine inserts and blimps over sporting events. That's real money in anyone's book, and it is now paying dividends in the numbers of eyeballs that are attracted to those sites and other job boards.

9. Convenience matters, especially for today's time challenged workers. Baby Boomers must deal with aging parents and teenagers. Gen Y parents are in the throes of raising young children. And for a growing segment of the workforce, the reality of dual working spouses means less time to stay on top of the job market and effectively manage one's career. One solution to this situation that is fast gaining popularity is the *job agent.* This handy feature is now offered on about 40% of all job boards and enables a person to turn their job search over to a computer. Basically, all one has to do is specify the kind of position they want or would like to consider; after that, they can return to dealing with work or family, and the job agent will search through all of the openings posted on the job board each day to find a match. When it does, it notifies them by e-mail. Even better, the message is confidential, so even if a person is employed, they can use a job agent to look for a better position. As a consequence, the job agent attracts a better cross section of the workforce to job boards (passive as well as active job seekers) and takes all of the hassle out of looking for a better opportunity. While some corporate recruitment sites have launched their own job agents in response, the only openings they check are those posted by that company. Job agents at job boards, on the other hand, search through the postings of numerous employers, thereby improving the likelihood of a match for the job seeker and, as a consequence, enhancing their propensity to use them.

10. Many job boards are nimble, while most corporate recruitment sites are not. With the exception of the major commercial boards and those sites owned by publications or associations, job boards are typically run by small, entrepreneurial organizations. They can (and do) react quickly to shifts in the workforce, workplace and job market, enabling them to align their content and employment opportunities more closely to workers' actual needs. Corporate recruitment sites, on the other hand, are normally controlled by the internal IT or Marketing Department and often cannot be changed without their approval and/or support. In other cases, changing the corporate site or any subsection of it (e.g., the recruitment area) requires the agreement of an oversight committee that meets irregularly and must consider a wide range of potential actions. As a result, the content at corporate sites is often static and does not reflect issues and concerns that are top-of-mind among workers. This inflexibility enables job boards to do a better job of serving their customers and ensures that they will remain popular among them. And if they remain popular among job seekers, recruiters will follow.

As indicated by the five reasons above (and the five others described in my previous postcard), there is often a logical alternative to a sure-fire prediction. As you may recall, for example, the early advocates of online recruiting forecast with absolute conviction that its capabilities were going to "disintermediate" recruiters, yet (happily) recruiters are still with us today and arguably more important than ever in winning the Talent Wars. The recent claims for corporate recruitment sites are, in my view, similarly hyperbolic and just as likely to be inaccurate. That's not to say that corporate recruitment sites aren't an important development; they are. In fact, they're a core element of any comprehensive recruitment strategy. They will not, however, change life as we know it on planet Earth or even radically alter the way that successful recruiting is accomplished ... despite the wishful thinking of their proponents. ■

■ A New Way to Shop

Historically, recruiters have had two options when shopping for an online recruitment site: a major department store, such as Monster.com and HotJobs.com, or a boutique specialty store, such as FoodIndustryJobs.com or MDjobsite.com. As with their commercial counterparts, the former tries to satisfy your every recruiting need—from senior executives and technical professionals to recent college graduates—while the latter strives to provide a deep inventory in a specific career field, industry or location.

Now, however, you have another choice for recruiting online. Think of it as the strip mall of recruitment sites. Called **NicheBoards.com**, it collects a group of independent specialty sites all at one place. Currently, there are a total of eleven sites in the mall, including:

- JobsinLogistics.com
- CallCenterJobs.com
- Jobsinthemoney.com (Finance)
- Jobscience.com (Healthcare)
- LatPro.com (Bilingual/Hispanic)
- Jobs4HR.com
- Computerwork.com
- MarketingJobs.com
- DestinyGroup.com (Veterans)

Combined traffic at the eleven sites totals over a million visitors per month. Don Firth, President & CEO of JobsinLogistics.com and the originator of the strip mall concept, says the idea is to find and connect non-competing specialty sites so that recruiters have a one-stop alternative to the larger department store sites. While it doesn't replace the need to find the best sites for each of your requirements, it can be a way to shop smart and save time for certain of your openings. ■

■ Sites Set for Hourly Workers

We should all be wary of predictions by analysts, of course, but a recent report by the "pundits" at Goldman Sachs indicates that demand for light industrial or hourly workers is likely to lead the recovery from the late, unlamented recession. If that's right, today's labor surplus may quickly become tomorrow's shortfall. Unlike in past recoveries, however, recruiters now have a growing number of online resources to use in their search for hourly employees.

Historically, online recruitment has focused on professional and managerial positions. That's changing with the launch of a growing number of sites that specialize in workers for pick and pack, construction, plumbing, transportation, janitorial, clerical and other hourly jobs. Take CareerWeb, for example (now called EmplolymentGuide.com). It and *The Employment Guide* are both divisions of Trader Publishing Company. The *Guide* is the free employment publication you see in stands outside convenience stores and other outlets. While it lists all kinds of jobs, the majority of its ads target hourly workers. And a lot of them read it. According to Trader, 4.5 million unique readers see it each month, a figure that compares favorably with even the most monstrous of recruitment sites.

EmploymentGuide.com (the site) and the print *Guide* have recently launched a product called JobWire. It enables a worker to respond to a listing in the *Guide* by calling a toll-free telephone number and answering a series of automated, pre-determined, industry specific interview questions. The resulting information is then transformed into a candidate profile that's sent via e-mail to the employer that listed the position. Candidates don't need to have a resume or even have access to the Web. In addition, the employer develops a master profile that is compared to all responses so that its sees only qualified applicants.

The JobWire service has been tested in 9 cities and is expected to be available in all 55 *Guide* markets by early 2003. As of this writing, it can only be used by direct employers, but a staffing firm variation may be available shortly.

A similar but less broad-reaching service is offered by The Center for American Jobs. It has launched a site called NowHiringTruckers.com that uses the telephone to acquire information from candidates and pre-screen them for an employer's jobs. The resumes of qualified candidates are forwarded to the employer via e-mail.

Finally, WEDDLE's *Directory* lists a number of sites that specialize in hourly workers, including:

Sites for Hourly Workers	
Site	**Industry**
Coolworks.com	Hospitality
Jobsite.com	Construction
Manufacturingjobsite.com	Manufacturing
Restaurantjobs.com	Food Service
Retailjobs.com	Retail Sales

■ If You Were ...

The Web is has always been a place where creativity flourishes, and that's particularly true in the names and URLs given to some sites. But beware. As the following quiz illustrates, there is often more to a Web-site name than meets the eye. (Hint: all of the sites are involved, in one way or another, with recruiting.)

If you were ...

... an undercover cop looking for sites promoting the use of marihuana, what site might you go to?

... an orphan looking for a parent, what site might you visit?

... a big fan of a popular television show about the lives and loves of several young women in New York City, what site might you visit?

... at the wheel during a family car trip and realized that you needed to find a gas station quick, what site might you think could help you out?

Answers (don't peek):

WeedJobs.com (a site specializing in graduate students and Ph.D.s in weed science),
GetAMom.com (a site that specializes in contract and telecommuting work for stay-at-home Moms),
SecsintheCity.com (a site specializing in secretarial positions in London, England),
GasJobs.com (a site specializing in anesthesiologists).

■ Online Recruitment Advertising
What is it? How Can You Do It Better Than the Competition?

■ What is a Job Posting Anyway?

With all of the resumes flooding into recruiter e-mailboxes these days, it's easy to get a bit cocky about the merits of our sourcing activities. That confidence, however, has a downside: it can cause confusion about the function of a job posting. And while such confusion may not be all that harmful right now, it is very likely to impede or even destroy an organization's ability to attract top per-formers, once recruiting picks up.

A job posting, of course, is nothing more than recruitment advertising online. As such, its role is to entice job seekers to apply for an employer's open positions. There is no universal enticement that appeals to all job seekers, however, so an organization must first be very clear about the specific kinds of candidates it wants to target and then tailor its advertising to those populations. The range of options is both narrow and obvious. There are only:

- active job seekers,
- mediocre workers,
- passive prospects, and
- "A" level performers?

Implicitly or explicitly, every organization chooses to focus it advertising on a subset of these cohorts

How do you tell which cohorts an organization is targeting? Understand what motivates each cohort and then evaluate the organization's job postings to determine which motivators they address. For example, active job seekers have bills to pay so they can't afford to be picky. Their career goals have to take a back seat to their financial situation. Mediocre workers, on the other hand, have low expectations and modest career objectives. They'll apply for just about any job with any employer because ... well, why not? A job posting that appeals to such desperate and indifferent workers tells you a lot about an organization's real recruiting objectives. It may as well say:

> Looking for a lousy job with a crummy employer?
> Well, your search is over!
> Our organization offers below market rate salaries,
> and it layoffs off workers regularly without notice.
> If we're the kind of company you seek,
> we want to talk to you.

Sure, I'm exaggerating to make a point. Sad to say, however, there are more than a few employers with job advertisements online that are not all that dissimilar. If you don't believe me, visit just about any job board or corporate career site and take a look at the postings. With rare exceptions, they are short on details, short on persuasion and long on off-putting language and demeaning requirements. And despite those attributes, thousands of people still send in their resumes. They are that desperate. Or indifferent. They are not, you can be sure, the best and brightest in the workforce.

If an organization wants to entice passive prospects and "A" level performers, it must write an entirely different kind of job posting. This alternative recruitment ad functions as **an electronic sales brochure**. It connects with top talent and influences their actions by answering their questions (before they even have a chance to ask them), addressing their issues and concerns, and focusing on their interests. It:

- provides comprehensive, detailed descriptions of the open position and the employer;

- includes a persuasive, compelling description of the value proposition offered by the organization's employment opportunity;

- addresses their key motivations for considering a change in employment (i.e., the factors that a passive prospect or "A" level performer will take into account when evaluating the merits of a job change); and

- comes across as "job seeker friendly" by using a language that is clear and meaningful to top prospects.

An electronic sales brochure has both the facts an "A' level performer needs to make an informed career decision and the persuasive power to get even the most passive prospect to apply. Or, to put it another way, a job posting—at least one that targets the best talent—is neither a classified ad nor a position description. The former is too short and the latter is too boring to sell anyone other than the desperate and the indifferent.

Further, a job posting is neither an assessment instrument nor a resume reduction tool. Some organizations, especially those that recruit IT workers, think that requiring job seekers to apply online helps them evaluate an applicant's capabilities. Anyone who doesn't know how to cut and paste a resume into an online application form, they reason, can't be much of an IT professional. It's a misguided view for at least two reasons:

- The ability to cut and paste a resume into an online application form is hardly a measure of someone's ability to program in C++ or to administer an Oracle database. One bears absolutely no relation to the other. Indeed, the use of resume posting knowledge as a screen for an IT job could be perceived by the Federal Government as inappropriate because it has nothing to do with actual job performance.

and

- The key to recruiting top talent is to sell them first. In other words, you have to convince an "A" level performer to apply, and only then, can you evaluate them. Until they have made the psychological commitment to toss their hat into the ring for an opening, they are fickle and easily turned off. Hence, any disruptive requirement, such as forcing them to apply online, can cause them to turn away instead.

Similarly, a job posting ought not to be used as a vehicle for reducing the flow of resumes into recruiters' e-mailboxes. If that flow is clogging an organization's communication or resume management systems, then those systems should be upgraded. Punishing job seekers by forcing them to register or take a quiz online in order to apply simply undermines an organization's brand as an employer. It creates an unpleasant candidate experience that conveys a negative image of the organization as an employer. When that happens, the organization will achieve a reduction in the applicant pool, but unfortunately, those who leave will be the passive prospects and "A" level performers.

It's easy to take job postings for granted right now. There isn't much recruiting going on, and the flow of applicants seems almost endless. However, if you're serious about reaching out to the best and brightest in the workforce and convincing them that their next move should be to your organization, then your postings should be rich with the information they want, attentive to their career goals and work-life concerns, and as convincing as possible for them. In short, all of the things that most job postings today are not. ■

■ For Whom Are You Advertising?

All candidates are not alike. Sure, it would be nice if they were, but they aren't. "A" level performers don't act like "C" level performers, and passive job seekers don't act like active job seekers. And those differences have a huge impact on the appeal of our recruitment advertising. In fact, an advertisement's reach into the candidate population is all but fixed by how well it is tailored to account for those differences.

If you do minimal tailoring—for example, you use a classified ad for the content of your job posting—you've implicitly adopted a strategy of advertising to the masses, and that's exactly whom you will attract: active job seekers and mediocre performers. They don't care that you've provided very little information about the opening or done nothing to sell them on its value proposition. They have two things that passive prospects and "A" level per-formers don't: a resume and low expectations. All they want is a job, and almost any job will do. In essence, they are ready to apply and more than happy to do so ... just take a look at those resumes pouring into your e-mailbox these days.

If, on the other hand, you tailor your message—for example, writing a detailed and compelling job posting that emphasizes the key motivators among top performers—that's exactly whom you will reach. "A" level performers and passive prospects almost always have a job and aren't really looking for another. They don't have a resume and do have very high expectations. Hence, they won't even look at an ad that does meet the following four criteria <u>within the first four lines</u>:

- It must offer a powerful, persuasive statement about why the opening is a "dream job." Top performers care a lot about what job they take, and they will only take one that they believe will support their continued advancement.

- It must offer an equally as powerful and persuasive statement about why the organization is a "dream employer." Top performers also care a lot about the organization for which they work, and they only want to work for winners because they believe that top organizations are more apt to support the advancement of top performers.

- It must offer the opportunity for a meaningful increase in compensation. Top performers care a lot about their compensation because they believe that it is a key measure of their advancement in their field.

- And, it must offer a commitment to protect the privacy of the applicant. Top performers are almost always employed, so applying for a new position involves the risk that their current employer may discover what they're up to.

The rest of the ad must go on to offer much more detail about each of these four points—and that detail must <u>prove</u> the initial statements—but the first four lines are what piques the curiosity of the top performer and gets them to read on.

Even this degree of tailoring, however, may not be enough. Why? Because "A" level performers and passive prospects are also different from one another. As a consequence, we must now adopt techniques that our marketing colleagues have been using for years: we must learn how to identify and analyze the different segments of our target customer population so as to determine what motivates them to "buy" an employment opportunity. These differences might be based on age (e.g., the benefits preferences of Baby Boomers are not at all like those of Twentysomethings) or on family matters or other factors. Whatever they are, we need to know the motivators of the key segments within our target top performers and then tailor our ads to emphasize those points.

How can you acquire this information? Conduct a focus group with some of the top performers in your organization in the career fields for which you recruit. Ask them why they decided to sign on and what they think would persuade others just like them to do so, as well. ■

■ Getting Step 1 Right

Everything that we do as recruiters—sourcing, assessing, selling, selection—it all begins with the expression of a requirement. If that's incomplete or inaccurate, then our work inevitably suffers. And worse, it's often we recruiters who get the blame. So, the first and most important precondition to making ourselves successful is a full and complete understanding of what an opening's talent requirements (both expressed and implied) actually are. From there, we can:

(a) assess their appropriateness (given market conditions) and

(b) accomplish our mission cost and time effectively.

The challenge, of course, is that we do not define the requirements; our clients—the hiring manager if you're an internal recruiter, your point of contact if you're a staffing firm recruiter—do. We (or our applicant tracking system vendor) may devise the format, but they provide the data, and we have all had to deal with clients who didn't have the time, inclination or communications skills to tell us accurately want they want.

There have been many proposed solutions to this problem. These include:

- The competency-based job description found in Michael Zwell's book, *Creating a Culture of Competence*;

- The performance-based job description found in Lou Adler's book, *Hire With Your Head*; and

- the job analysis methodology found in Herb Heneman's textbook, *Staffing Organizations*.

While all of these approaches have merit, I've devised a different formula that combines the best of all three. It's based on the Ranger Patrol Order, a planning guide used by the U.S. Army's elite soldiers before going into combat. Since we are now in a War for The Best Talent, it seems only fitting to draw on a battle-tested device that is designed to uncover and address every detail required for mission success.

The Talent Search Order
(adopted from the U.S. Army Ranger Handbook)

The Order is divided into 5 paragraphs. Each paragraph identifies a subject that must be discussed by those involved (the recruiter and their client) and for which realistic plans must be made in order for the mission—in this case, a search for talent—to proceed.

What should you do with the Order, particularly if your organization already has a requirements document and process? The Order is a versatile and complete guide, so you can use it as a cross-check to make sure that:

(a) your client is clear in their own mind about what they want and why;

(b) you thoroughly understand what the client wants, whether it is articulated or not; and

(c) you and your client are on the same page about both the details of the requirement and how realistic they are.

The 5 paragraphs of the **Talent Search Order** are:

☑ **Situation**

(a) Friendly

    (1) What is the current position's title and location?

    (2) What is the state of the business unit where the position is located?

    (3) What is the morale of the team that includes the position?

    (4) Are there any expected changes in (1) or (2) due to either desired improvements or situational adjustments (e.g., relocation, budget cuts/increases)?

(b) Enemy

    (1) What is the supply of talent qualified to compete for the position within the company, the local geographic area and nationwide?

    (2) What are competitors offering to attract such talent into their organizations?

☑ **Mission**

(a) The strategic role of the position (its expected contribution to the goal of the enterprise)

    (1) What are its primary and supporting responsibilities at the strategic level?

(b) The tactical roles of the position (its expected contribution to the goals of the team and business unit)

    (1) What are its primary and supporting responsibilities at the unit/team level that enable the position to play its strategic role)?

☑ **Execution** (of the job)

(a) Concept of operation

    (1) What are the tasks to be performed (what the new hire will do)?

    (2) What problems must be solved, what issues addressed, what constraints overcome?

(b) Coordination instructions

    (1) What are the expectations (when, how and where the new hire will do the job) of the direct supervisor? The next higher manager?

    (2) Are there any planned changes in expectations?

☑ **Administration & Logistics**

(a) What is required for successful mission accomplishment (i.e., the KSAOs (knowledge, skills, abilities & other attributes) required to perform the tasks and meet the expectations identified in Execution)?

    (1) What specific on-the-job accomplishments would indicate the desired level of capability in each KSAO?

(b) What job spanning or cultural competencies (e.g., teamwork, group work) are required to perform the tasks and meet the expectations?

(1) What accomplishments indicate capability?

☑ **Command & Signal**

(a) Signal

(1) What is the definition of successful on-the-job performance and how will it be communicated?

(2) What specific objectives must the new hire accomplish within the next 6, 12, 24 months (e.g., Intel now includes each new incumbent's expected deliverables within the first 12 months in it recruiting requirements documents)?

(b) Command

(1) What other performance measures will be used to assess the contribution of the incumbent?

(2) Who will evaluate the performance of the new hire (i.e., to whom will they report)?

(3) When will the evaluation be performed and how? ■

■ The "DP" Job Posting

O.K., every recruiter with more than 15 minutes experience knows that the trick to recruiting in a War for the Best Talent is to reach out to and mobilize the passive job seeker. Focusing on active job seekers limits your reach to just 16% of the American population, according to the U.S. Department of Labor. In order to recruit among the other 84% of the workforce, however, a recruiter must "de-passify" the "employed-but-willing-to-consider-a-better-position" job seeker. That's the purpose of the **"DP" Job Posting**.

The "DP" job posting has five distinct sections:

- a lead-off Summary
- Advantages
- Benefits
- Capabilities
- a concluding Sign-Off.

Hence, I describe its structure as S-ABC-S. All of the sections but the Summary should begin with their title, which is left justified and appears on its own, separate line in the posting.

The content of a "DP" posting is written in the second person, as if you were addressing the job seeker personally. For example, "This position will enable you to acquire and hone new skills in your field." It is also written in the language of job seekers (that is, it describes "opportunities" rather than "responsibilities") in order to better resonate with them. And, as much as possible, the text is presented in bullets so that it can be quickly scanned and easily absorbed.

The guidelines for each individual section of the posting follow:

The Summary

This section should run no more than five lines and include the following 4 elements in the following order:

- A forceful statement about why the opening is a "dream job;"
- An equally as forceful statement about why the organization is a "dream employer;"
- A salary figure or range. Terms such as "Competitive salary" or "Salary commensurate with experience" will not work with passive prospects and "A' level performers; and
- A short, but emphatic statement regarding the organization's commitment to protecting the privacy of the candidate.

The order in which these statements appear is important because it places the right information up front should a commercial site include the first 1-2 lines of your job posting in the results of a job database search (as some now do).

Advantages

This section should describe the opening to the passive job seeker by telling them:

- What they will get a chance to do on the job.

- Who they will have the opportunity to work with. [the team as well as the supervisor]

- What they will be able to learn in their work.

- What contribution their efforts will make to the organization's success.

- What they can achieve personally and professionally from the position.

Benefits

This section should describe the benefits of working for the organization and in the position, tailoring the presentation as much as possible to the job seeker. For example,

- What can they earn in salary, bonus and other forms of compensation (e.g., options)?

- What other support and assistance will they receive from the employer?

- Where will they get to work (the culture and stature of the employer as well as its facility, if it is particularly attractive or supportive)?

- Where they will get to live (if the job is located in an interesting or fun place)?

Capabilities

This section should describe to the passive job seeker what it will take for them to continue their career success in the position. Specifically, it should tell them:

- What skills, experience and education they'll need to be successful.

- What kind of outlook and personality they'll need to feel comfortable in the organization.

Sign-Off

This section gives the job seeker multiple response channels by which they can apply for the position. These should include:

- e-mail, with complete instructions on how a resume should be sent (e.g., Send your resume as an Attachment to an e-mail message addressed to jane.doe@bestco.com).

- postal mail

- fax

- online Application Form (for those without a resume). The form should ask for no more than seven pieces of information, one of which should be the person's e-mail address.

In addition, this section should give the applicant an opportunity to:

- **Refer** the opening to a friend or colleague if they, themselves, are not interested; and/or

- **Opt-in to an e-mail program** through which you will keep them informed about your employer and its future openings that may be of interest to them.

The "DP" job posting takes full advantage of the Web to focus on the needs of passive job seekers. It uses the medium's lack of space constraints—most commercial sites accept postings of up to 1400 words—to offer a full description of an opening's value proposition. By answering all of the questions job seekers might have about an opportunity before they have to ask them, the posting provides <u>the information they need to determine what a new job can do for them</u> ... and that's the way to "de-passify" them. ■

■ Your Job Posting To-Do (And Don't) List

☑ **Do:**

1. Write a powerful, persuasive title. Include the position's location, principal skill or function (e.g., Technical Sales, Project Manager) and a differentiating trait ... some sizzle that will set it apart from other similar position openings.

2. Get the first five lines right. Most job seekers won't read any further if the posting doesn't have the following elements in the following order:

- A hard-hitting statement that explains why the opening is a "dream job."

- A hard-hitting statement that explains why the employer is a "dream employer."

- A salary range for the opening.

- A statement about the organization's commitment to protecting the privacy of applicants.

3. Use the right format. People don't read online; they scan. Therefore, format the body of your posting with headlines and bullets so that it can be reviewed and understood at a glance.

4. Answer candidates' questions. As a minimum, tell them:

- What they will get to do

- Whom they will get to work with

- What they might be able to accomplish

- What they will be able to learn

- What compensation they can earn

- What benefits they will receive

- What skills and experience they must have to be successful on-the-job.

In the old days of a surplus labor market, this information was typically presented as "requirements and responsibilities." Today, it should be introduced as "advantages, benefits and capabilities," ... in other words, the facts that candidates need to evaluate a job's value proposition for them.

5. Give applicants multiple ways to respond. Provide an e-mail address, a fax number, a postal address and an online application form (for those who don't have a resume—that's often your passive prospects and "A" level performers). Also offer a way for the reader to refer the opening to a friend or colleague.

☒ Don't:

1. Use internal position titles or requisition numbers in the title of your job posting. A posting is an "electronic sales brochure," not a bureaucratic document.

2. Use vague language or stint on details in describing the value proposition of your opening. According to WEDDLE's surveys, the #1 complaint among job seekers is job postings without enough information. Give them what they want, and you'll increase their interest.

3. Assume your prospective candidates know how to send their resume to you online. You'll increase your yield if you offer them some help in your posting (i.e., instructions that are brief, but not condescending, on how to cut and paste a document into or attach it to an e-mail message). Remember, the people you most want to reach—passive prospects and "A' level performers have the least experience applying for a job online, so help them out. They'll appreciate it and your response rate will go up.

4. Treat "A" level candidates and passive prospects as second class applicants. They don't have a resume, so using that term in your postings (e.g., *Submit Your Resume* rather than the more inclusive *Apply Here*) is the online equivalent of telling them to stand in the corner.

5. Use a generic term in the e-mail address you provide for submitting resumes. People mistrust machines so personalize the address by including a name, even if it's not actually for a real person (i.e., janicedoe@yourco.com, rather than the ever popular but off-putting resumes@ yourco.com. ■

■ Job Posting Tips

Even in a slow economy, there are plenty of job postings on the Web competing with yours for the attention of that elusive top-flight candidate. How can you give your postings an edge? The following tips will help you out:

🍄 **A well written title** can separate your posting from others and entice even the most passive job seeker. Great titles have three elements:

Location--Skill--Sizzle.

- **Location** is the state or city in which the job is located.

- **Skill** is the term that most prime candidates would use to describe themselves in the job. In other words, do not use bureaucratic terms or requisition numbers to describe a position (e.g., the designation *Systems Analyst I* may mean something to your HR Department, but it means nothing at all to an external candidate). Hence, it's better to use words that are significant to your target candidate population; they think of positions as the skills they bring to the job (e.g., they are a C++ programmer or a project manager or a civil engineer).

- **Sizzle** is a key motivator for your target candidate population. To be successful, therefore, you will have to know what motivates the best and brightest to accept an employment opportunity with your organization. How can you find that out? Conduct a focus group with some of the organization's best employees in the field for which you are recruiting. Ask them why they came to work for your organization and emphasize those motivators in your posting title (as well as the body of the posting, itself).

The key to an effective title is to express those elements with words that your prime candidates will relate to and understand. Don't overdo slang or trendy words, particularly if they can cause confusion. One recent posting used the phrase "Minister of Buzz" to describe an opening for a Director of Communications. What kind of candidates did it attract? Well, one of the resumes, at least, was from a Baptist Minister.

🍄 **The first five lines or Summary** of a posting are critically important. If you don't get those right, research shows that most job seekers—and especially "A" level performers and passive prospects—won't read any further. One of the most important elements in the Summary is salary. A recent study by Yahoo! found that postings that include a salary figure or range attract 100% more responses than those that are silent about salary or use such say-nothing terms as "Competitive."

🍄 **Beware the use of HTML** in job postings. Using the programming language of the Web in your postings does enable you to spice them up with your logo, color frames and other features that have genuine eye appeal. Graphics and images, however, significantly increase the time required for a posting to open on a candidate's computer. Most people are still accessing the Web with a dial-up modem, so be sure that you test any HTML posting with that kind of connection <u>before</u> you post it. If it takes more than 14 seconds to download, you're going to lose a lot of prospective candidates, and especially those impatient "A" level performers and passive prospects. In short, color is fine, but great content that is easily accessed is better. ■

■ Little Known Secrets of Job Posting Pros

What day is best for posting an ad online?

According to Nielsen/NetRatings, the most active Internet usage occurs on Monday, when 74% of the total U.S. Internet population at work and 48% of the population at home is connected. Hence, the best time to post an ad is ... Friday.

At that point, the ad has the potential to be seen by the sizable population that will log on over the weekend (according to *Business 2.0*, users will visit 14 sites and spend almost 6 hours online each weekend), but more importantly, be ready for viewing by the biggest audience, when the crowd arrives at work Monday morning.

Then what?

Post as early as necessary on Friday (for the sites you have selected) to ensure that you have the time to see and proof the ad once it's online and make any necessary changes before the close of business. (Errors do occur during any site's posting process, so always proof your ad once it appears online.)

And don't forget to re-post the ad every week (on Friday) during your entire posting period. That way, it will be identified as a new ad each week, and the computer will include it in the search results for any job seeker who looks at only the latest postings.

And then?

In one recent survey of job seekers, 52% of respondents described online resume submission as the "black hole syndrome." To avoid tarnishing your employment brand with that kind of reputation, be "candidate friendly." Use an auto-responder—a feature that is included in most candidate management systems today—that will automatically acknowledge the receipt of each applicant's resume and tell them what happens next in the review and assessment process.

That simple courtesy will cut down on the e-mail and phone calls you get from applicants inquiring about receipt of their resume and, even more important, treat them to a much more pleasant initial experience than that provided by many employers. And in the War for the Best Talent, such a positive first impression is half the battle in selling the best and brightest. ■

■ A Triple Whammy

Who isn't on the receiving end of a torrent of resumes these days? If you have an employment Web-site or post jobs on a commercial site, you can expect to be inundated with resumes from job seekers ... whether they're qualified or not for your openings. But there's the rub. According to one recent report, as many as 60% of the resumes you receive are duplicates. Sure, they don't take up file space the way paper resumes do, but these copies of copies of copies gobble up processing resources and potentially diminish your ability to find qualified applicants in your resume database.

So, what's to be done? I like the following three-part strategy because it not only helps to cut down on duplicates, but it can also help you collect appropriate data for the Equal Employment Opportunity Commission and enhance your retention rate among new employees. In short, I think it's a triple whammy!

Eliminating duplicates. The key to weaning candidates off of duplicate resume submissions is early information. Candidates tell us that they hit the Submit button 3, 4 or 5 times because they are uncertain:

(a) that their resume has, in fact, been transmitted from the job board or career area of your Web-site and/or

(b) that the resume has actually been received at the other end by you.

Therefore, tell them, in the text of your job postings, that you will notify them by auto-responder when you have received their resume. Also tell them, that they should send a second resume if they have not heard back from you within [give yourself a reasonable period of time taking into account the pace at which your recruitment process works], but that sending another copy before that time or after receipt has been acknowledged will actually hurt their chances of employment. Place this statement above the Submit button in the posting, so that it's difficult to miss. This approach takes the "black hole" feeling out of a candidate's resume submission and gives them the sense that you really do want to receive their credentials.

Meeting EEOC guidelines. The key to defining who is and who is not an applicant—and, as a result, about whom data must be collected—is an employer's definition of its application process. Every employer has the right to delineate the steps in its process so long as those steps pertain to every-one and are fairly administered. Moreover, the statement you use to define your process can also help you eliminate duplicate resumes. How? By including in it the notification that you will be using an auto-responder (see above) and that the auto-responder message will pose several questions that must be answered for a person to be considered an applicant for an opening. There should then be two sections to the questions:

(1) a mandatory section that acquires additional skill or attribute data about the candidates, and

(2) a voluntary section that collects EEOC data.

The questions will act as a screen to discourage continued activity by "graffiti applicants," thereby constricting the pool of people who must be counted and tracked as applicants, and the answers to the questions will provide additional data for candidate assessment.

Improving retention among new hires. In addition to the skills assessment (which you can do with questions devised by the hiring manager or other in-house experts or by using an outside resource such as TopCoder.com which provides "contests" for IT pros), expand the mandatory set of questions to include those that will give you a fix on an applicant's likely post hiring commitment.

Retail recruiter Unicru says that it has correlated the answers to certain—well, out of the ordinary questions—to a person's likely retention. What are those questions? Unicru claims that it can predict, with up to 80% accuracy, an applicant's tenure within two months by asking:

- The name of the applicant's supervisor from two jobs ago. (If they can't remember, they won't be around long, says Unicru.)

- The total number of mornings an applicant is willing to work. (The lower that number, the shorter their retention).

Whether you use those variables or others that you have identified, the auto-responder is the right place to start getting a fix on the likely tenure of an applicant. That factor, as much as their skill and experience, will determine the success of your recruiting efforts. ■

■ Gas Up Your Auto-Responder

For most organizations, an auto-responder is simply an automatic message the computer sends back to job applicants to acknowledge the receipt of their resume. It's an easy way to say thank you and to fend off some of the normal deluge of follow up telephone calls. While that is certainly helpful, this feature can do much more for you and your organization ... if you gas it up.

You can put horsepower in your auto-responder by using the following formula:

G -give candidates more information.
In addition to saying thanks for the resume, make sure your auto-responder includes the following key elements:

- A timeline for the review of their credentials

- An explanation of what will happen next if they are found to be potentially qualified for your opening

- An explanation of what will happen to their resume if that are found not qualified for the opening

And of course, keep the message positive and upbeat.

A -add information to each candidate's record.
As soon as you have finished your initial review of submitted resumes, send out a second auto-responder message to those candidates deemed to be potentially qualified. This message should ask for the following additional information:

- Their availability date;

- Their current salary, including bonus and other forms of compensation;

- Their current location (if relocation assistance is not provided); and

- Their willingness to travel if that is a part of the job (particularly by air, as that has become difficult for some after 9/11).

The Secret: This information is the equivalent of that captured by telephone screening calls in many organizations. The research shows that candidates will provide this information by e-mail, as well, if your message contains a strong statement underscoring your organization's commitment to protecting their privacy.

S -separate the "A's" from the "C's".
Send a third auto-responder message to those who provide all of the information requested by the second message. In this last message, present a key task or function that must be accomplished by the person selected for the open position. Then, ask the candidates to describe how they have

handled a similar task or function previously in their career or, if they haven't, how they would perform the task in the future. Limit their response to 150 words or less:

(a) so you don't have to wade through novel-length answers and

(b) to see how concise and precise they can be in their presentations.

Use the information you receive to separate the "A" level performers from all of the rest and then focus your subsequent recruiting efforts on them.

A gassed-up auto-responder can save you time and improve your selection results by increasing the range and depth of information you have for candidate evaluation. So, give it a try. It just might make your employer, the "Leader of the Pack." ■

■ Value-Based Advertising Copy

In the dark ages of recruiting—you know, way back in the 1990's—recruitment advertising had a single purpose. Its role was simply to notify job seekers of an employment opportunity. That's all it had to do because there was a surplus of labor and, with even the stingiest description of an opening, candidates would apply. Indeed, the traditional classified ad set the standard for tight-lipped advertising. It contained barely enough information to determine the nature of the job and the identity of the employer.

Today, of course, it seems as if that fabled time has returned. Despite demographic facts that have not changed, there now appears to be no end to the candidate supply. Recruiters who, just six months ago, were desperately trying to pen recruitment ads with enough sizzle to attract increasingly choosy candidates are now back to dashing off your basic classified job notice and watching it attract hundreds or thousands of job seekers. This turn of events wouldn't be a problem, except that such behaviors become habits and when they do, they set an organization up for disaster, once the economy recovers. When that day arrives—and we all know that it's a matter of when, not if it will—the demographic constraints that are currently masked by layoffs and downsizing will reassert themselves with a vengeance. And when they do, those recruiters who source with advertising designed for a labor surplus market will find themselves all but ignored.

How can you avoid such a lonely situation? Learn the skills involved in writing value-based advertising copy. This very non-traditional employment message is based on research conducted by McKinsey & Company in the latest update to its classic work, *The War for Talent*. It found that the best performing employees seek a combination of advantages in a new job. No one advantage is sufficient to "sell" the position, so all of them must be addressed in advertising, or top notch candidates are unlikely to notice or apply. Further, the description of the advantages in the advertising must be informative and compelling. In other words, enough must be said about each advantage, and that expression must be persuasive enough to establish a "value proposition" that will attract and engage even the most passive members of the target candidate population.

What are the advantages that must be addressed in value-based advertising copy? They are:

- Exciting work
- A great employer
- Personal development
- Wealth and rewards.

McKinsey found that top performers are most interested in interesting and challenging work. After that, they want to perform that work for a highly regarded company, where they will be recognized and rewarded for their contribution and can advance their career.

How can that information be arrayed in a job posting?

First of all, unlike the notification approach of a classified ad, the value posting <u>persuades</u>. To do that, it must not only say the right things (that's the value proposition), but it must say them several times. I recommend that, as a minimum, the advantages of a particular job be mentioned in a lead-in summary of 4-5 lines and then described in detail in the body of the ad. Most commercial recruitment Web-sites permit job postings to run 1,400 words or longer (the equivalent of two typed pages) so there is unlikely to be any restriction on the space you need to make your case.

Second, make sure that the advantages are described with details that will <u>sell the position</u>. For example, in each of the four areas identified above, McKinsey found that the following characteristics are constituent elements of the value proposition:

Exciting work:

- It's work they can feel passionate about,
- It's the knowledge that they will be listened to,
- It's the ability to show initiative, and
- It's the assurance that they will have the freedom and autonomy to get the job done in the way they think best.

Great employer:

- It's an organization that is well managed,
- It's the chance to work for a great boss who is someone they can admire,
- It's an organization with a culture and values they can respect, and
- It's an organization where senior management is worthy of trust and does not tolerate bureaucratic indifference, incompetence or mediocrity.

Development:

- It's a job where they can hone skills that will advance their career in the near and the longer term,
- It's an organization with senior managers who will take an interest in and support their advancement, and
- It's an organization that is committed to identifying and promoting high performers.

Wealth and rewards:

- It's a job that has the potential to create substantial wealth for them, and
- It's an organization that pays high performers more than average performers and does so with high cash compensation.

Finally, don't forget the family. Over half of all those polled by McKinsey listed the ability to "meet my personal/family commitments" as a key element in their evaluation of a new employment opportunity. Hence, it's important to include in the posting any "family friendly" benefits or programs that your organization offers. These might include on-site child care support or financial assistance, flex time scheduling, a policy that permits sick days to be used when a child is ill and support for employee participation in the National Guard and Reserve. Such programs and policies are traditionally not introduced until the candidate is well into the interviewing process and/or has been hired and is going through orientation. While that approach may work in a labor surplus market, it's a ticket to disaster in a market where you have to sell candidates just to get them to pay attention.

Value-based advertising copy can't turn a lousy job into a dream opportunity, but it can ensure that candidates know the best about an opening. And putting the best about a job forward (where candidates can see it) is the only effective way to recruit when the economy is growing and labor is short. According to most economists, that means you have, at most, about 3-6 months to hone your skills as a writer of value-based advertising copy. ■

■ Using Search Engines

With layoffs and unemployment rising and all of the media buzz about the sputtering economy, you would think that job-related words would be among the top search terms at search engines. Well, guess what? According to a survey conducted by Alexa Research, the most frequently used term is ... "sex." That's right! Employment-related words don't even rank in the top 20, unless you consider "horoscope" to be a form of career planning.

All is not lost, however, because the top 50 terms accounted for just 2.73 percent of all searches. In other words, there is considerable diversity in the range of subjects that people search for on-line. And since that's so, is there any way that recruiters can put search engines to work for them? Sure there is. But to have any success at all, you'll have to adopt the following guidelines:

■ **First, don't use them for job posting.** People use search engines to go someplace else. They don't hang around at these sites and read their content. Instead, they come, they search, and they leave. The time they spend on the sites is devoted to searching their directories or indexes, not to looking at job postings. That's why our Annual Survey of Best Recruiting Practices Online has consistently ranked posting jobs on search engine sites among the least effective techniques.

■ **Second, do use them for targeting messages to a specific candidate population.** While people may not use generic employment terms on search engines (i.e., "jobs" "openings"), they are starting their job search campaigns there. The way they search, however, is very idiosyncratic. In most cases, they use search terms that are specific to their career field, industry, geographic preference and/or the organization of interest to them. To put this pattern to work for you, therefore, you have to:

(a) determine what nouns and phrases are likely to be used in a search by your target candidate population(s), and then,

(b) devise a way to make your opportunities visible when those terms are used in their searches.

The former can be accomplished with a focus group among your recent hires and/or the high performers in your organization. The latter can be achieved with either of two strategies:

① For openings you are always trying to fill, it may make sense to register the postings on those search engines where you can purchase a higher placement among the results of a relevant search. In other words, instead of your posting appearing as #372 out of the 1,300 documents identified by a prospective candidate's search, the site will sell you the right for it to appear as #1 or 2. For this strategy to work, however, your posting must be rich with the search terms (i.e., keywords) identified by your focus group.

② To draw prospective candidates to your own site (where they can see more than a single posting), you might want to try Yahoo's new Sponsored Site program. Yahoo was recently cited as the second most heavily trafficked property on the Internet by Nielsen/NetRatings. It draws almost 70 million visitors each month. Its Sponsored Site program enables you to have a full color Web ad appear for you site whenever a relevant search term is used on the search engine. For example, if you're looking for engineers and purchase the word "engineer" on Yahoo!, every time someone enters that word in a search, your ad will appear at the top of the results page. And according to a Yahoo! spokesperson, you can buy such visibility for as little as $25 per month.

Nine out of ten Web users visit a search engine, portal or community every month. They also visit these sites regularly, averaging just under five visits per month. The strategies described above can help you capitalize on that traffic and effectively turn their searches into highly targeted ads for your employment opportunities. ■

■ **Sourcing Candidate Resumes & Information Online**
How Should You Do It? Where Will You Get the Best Results?

■ Cherry Picking Top Talent

Sure, you have more resumes than you can use right now, but are they from the candidates that you most want to hire? The key to winning the War for the Best Talent is preparation. Now, is the time to target top prospects—find them, connect with them and build a relationship with them so that when recruiting picks up again, you have an inventory of All Stars ready to make the jump to your team.

One of the most lucrative pools of talent in which you can source is a competitor or target company. Now, for staffing firm recruiters, sourcing from a specific company has long been an accepted practice. I do, however, recognize that the strategy may make some corporate recruiters just a bit uncomfortable; so, if you're in that group, please consider this: surveys show that 30% or more of most companies' workers plan to move to another employer as soon as they deem it is safe to do so (i.e., when a recovery makes jobs more prevalent and easier to get). If you can capture some of that flow (and not lose any top workers yourself), you will not only have acquired needed talent, you will have also made it more difficult for your competitor to keep up in the marketplace.

How can you search for your competitor's talent or for the talent of a target company?

■ One obvious place to look is among the sites frequented by the kinds of workers you seek. Check the resume databases at appropriate alumni organization, association and trade group sites using the names of your competitors/target companies as search criteria. For example, if you work for Ford and find that University of Michigan graduates make some of your best performers, visit the university's alumni site at www.career.umalumni.com and search its resume database using General Motors as one of your keywords.

You'll find a free directory of college sites (from which you can connect to their alumni area or portal) at www.google.com/ universities.html. You'll find free directories of association and trade organization sites at www. weddles.com (U.S. and international) and the American Society of Association Executives site at www.asaenet.org/gateway/OnlineAssocSlist.html (U.S. only).

■ A second way to cherry pick the competition and target companies is by searching their own Web-sites. For those of you who have been recruiting online for awhile, you'll remember a technique called "flipping." It's a way of searching sites for documents that have been linked to those sites. The documents are not visible to site visitors, and often cover a wide range of topics, from environmental statements and product catalogs to ... yep, you guessed it: resumes. Why would anyone link a resume to their employer's site? Basically, for convenience. It's a safe place to store your resume—since most companies do not regularly review what's been linked to their site—and the link makes the resume readily available for you to use whenever you need it.

Flipping is not hacking; it only uncovers documents that are linked to the public area of a site. On the other hand, it does reveal prospective candidates that, in all likelihood, the competition or a target company doesn't know or even suspect are in the market.

How do you flip a competitor's or target company's site? Follow the 5-step process below:

① Go to HotBot.com. While any search engine will allow you to flip a site, I've had the best luck with HotBot.

② In the search criteria box in the center of the HotBot home page, enter the complete URL of your competitor's/target company's site (e.g., http://www.gm.com).

③ Open the drop-down window entitled *Look for:* at the top of the tool bar on the left side of the home page and click on "Links to this URL."

④ Click on Search. If your results include too many non-resume documents, return to the HotBot home page and click on the Advanced Search link located in the middle of the tool bar on the left side of the home page.

⑤ When the Advanced Search page opens:
- Scroll down to the Word Filter
  - do not change the default settings (i.e., leave the entries "must contain" and "the words" as they are)
  - in the first keyword box, enter the word resume
  - in the second keyword box, enter the skills for which you are searching
- Scroll down to Date and adjust, if necessary
- Scroll down to Region and change the drop-down window entry to North America (.com)
- Click on Search

Steps ④ and ⑤ will remove most (but not all) of the extraneous documents from your flipping results and thus let you focus on the resumes of prospective candidates waiting for you to cherry pick them from the competition or target company.

- A third way to hunt for competitors' or target company talent is to search the online archives of magazines for articles that have been authored by or mention their employees. There is a free archive of articles that have appeared in over 300 magazines and journals at www.findarticles.com.

To make best use of this resource, use the following search tips:

① In the search criteria box, enter the skills you are seeking (e.g., Oracle, engineering)

② In the same search string, add the names of competitor organizations using the plus sign as your Boolean operator (e.g., Oracle +GM +Chrysler)

③ When searching for multi-word skills, use quotation marks to signify the phrase (e.g., "Oracle database administration" +GM +Chrysler)

Recruiters, today, have a choice when sourcing candidates: they can sit back and sift through the torrent of resumes flooding their e-mailboxes—many of which are from persons in transition—or they can proactively search for talent where talent works and cherry pick the best. Which choice will you make? ■

■ Top Talent Targeting

To win in the War for the Best Talent, recruiters must be proactive. We cannot afford to sit back and wait for top talent to come to us, via the corporate recruitment site or job postings anywhere else on the Web. Instead, we must initiate early and continuous efforts to find those passive prospects and "A" level performers who can make a difference for our organization. That's what top talent targeting is all about: finding the best workers where they live, work and play online.

As you might imagine, there's a whole toolbox of techniques for targeting top talent on the Web. Elsewhere in this book, I explore such methods as e-networking and searching home pages in virtual communities. What follows is another technique, one that is designed to help you find top candidates at the executive level.

This technique uses a search engine to probe a corporate Web-site for information about a specific category of employee, in this case, its executives. Start at the search engine Google (www.google.com). Obtain the URL or Internet address of the corporate site(s) you would like to search. (If peeking inside another company's site is making you feel slightly uncomfortable, remember two things: first, any information on the site is in the public domain and second, what you're doing is simply the electronic version of what executive recruiters have always done.)

Next, enter the following search string into the search criteria box on Google's home page:

site:thecompany.com intitle:executive

This search string will identify any page on the site that refers to executives and may even uncover a roster of all of the organization's top executives. If you're looking for a specific person, and they do not turn up in the search results, check to see if they work in a subsidiary of the company whose site you checked. If they do and that subsidiary also has a site, you can search it, as well, with this technique.

The final and most important step involves your initial contact with the executive. Whether you use e-mail or the telephone (see Making Contact), always ensure that your message is discrete, personal and complimentary. You are, after all, communicating with a winner. Make sure they know you know that. ■

■ URL Peeling

Peeling is one of those Internet search techniques that helps you find gold in spots that others walk right past. As with flipping, it does not involve hacking or breaking into protected information on a site. Instead, peeling is a way of picking out and looking into the "file cabinets" that are used to organize the public information on a Web-site. Here's how it works.

Let's say you've identified an association where many of your targeted candidates are members. (See WEDDLE's free Association Directory at www.weddles.com for a list of over 10,000 association sites) You visit the site and flip it using the Advanced Search feature of the HotBot search engine. (For an introduction to flipping, please see the first postcard in this chapter). In the Word Filter box, you specify certain skills for which you are looking. When the search results come back, you see a page entitled 2001 Conference Fact Sheet. Its URL is shown below:

www.theassociation.org/memdirectory/annconf/details2001.

When you open the page, all that's there is a list of people serving on the organizing committee for the association's annual conference. At that point, many recruiters would simply close the page and move on. The more expert searcher, however, would check the URL and note that embedded within it is the term "memdirectory." By peeling back or removing the two elements that follow that term (i.e., "annconf/" and "details2001") and then visiting the page at the new address (www.theassociation.org/memdirectory), you might just find a document that is—as its name suggests—the entire membership directory for the association.

Obviously, not every page on the Web will lead you back to such a wonderful horde of prospective candidates. But some definitely will. What clues should you look for? Keep an eye out for any of the following terms, alone or together, in the body of a Web page address:

Addresses	Employee
Directory	Member
Listing	People
Roster	Staff

■

■ The Recruiter's Nightmare

As the economy continues to sputter, candidate resumes are pouring into employers' resume management systems and the resume databases on commercial recruitment sites. By one estimate, more than 4 million resumes have been posted in the last 3 months alone. And that tidal wave of candidate records has created a new nightmare for recruiters: the possibility that they may overlook the perfect candidate for an opening as they search through the data morass.

How can you avoid missing dream candidates in the resume databases you use? There are two key principles involved in conducting an exhaustive search that overlooks no one:

- Use the right keywords
- Use the right search strategy.

Use the Right Key Words

The search engines in your typical resume database simply look at every word in every candidate record and compare them to the words you list as your search criteria. Computers are dumb as dirt, so they will not recognize the synonyms of your listed criteria or even the same word if it is spelled differently or incorrectly. Hence, the only way to conduct a thorough search of a resume database is with your target candidates' vocabulary: the <u>exact</u> nouns and phrases they use to describe their skills and experience.

How can you acquire those search criteria? The following suggestions will get you started:

- Use your intranet or e-mail to solicit the input of your organization's top performers in the fields for which you are recruiting. Ask them to list the words <u>they</u> would use to describe them-selves as a candidate.

- Use the same approach to solicit the input of hiring managers. Ask them to list the words that describe their ideal candidate. (Using the Web to acquire their input rather than a face-to-face meeting increases the likelihood that you'll actually get the information you seek.)

- Create a "key word taxonomy" that is available to all recruiters. Use it to display your input from top performers and hiring managers and add to it the criteria your fellow recruiters have found to be most effective in their searches. As the range and depth of this resource grows, it will:

  - save time and improve search productivity,

  and

  - become the institutional memory of your recruiting staff and thus diminish the knowledge lost through turnover.

Use the Right Search Strategy

Whether you're searching your own, internal candidate database or the database at a commercial site, success depends upon your linking the right key words in an effective Boolean search string. Such a string puts you, rather than the computer, in charge of determining who will be an acceptable candidate. The following principles should guide your strategy:

① Identify the required categories of criteria for the optimal candidate (e.g., skill, skill level, location, experience); separate the categories with the Boolean operator AND.

② Determine the synonyms used in each category (e.g., for skill level: director OR manager); separate the synonyms with OR.

③ Include no more than 3 categories (ANDs) with no more than 2-3 synonyms (ORs) in each category in your first search iteration; begin with the most important criteria:

(director OR manager) AND (Connecticut OR CT) AND (engineer OR "structural design")

④ Alternate adding one AND (required criteria) and two ORs (their synonyms) with each search iteration

2nd run:

license AND (director OR manager) AND (Connecticut OR CT) AND (engineer OR "structural design")

3rd run:

license AND (director OR manager OR "project manager") AND (Connecticut OR CT OR 06902) AND (engineer OR "structural design)

Continue iterating your database search until you have identified a pool of qualified candidates that is large enough to provide adequate choice but small enough for efficient review. ■

■ Combing Communities

Virtual communities are gathering spots on the Web where people come together to share a bargain or an interest. Given the size of their total population—collectively, it's probably in excess of 30 million people—and the fact that most of those who join are "passive job seekers," they represent a very lucrative recruiting destination. How can you comb the candidates in virtual communities? The following guidelines will get you started.

Rule #1: Take the easy way out. While it's true that you can use a search engine to x-ray the contents of a virtual community, the four largest sites actually provide a free search feature right on their home pages. These sites are:

- AmericaOnline Hometown atwww.hometown.aol.com,

- Angelfire at www.angelfire.com,

- Yahoo! Geocities at www.geocities.com, and

- Tripod at www.tripod.com.

Now, what exactly are you searching? Most of the members who join a virtual community do so because they provide free home pages or personal Web-sites. While these pages are not resumes, they often contain considerable information about their owner's work experience and credentials. In addition, many people also attach their resume to their home page which, of course, makes your job even easier.

How do you get the best results from the search feature on these sites. Use the following Boolean strings:

- If you only want to see home pages with resumes attached:

resume AND (the key skills you want, each separated by AND) AND (the industry or work experience you're looking for)

- If you're willing to look at home pages without resumes attached:

(the key skills you want, each separated by AND) AND (the industry or work experience you're looking for)

Rule #2: X-ray if you must. This technique enables you to peer into the pages of a virtual community that does not provide a free onsite searching feature. In other words, you get to see what's on the site just as if it had a Table of Contents for you to review.

How does x-raying work? First, you have to identify one or more virtual communities whose members might be prospective candidates for your openings. I suggest you try the following:

- TopCities at www.topcities.com,

- Family Shoebox at www.familyshoebox.com, &

- MaxPages at www.maxpages.com.

Next, you have to find a search engine that yields good x-ray results. Although some prefer Northern Light (www.northernlight.com), I've had the best success at AltaVista (www.altavista.com). To x-ray with AltaVista:

(1) Click on the Advanced Search icon on its home page.

(2) In the Boolean box on the Advanced Search page, enter the following search string:

host:site.url (for example, host:topcities.com) AND (the key skills you want, each separated by AND) AND (the industry or work experience you're looking for)

Although x-raying a site will bring back some irrelevant pages, it will also often uncover a gem candidate or two that the competition will never find and that yield gives you a genuine competitive advantage. ■

■ Online Recruiting Power ✷ Tool Box

Power ✷ Tool: Passive Candidate Drill

America Online has 33 million members and more sign on every day. Recent studies indicate that the first thing 90% of all AOL users do when they start up is launch a home page. Even more interesting, these same studies reveal that 85% of those home pages incorporate a resume. How can you drill into this pool of mostly passive job seekers? Visit **http://hometown.aol.com**. In the Search & Explore dialogue box on that page, enter the skills for which you're recruiting. If you only want to look at home pages that include a formal resume, then simply begin the skill word string with the word, resume.

Power ✷ Tool: Web-Site Crowbar

There are two ways to probe a Web-site. The most obvious, of course, is to visit the site and look around. If you're a corporate recruiter who is searching a competitor's site for candidates (good candidates, after all, are those with the right skills, but the best candidates are those who have the right skills and are willing to work for your employer rather than the competition), you might look for organization charts or rosters and directories for specific business units. If you're a staffing firm recruiter looking for points of contact for a prospective client, you might look for the names of recruiters mentioned in job postings or for HR Department rosters and directories.

In some cases, these efforts will be successful, but in other cases, the organization operating the site will have learned about the vulnerability of such information and removed it from the site. What can you do then? Probe the site a second way by going back into the past. That's right; there's now a site called the **Wayback Machine (http://web.archive.org)** that enables you to pry open previous versions of Web-sites, dating as far back as 1996. Back in those days, site webmasters weren't as concerned about the visibility of corporate information online, so you just may find the name and telephone number or e-mail address of that key contact you're looking for.

Power ✷ Tool: Technical Term Manuals

Despite all of the retrenchment in corporate IT Departments during the past year, there is still demand for technical talent. What's different, however, is the degree of precision required by hiring managers. They want very specific skills and a much deeper degree of specialization than was the norm in the past. That means searching for candidates with ever more esoteric skills identified by acronyms and names that sound more like gibberish than English. How can you translate this techno-talk into something you can work with? Use one or more of the **dictionaries of technical terms** found online. They include:

- AcronymFinder (www.acronymfinder.com). It lists 227,000 acronyms and abbreviations;
- The Techencyclopedia (www.techweb.com/ encyclopedia). It lists more than 20,000 IT terms;

- WhatIs (www.whatis.com) is a part of the TechTarget Network. It permits you to search for a word or term by keyword, alphabetically or by category (e.g., software, Internet);

Webopedia (www.webopedia.com) from Internet.com. It is a database of computer and Internet terms searchable by keyword and category. ■

■ Sourcing Those Who Serve

Each year, several hundred thousand men and women leave the United States Armed Forces and the Peace Corps to begin careers in the private sector. In most cases, these individuals have:

- learned to work in culturally diverse environments;

- been trained on some of the most advanced technology available for engineering, logistics management, information processing, operations management and other functions;

- acquired and honed supervisory and leadership skills; and

- demonstrated personal responsibility and an understanding of teamwork in even the most pressure-packed situations.

Such attributes, in and of themselves, make these individuals very attractive candidates. But these men and women have also volunteered to serve their country in a difficult time, and that fact speaks to the quality of their character and burnishes their credentials even more. In short, there are no better candidates in the War for the Best Talent than those who have served in the nation's Armed Forces and Peace Corp.

How can you recruit these veterans and volunteers? The following list of sites will get you started; it's drawn from *WEDDLE's 2003 Directory of Employment-Related Internet Sites*:

Site Name	URL
Blue-to-Gray	www.bluetogray.com
Classified Employment Web Site	www.yourinfosource/CLEWS
Connecting Corporations to the Military Community	www.vets4hire.com
Returning Peace Corp Volunteers	www.peacecorps.gov/rpcv/ hotline/postjobs.cfm#submit
Transition Assistance Online	www.taonline.com
VetJobs	www.vetjobs.com

And for those of you who may need a little help translating the military jargon and acronyms you might see on a veteran's resume, try *Janes* (www.james.com/defence/glossary). It covers 20,000 terms, which is good, but only scratches the surface of what the military has created. ■

■ Finding & Contacting "A" List Candidates

The best candidates—those "A" level performers whom everyone wants (including their current employer)—don't act like your typical job seeker. To put it more bluntly, they don't put their resumes in resume databases (in fact, they normally don't have one) and don't respond to job postings. There's no need to; they know that employers will come looking for them.

That self assurance, in turns, means that we recruiters must hone two sets of skills:

- the skills of identifying and locating the All Stars online and
- the skill of contacting them so as to make a positive first impression.

The first skill set is essentially a research activity; the second sets up a wooing process. In both cases, the unique attributes of the "A" level person play a significant role in shaping exactly what we do and how we do it, when we set out to recruit them.

Research: Finding the All Stars

"A" Level Attributes:

While some "A" level performers may actually look for a job from time-to-time (because they too can get caught up in layoffs at sick companies), I think the majority do not. Why? One key reason is probably that they don't have a resume and don't want to take the time to create one.

If they're curious about or need to take a look at what's available in the job market, therefore, it's more likely that they will sign up for a job agent. This software feature is available on about 40% of all recruitment sites and is designed to keep a person privately informed of any positions in which they might be interested. Which of these agents are they likely to use? Unlike the vast majority of job seekers, who will normally use the agents at the biggest and best known sites, top talent will gravitate to those provided at sites they trust: the ones that are operated by their professional association, alumni group and select commercial organizations (e.g., CareerJournal.com from *The Wall Street Journal*).

These attributes (or eccentricities?) of top talent necessarily shape our sourcing strategies online. For the best results, I suggest you adhere to the following guidelines:

- Don't purchase a long-term contract for resume search at any site without first making sure that its database holds more than the records of active job seekers. How can you tell? Conduct a trial search for a couple of your openings.
- Select sites that are likely to be visited by the best of your target demographic and then only post openings on those sites that offer job agents.
- Visit the online discussion boards and other networking areas on your targets' favorite sites and look for the individuals who stand out.

- Consider using a research service such as that provided by Eliyon (www.eliyon.com). Its software crawls around the Web and looks for references to people (e.g., a press release, a paper presented at a conference). It then extracts relevant information (e.g., name, title, employer) and organizes it into a database that can be searched for a fee. Currently the site claims to have over 7.5 million records from people at almost 3 million companies.

Contact: Beginning the Wooing Process

<u>"A" Level Attributes:</u>

While "C" level performers and active job seekers may not mind an initial contact by e-mail, the vast majority of "A" level performers look for something different. They want to hear a human voice. And if they can't hear a human voice, they expect any communication from a recruiter to be much more personal than a form e-mail message. In short, the best and brightest like to be (and rightly should be) treated as "preferred customers."

In addition, "A" level performers aren't interested in open jobs; they don't even care about dream jobs. What they want—because they've always had it and because it's what they believe has enabled them to be "A" level performers—is a dream job with a dream employer. To put it another way, "A" level performers don't look for a job; they look for a career opportunity.

These two attributes, in turn, dictate that we adhere to the following guidelines when contacting "A" level performers online:

- If possible, always contact the "A" level performer first by telephone and always call them at home. How do you find their telephone number? Try The Ultimates (www.theultimeates.com) or the phone book at Google. To make best use of the Google directory, use the following command in the search criteria box:

  rphonebook:last name of person, city of residence

For example,

  rphonebook:Miller, Boston

The "rphonebook" command directs Google to look up all Millers in the city of Boston with a telephone number listed <u>in its residential phonebook</u>. In some cases, this directory even includes telephone numbers that are unlisted in traditional telephone books.

- Always have a script ready that:

  (a) acknowledges the person's success to date,

  (b) introduces your opening <u>and</u> your organization, and

  (c) describes how both will be advantageous to them and their career.

  If you cannot reach the person by telephone, use the Best Practices in e-mail communications to try and connect with them (see Making Contact).

- If the prospective candidate is interested in your position, ask if you can e-mail them addition-al information about the position and your organization and invite them to visit its Web-site (if it's any good). If they aren't interested, ask if you can e-mail them some information about your organization. In either case, you'll acquire their personal e-mail address and be able to begin the wooing process. ■

■ Regarding Passives

Standard Web sourcing techniques work just fine for active job seekers, but seldom uncover significant numbers of "A" level performers and other passive prospects. Many of these best and brightest are unmoved by even the most persuasive job posting. And most do not have a resume to archive in an online database. Therefore, if you want to find such candidates online, you'll have to find another way. Consider this …

Virtually all Internet users correspond by e-mail. Some of this communication is personal, but much comes from a work e-mail address and is devoted to professional and/or business topics. Typically, the latter involves postings to online discussion boards on sites hosted by professional associations, trade organizations, alumni groups, newsgroups and listservs. This e-mail expresses the author's knowledge, experience, personality and other attributes and is in the public domain. In other words, these messages would offer a great window into the passive population, if you could only find and access them.

Well, now you can. Here's how the technique works:

Step 1: Conduct a focus group with appropriate managers and staff to identify the employers where top prospects in specific occupational fields tend to work.

Step 2: Go to the search engine Google.com.

Step 3: Conduct a "Regarding" search using the following command:

Re: @companyname.com

This search will uncover postings to forums, discussion boards, newsgroups and other sites by the employees of the target company. For example, we ran the search Re: @ti.com and found hundreds of postings by Texas Instruments employees on topics ranging from OS/2 to brine shrimp eggs.

Step 4: Make the right first impression. Send an e-mail that will impress and pique the curiosity of the best prospects you identified in Step 3. That's more of a challenge than you might think as recent research indicates that over half of the impact of our communications comes from our physical appearance, mannerisms and eye contact—the attributes we cannot easily express in a written message.

So, what can you do? I suggest that you adopt *elegantly casual* language for your e-mail messages. These are words and expressions that will convey a tone of class, confidence and caring. For example, begin your messages with the phrase "Hello First Name" rather than "Dear Jim" (too formal) or "Hi Jane" (too casual). Also avoid slang, business or in-house jargon and "flowery" or overly ornate words. Keep your sentences relatively short, with each sentence clearly focused on a single subject. Most of all, make sure your messages have enough detail and sizzle to interest and intrigue even the most passive of prospects. ■

■ Nabbing Networkers

Checking the postings at recruitment Web-sites is fast becoming a core component of what job seekers do. That activity holds less appeal, however, for those who aren't actively looking for a new or better job. Such passive job seekers (including most "A" level performers) tend to explore opportunities the old fashioned way, even on the Web. They integrate their search into the networking they do almost every day.

As in the real world, people network for many different reasons on the Internet. They connect with others to upgrade their skills, contribute to the development of their field, and enhance their visibility and stature among their peers. They also do it to keep tabs on the job market, to make sure they don't miss out on a great opportunity.

How does all that happen? Networking online occurs via e-mail, so they add a resume to their messages and ask their correspondents to help them out. And it's that very natural step that enables you to nab them.

Networking occurs all over the Net, of course, but newsgroups are probably the largest single venue for such interactions. There are over 100,000 of these free discussion boards. They address everything from archeology to zoology, including a wide range of business and occupational topics. They are all accessed through Google, the search engine at www.google.com.

To begin your search, click on the Groups button on the Google home page. Once the Groups page opens, enter the following Boolean string in the search criteria box:

keyword keyword keyword my insubject:resume

This string will search the 600 million newsgroup posts archived by Google and identify those with resumes attached that contain your keywords. For best results, use three keywords, varying them until you find those resumes with the right set of attributes for your requirement.

This technique is limited, of course, because many passive prospects never attach a resume to their networking posts. Indeed, while there is no accurate estimate of how many resumes are attached to newsgroup posts, the figure is almost certainly less than the percentage of individual home pages with resumes attached, and that's estimated to be just 40%. So, how can you find passive prospects who are networking in newsgroups, but don't have a resume or won't put one online? Focus on what they have to say in their posts; or, to put it another way, take a peek over their shoulders.

The best way to pinpoint expertise in postings is a Re: search. The Boolean string looks like this:

insubject:re: keyword keyword keyword

As with the previous string, do not use more than three keywords at any one time. Simply vary the keywords until you find posts that reflect the kind of knowledge or background you seek in a candidate.   The process will clearly take a bit of time, but is likely to help you nab networking talent that your competitors would never, ever find. ■

■ Culling Corporate Alums

If there is a silver lining to all of the layoffs over the past couple of years, it is the growth of corp-orate alumni sites. Former employees of organizations ranging from Yellowstone Park and Arthur Andersen to eToys and Miracle-Gro have established these spots online to stay in touch, trade war stories and updates on litigation and to help one another find another job. And it's the last point, of course, that makes these sites interesting to recruiters. In essence, they enable you to cherry pick some of the top talent from a struggling competitor or to find those with scarce skills who would not normally be in the job market.

By my estimate, there are over 300 corporate alumni sites now in operation. Some attract hun-dreds of participants each month, while others seem to be nothing more than a virtual version of five or six people meeting at the water cooler for gossip.

The sites also differ widely in their sophistication and content. For example, the alumni site for former employees of Digital Equipment Corporation is a stand-alone Web-site that offers net-working and posts job openings and advertisements. The Ozark Airlines site, on the other hand, is set up as a free e-mail group on Yahoo! and basically acts as an address exchange. The Ernst & Young site is a great example of a company-owned alumni site that helps departed employees stay connected with their former employer (in case they want to return at some point or, better yet, refer business to it), while the Worldcom site (www.worldcombombs.com) is—not surprisingly—a reservoir of ranting.

With all of these differences, how can you find alumni sites and what should you do once you locate them? Let's deal with each of these questions in turn.

There are three ways to search for alumni sites:

- **Check e-mail discussion groups** at YahooGroups (www.groups.yahoo.com), Topica Ex-change (www.topica.com) and Groups@AOL (www. groups.aol.com). When I checked Yahoo, I found 117 groups ranging in size from under 5 members to over 100. They included groups of alumni from the Splash Dive Company and the New York City Office of McKinsey & Company.

- **Use search engines.** For example, when I used the search term "former employees" at Google, I found 1,630,000 listings, including corporate alumni sites for Harry's Chocolate Shop and Enron.

- **Check virtual communities** such as YahooGeocites, Tripod and Angelfire. When I checked Yahoo Geocites (www.geocities.com), I found 25 group homepages including those for AST Research and Tyco.

What should you do on these sites? First, be careful. Make sure that you do not violate the norms of the site. Look for the group/site administrator and ask them how you should offer job opportunities to the group. Then, follow their guidance. ■

■ Previously Employed Employees

By now, most of us have heard of "boomerang employees," the ones who leave an organization to work someplace else and then return to work for their original employer. Well, now there's also "previously employed employees;" they're the ones who get laid off, but are subsequently hired back when conditions permit.

With business conditions still unsettled, staff reductions are continuing at a pace not seen since the 1991-92 recession. Even as they lay off employees, however, organizations realize that labor shortages aren't going away and as a consequence, the battle for new hires will be fierce, once the economy picks up steam. To prepare for this next stage in the War for Talent, some employers are now actively courting the very same people they are laying off. They are hoping that they will retain their interest in the organization and agree to become "previously employed employees" when offered the chance in the future.

Cisco, for example, has offered its 6,000 laid-off employees one-third of their salary and stock options for a year if they will stay near by and in touch with the company by working for a non-profit associated with Cisco. Charles Schwab, on the other hand, has guaranteed each laid-off employee a bonus of $7,500 if they accept an offer to return to work with the company within 18 months.

These initiatives are designed to operate as ties that bind previously employed employees to their original employer. The jury is still out, however, on whether they deliver any real holding power among top workers. And since every investment must count these days, it makes more sense to pursue this strategy in a way that costs less and reduces risk. That's where the Internet can help.

The Virtual Ties That Bind

Staff reductions are often viewed as permanent separations. This sense of organizational divorce can be reduced by offering affected individuals assistance, connection and friendship despite the change in their formal employment status. This support can help heal the shock of termination, reinforce ties that bind people to the organization and be cost-effectively delivered through the operation of a special Web-site, designed especially to serve former employees. The purpose of this site is not outplacement; rather, it is to retain previously employed individuals as candidates for re-employment by the organization.

What features might such a Web-site include? The following ideas are food for thought:

- **Continuing education programs** that are free, open to all former employees and delivered online. The programs should focus on developing those skills that the organization has historically had a difficult time acquiring. It could include second language skills for supervisors or written communication skills for those in technical fields.

- **Access to certain resources and services** that provide a special benefit for current employees. These might include air travel discounts, reduced fees at local stores, tax preparation assistance, even special bargains on house and garden services. Making these resources and benefits available to displaced employees demonstrates the organization's desire to stay connected with them <u>and</u> its commitment to helping them out.

- **A Q&A feature** with a senior executive where displaced employees can ask questions and get straight answers about the organization's status and efforts to weather the economic downturn. This is not meant to be a forum for personal complaints or for corporate cheerleading, but a source of candid information about the employer.

- **A virtual newspaper** that details the activities of current employees. This publication should be designed to help former employees stay in touch with their friends and colleagues in the organization. It's about the softball and bowling teams and the volunteer Habitat for Humanity project, not corporate press releases.

In a War for the Best Talent, recruiting programs should not be limited to focusing on strangers (i.e., new prospects), but should also involve those former employees you know well. Reinforcing the ties that bind displaced workers helps retain their allegiance and their willingness to return as "previously employed employees" should that be appropriate in the future. ■

■ **Making Initial Contact With Prospects**
How Should It Be Done? What's the Goal?

■ Making Pre-cruitment Work

Pre-cruitment is the art and science of being prepared in recruiting. It is a way of stepping out of our traditionally reactive, inefficient, frantic and frustrating paradigm and into an operating mode that gives us a much better chance of finding and acquiring <u>the one best candidate</u> for an opening, rather than the best available one. (Please see Your Recruiting Process for a more detailed explanation of pre-cruitment.)

How does that happen? There are, of course, a range of tools that can help you implement pre-cruitment. One of the concept's key principles is "top talent targeting," finding the best talent for your openings <u>before you need them</u> so that you have the time to pre-interview, pre-qualify and pre-sell them on your organization.

Top talent can be identified by your employees and hiring managers and by your own networking. Once you've identified these prospects, the trick is to find a way of contacting them, and that's where online employee directories may be helpful. Use the following technique to uncover thousands of employee directories that are open and accessible to the public on the Internet.

① Go to the search engine AltaVista (www.altavista.com).

② Click on the Advanced Search link at the top of the site's home page.

③ In the Boolean search criteria box on the Advanced Search page, enter the following string:

host:*.com AND "employee directory"

When I ran this search, I found over 5,500 employee directories. To find a specific directory for a specific company (where you have targeted some top talent) simply add the company name as another criterion (e.g., host:*.com AND "employee directory" AND Merck).

If you are just probing for talent, however, you can also add a specific skill or industry (e.g., host:*.com AND "employee directory" AND Skill/Industry). Here's what I found, for example:

Nursing	74 directories
Engineering	393 directories
Healthcare	121 directories
Packaging	51 directories

As with any Web tool, however, you should not expect perfect results. For example, my Pharmaceutical search listed a directory for Miramar Nurseries ... "San Diego's leading supplier of landscape materials." ■

■ Getting Past Go (Away)

You've identified the perfect candidate for a key position. Through networking, you know that this person is truly among the elite ... a genuine "A" level performer. And because they are, you also know that your approach must be perfect or you'll never get past go (away). So, how do you connect with them online? Try the following tips:

1. Give your message the right subject. Don't overdo it, but include enough information in your subject line to let the recipient know that:

(a) your message is about an employment opportunity, not a sale for used computer parts; and

(b) you've done your homework on them.

For example: The Best Next Move for a Successful VP of Sales.

2. Start with a compliment. Once again, don't overdo it, but use a compliment to put your message in the recipient's frame of reference. They know that they're a winner, and they must know that you know it too. Convince them of that, and they'll be much more likely to take you seriously.

3. Keep the first message short. Provide just enough information for the recipient to evaluate their potential interest. "A" level performers are used to being in charge of their careers, so don't try to sell them in your first e-mail. Let them decide to be sold, and then, do just that. ■

■ Making Contact By E-Mail

Proactive sourcing is a multi-step process. It includes:

- Locating high potential pools of your target demographic (Please see Sourcing Candidate Resumes & Information Online);

- Identifying key prospects; and

- Making initial contact with those prospects in a way that induces them to ask for more information about your opportunity and/or agree to stay in touch with you.

Each activity has its own set of challenges, but for many recruiters on the Net, it's the last step — making the right first impression—that causes them the greatest problem.

There are two key elements to a well written e-mail message to a prospective candidate: its title and the body of the message, itself. Let's take a look at each of them.

The Message Title

Most top prospects get employment inquiries on a regular basis. Even if they don't, the messages they do receive from recruiters are often indistinguishable from the thousands of commercial messages that are dumped into their e-mailboxes daily. To avoid getting deleted with the trash, therefore, your message must have a title that sets it apart.

The purpose of the title is to pique the curiosity of the reader. It must be intriguing enough to get them to stop and read the message. To accomplish that goal use the following guidelines:

- Never include internal position titles (e.g., System Analyst I) or requisition numbers in the title.

- Personalize the title using the second person and information you have collected about the candidate (e.g., You're a Successful Project Manager; Take a Look at What Your Future Could Hold)

The idea is to create the (true) impression that the message is not a form letter or a shot in the dark, but instead an individual communication with a very important subject: the advancement of their career.

The Body of the Message

Format & Style

- Use short paragraphs;

- Use short, clear, hard-hitting sentences within each paragraph;

- Write in complete sentences (i.e., with a subject and a verb); do not include a long laundry list of points in bullets;

- Use the second person (you) and speak to the recipient as a professional colleague;

- Do not use internal terminology and only use professional jargon if it is widely accepted and understood;

- Do not include the position description or a job posting in the body of the message; do attach it to the message, if it is complete and well-written;

- Eliminate all spelling, typographical and grammatical errors.

Content

The content of your message should be organized into three sections with the acronym ABC:

- **A = Attention Getter.** The purpose of this single paragraph is to get the recipient to read on. Hence, it must:

   (a) be tailored to them, proving that you've done your homework and truly want to connect with them, and

   (b) make a clear, compelling statement about what's in it for them (i.e., how will this position advance their career).

- **B = Body.** The body of the message provides detailed evidence that supports and proves the value proposition expressed in the first paragraph. Don't try to tell the recipient everything, however; instead, prioritize and focus on three main points in short, separate paragraphs.

- **C = Closing.** The definition of success for a contact e-mail is a response from the recipient that says either:

   (a) tell me more or

   (b) I'm not interested right now, but stay in touch.

   Therefore, close with a call to action and a deadline (e.g., This is a very important position, so I must identify top candidates right away. If you're interested, please let me know by _____. If you're not, please let me know if I may stay in touch with you about future opportunities with our organization.) ■

■ E-Mail Etiquette

A recent survey by Vault.com found that many people do not feel comfortable using e-mail to discuss sensitive and/or personal matters. For example, of the poll respondents:

- 96.4% said they would prefer to ask for a raise in person; only 2.1% would address the subject by e-mail.

- 70% said they would feel uncomfortable notifying an employer of their resignation by e-mail; just 3.5% said that e-mail was fine for such a communication.

- 64.9% felt it was best to praise a co-worker in person, while 30.5% felt it was O.K. to do so by e-mail.

Does this mean that e-mail is not the right medium for discussing a person's interests in an employment opportunity? I don't think so. However, there are some steps you can take to ensure that your messages don't inadvertently cross into someone's discomfort zone.

Step 1: Employees are now well aware that their employers have the right to surveil their e-mail received on-the-job. Hence, they may consider any message received at work about a potential job change to be risky. That is probably one of the reasons behind another interesting finding in our latest survey of online job seekers. For the first time, more people used job search Web-sites from home than from work. Therefore, wherever possible, use non-work related e-mail addresses to send your messages to prospective candidates.

Step 2: Begin your message by telling the recipient how you got their name, especially if you contact them at work. If they are not in the job market, noting that you are contacting them on your own initiative (e.g., "I recently saw your posting on the XYZ newsgroup.") will help defuse their anxiety about receiving the message. And, if they are engaged in an active job search, saying something like, "I recently discovered your resume in the database at the XYZ site." will reassure them that their personal information is being used as they intended.

Step 3: Leave out of your message any personal information that you may have collected elsewhere on the Web about a prospective candidate. Even if that information is in the public domain (e.g., home address, telephone number), recipients who see such public visibility as an invasion of privacy are as likely to blame the messenger as the original source. And that can only hurt your recruiting efforts.

Step 4: Give the recipient a way to respond to you other than e-mail. Not only are people often uncomfortable discussing sensitive or personal matters by e-mail, but e-mail itself is still not the preferred communications modality for many Americans. According to a survey of AOL users last year by *Fast Company* magazine, the most popular form of communication is the telephone, followed by face-to-face meetings and, then, by e-mail. By giving people the choice, you are allowing them to respond to your message in a way that is most comfortable for them ... and that can only increase your yield. ■

■ Voice Mail Victory

Voice mail. If you're in recruiting, you're leaving a lot of it. Even so, why would a book about Internet recruiting resources bother to address it? Well, consider this:

- Recruiting online in no way negates the use of traditional recruitment communications tools. Indeed, online recruiting is most successful when it is fully integrated with the telephone and face-to-face interactions.

- According to voice mail guru, Thomas N. Hand, 75% of all business calls end up in voice mail. Hence, no matter how good you are on the Web, if you blow it with your voice mail, your yield will suffer.

How can you turn your voice mail messages into hiring victories? I've developed the following primer to help you out. It's based on content developed by Mr. Hand.

YOUR VOICE MAIL PRIMER

Rule #1 Use an empathetic tone of voice. Don't sound like an answering machine or like a used car salesperson. Instead, modulate your voice to sound friendly, but professional.

Rule #2 Treat people as individuals. The person you call is more likely to remember your request for a return call if you include their name. For example, "I look forward to hearing back from you, Janice."

Rule #3 Thank them for listening to your message. (They're busy, just like you, and listening to your message takes up some of their time.) For example, "I look forward to hearing back from you, Janice. And thanks."

Rule #4 Don't rush. Insert pauses at strategic points in your message. These pauses should last about a second and be used:

(a) after your greeting and self-identification,

(b) before and after you state your telephone number,

(c) whenever you want to emphasize a point, and

(d) just before your last words.

For example, "My telephone number is [Pause] 203-964-1888. [Say the numbers slowly, then Pause] I look forward to hearing back from you, Janice. [Pause] And thanks."

Rule #5 Get the beginning right. The research shows that most messages are deleted within their first 20 seconds. Hence, the professionalism, confidence and courtesy of your first two sentences are likely to have a huge impact on the success (or not) of your voice mail. For best results, use a moderate pace and:

(a) greet the person by name and

(b) identify yourself.

For example, "Hello, Janice. [Pause] This is April Miller from Lamis Furniture in McLean, Virginia." [Pause]

Rule #6 Avoid leaving overly long messages. About 30 seconds is best; that's enough time to get your point across, but not so long as to intrude on the listener's time. The goal is to get the person to call back promptly. Hence, hone your message so that it quickly focuses on a "hook," such as:

- A previous conversation during which the listener asked you or gave you permission to call them back

- A previous introduction you had to or meeting you had with the listener

- The name of a person who knows the listener and referred you to them

- A previous connection you made with the person, including a conference presentation they had made, a published article they had written or a resume they had sent to your employer or posted at an online site.

Rule #7 Practice and then practice some more. For most of us, leaving great voice mail messages is an acquired skill. Don't, however, practice on prospects. Instead, call yourself and leave a variety of messages. Listen critically to all of them, select those that seem most persuasive to you, and continue to hone those messages even further. When you think you've got one or more really good scripts and presentation, call a colleague, leave your message(s) and ask them what they think. It's only when you and they agree that your message sets the right tone, conveys the right information and gets the listener to take the right action that you're ready to call prospects.

Rule #8 Follow-up with an e-mail message. As part of your integrated communications strategy, use e-mail to tell the prospect that you've left a voice mail message and look forward to their response. The e-mail will build your name recognition and encourage them to call you back. ■

■ **Building Candidate Relationships Online**
Why Bother? How Is It Done?

■ Fast Food or Gourmet Recruiting?

The concept of just-in-time recruiting has taken the Human Resource profession by storm. Its promise of providing robust pools of qualified candidates the minute that position vacancies occur seems to herald a new era of productivity and effectiveness for recruiters. I mean, who wouldn't be entranced with the possibility of laying a slate of highly qualified candidates on some pushy hiring manager 24 hours after they dropped their requisition on you without any warning? It's every recruiter's dream.

The dream, however, could actually be a nightmare. While the concept's underlying theme of operating efficiency makes eminent good sense, the translation of that idea into day-to-day activities can easily go astray. Indeed, I would argue that the manner in which just-in-time recruiting has been implemented to date has done more to hurt than to benefit the recruiting function.

The concept of just-in-time recruiting arose in conjunction with the development of the Web as a recruiting resource. In fact, its early proponents suggested that it was the Web that made the concept feasible. Why? Because the key to being just-in-time, they opined, was speed, and the Web, of course, enabled everything—but especially candidate identification—to move more quickly. In essence, just-in-time recruiting was implemented as warp speed sourcing. Or, to put it another way, it was the "fast food" approach to recruiting.

The idea was simple enough: staffing requirements would come into recruiters who would, turn:

- roar around the Web posting jobs at recruitment Web-sites and data mining like crazy for candidate resumes archived online

and

- zap the information they collected about appropriate candidates to hiring managers via Web-based applicant tracking systems.

The faster you went, the more just-in-time you would be. Speed was the rule.

Well, speed may have it advantages, but it can also blur your vision. In other words, sourcing fast when a requirement comes in simply ensures that you will identify those candidates who are available at that point in time more quickly. Unfortunately, this approach limits who you can see to just half of the workforce, and not necessarily the best half at that. Here's what I mean:

- According to the U.S. Bureau of Labor Statistics, approximately 16% of the U.S. workforce is actively looking for a job at any point in time. These active job seekers are the only people in the workforce who have a resume and thus are the only ones who can be found by data mining for resumes on the Internet.

and

- According to conventional wisdom, the rest of the workforce is composed of "A" level performers and passive prospects. Our best performers, which I estimate at about 16% of the

222

workforce, are almost always employed and almost never look for a job. You won't find them reading the postings at job boards or archiving a resume—which they don't have, anyway—in a resume database. Passive prospects, on the other hand, comprise the remaining 68% of the workforce and are about evenly split in their behavior. Half or 34% act like "A" level performers and never look for a job, and half or 34% act more like active job seekers and will occasionally take a peek at a job posting.

Add active job seekers at 16% of the workforce to the active half of the passive prospects at 34% of the workforce, and you get my estimate of 50% of the workforce reached by warp speed just-in-time recruiting. That limitation hits recruiters two ways: it causes us to exclude 50% of the workforce population from our sourcing, and it eliminates altogether the one cohort we most want—those "A" level performers who spell the difference between excellence and mediocrity in organizational performance.

So, what's to be done? I think we should shift from just-in-time recruiting with its focus on being fast to **real time recruiting** with a focus on being prepared. This alternative also relies on the Internet, but for <u>its reach rather than its speed</u>. Hence, real time recruiting begins with demand forecasting, the determination of an organization's requirements 6, 12, and 24 months from now. Once those needs are known, a range of strategies, including online headhunting and electronic networking, can be used to identify and connect with high quality prospects before they are needed for these open positions. This advance interaction provides us with the time we need to collect additional information from these prospects, pre-sell them on the value proposition of employment with our organization and pre-qualify them for its expected openings. In short, it enables us to do what we do best: build relationships with great talent.

Since most "A' level performers and passive prospects don't have a resume, this relationship-building effort is based on the notion of pre-interviewing, rather than resume acquisition. Typically, it involves a communications campaign that:

■ is tailored to each individual by data that are already collected in a talent database (even if that's initially nothing more than their e-mail address, occupational skill and skill level)

and

■ continuously expands the contents of the database through e-mail messages that both provide useful information to the individual and ask for additional information about them.

This strategy of progressive data collection via communications that provide value to their recipients is also known as "permission marketing." It enables the organization to nurture familiarity, trust and confidence among high quality candidates while simultaneously acquiring detailed insights about their capabilities, experience, preferences and goals.

The resulting data-rich talent database is at the heart of real time recruiting. When new position vacancies arise, the recruiting function is able to respond in real time because it can draw on a database that has been pre-stocked with the right talent and the right information for accurate hiring decisions. Sure, the process is fast—instead of roaming around the Web at large looking for needed talent, recruiters search the database on their own desktops—but more importantly, it biases the organization's recruiting toward the finest talent there is for its openings. There's no need to rush selection or accept the best available candidate because recruiters have already prepared the talent their organization most wants, and that talent is ready to serve. I call it the "gourmet" approach to talent management, and it is the fundamental difference between real time and just in time recruiting. ■

■ Database e-Marketing

An earlier postcard introduced Weddle's Law (please see Your Procedures for Online Recruiting), an extrapolation from the time-proven prediction of computing power's exponential growth enunciated by Intel founder, Gordon Moore. Weddle's Law holds that the number of high quality candidates who have records in your resume database <u>and</u> are willing to consider your organization's employment opportunities will double with every 18 months of <u>effective communications</u> between your organization and those candidates. With most employers now acquiring just 5% of their new hires from their candidate database (according to a study by Hire Ability), the law offers a reasonable and viable strategy for upgrading this important corporate asset.

But what are these "effective communications?" I've received a number of calls and e-mails asking for more information about the design and operation of a database communications campaign. Here are some suggestions to get you started:

- Every campaign must be tailored to the organization and the talent it recruits. Perhaps one of the most effective ways to design your message content is to ask recipients what kinds of information they would find most interesting and/or useful. This approach will ensure that your messages are welcomed and give candidates a sense of involvement in the company—a taste of what it will "feel like" as an employee even before they are.

- Treat every message as an exercise in permission marketing. In other words, each message should both give the recipient information they will consider valuable (identified in #1 above) and ask for information the organization considers valuable (in evaluating them).

- Send a new message to candidates every 6-8 weeks. Begin every message with a standard prefix in the Subject line so that they will come to recognize it as a communication from your organization and pay attention to it (assuming you have done #1 well). Just as online advertisements often begin their Subject lines with ADV:, begin yours with your company's name (e.g., INTEL: Latest News on Chip Industry Prospects in 2003).

- There are any number of subjects that you might suggest to your candidates (in the first bullet above) and thus cover in your messages. These include:
    - News about the company's major announcements and successes. Do not, however, send marketing or promotional messages about your products and services.
    - Updates on your organization's industry. This information should address the state of the industry and major developments, but not lobby for support of legislation or regulatory change.
    - Updates in key occupational fields for which you are always recruiting. This information should not get into personalities or controversy, but instead focus on topics that will contribute to a person's professional development.

- Invitations to chats and other presentations conducted by your organization's employees and addressing topics of interest to specific occupational fields and/or to everyone in the industry.

■ Every message should also include:

- a Privacy Protection Warranty for all information requested of candidates, and
- the opportunity to opt-out of receiving future messages. ■

■ Employee Relationship Management

Well, it's finally happened. All of the hype about Customer Relationship Management and Candidate Relationship Management has now lead to a new genre of tools for Employee Relationship Management. Brought to you by Siebel Systems—the folks who created the Customer Relationship Management frenzy—this software product is supposed to help you direct, inform and track your employees. According to Siebel, the idea is for employers to apply ERM (yes, it already has its very own acronym) "to the problem of increasing return on investment in human capital."

Sounds good, but how does Siebel envision the use of its software in the workplace? According to one report, here's what happens:

- The CEO sets objectives for the company.

- Managers set objectives that support the objectives set by the CEO.

- Employees set objectives to deliver on the managers' objectives so that they can keep the CEO happy.

- Supervisors conduct reviews of all employees each quarter to check on their compliance with the CEO's objectives.

- Employees who are out of compliance are given guidelines and a deadline for fixing their performance.

- Managers monitor employee compliance on a day-to-day basis with a desktop dashboard.

Evidently, Siebel considers the dashboard the heart of its system, and there's the rub. This nifty electronic report card is essentially the only real difference between ERM and traditional performance appraisal systems. The difference, however, is huge. You see, the dashboard enables managers to peer into employee activity from afar in order to monitor their behavior and progress toward the CEO's objectives. There aren't spy cams in the corridors (at least, Siebel isn't promoting them), but managers can significantly reduce their interactions with employees because they—the managers—have all of the information they need to know about their employees right at their fingertips.

It's elegant technology, I suppose, but the relationships it promotes are brutish. They are nothing more than top down commands and follow-up compliance reports that leave employees feeling as if they are proles, laboring away for the CEO's mighty machine. That vision of management may stroke the boss's ego, but it hardly builds trust, commitment, a willingness to sacrifice and loyalty—all of the human ingredients that separate a world class corporation from the rest of the pack. In fact, the ERM software doesn't manage relationships, at all. It perverts them. It substitutes keeping track of people for leadership. Why? Because leadership involves getting your hands dirty. It's the actions a person—the leader—takes on the shop floor and in the office suites to earn the respect and trust of other people. And you can't take those actions by playing Big Brother with some stupid piece of software.

All of which brings me back to Candidate Relationship Management, another software genre that is quickly becoming the tool of choice among employers. We all know what's driving this train; it's the unending torrent of resumes from applicants that pour into our Web-sites and e-mail boxes. In other words, many of us are turning to CRM software to manage electronic paper. And unfortunately, that's where it stops. We collect the resumes, stuff them into a database and search the database whenever we have an opening. We have automated the administrivia of e-paper collection and storage and virtually ignored the people behind the resumes. The net result is similar to the output of ERM: lousy relationships.

You don't believe me? Here's some of the evidence:

- Countless surveys show that the vast majority of job seekers feel as if the experience of submitting their resume to an employer online is akin to wandering into a black hole. All too often, the CRM system is not used to acknowledge the receipt of a resume or, worse, the acknowledgement that is sent provides precious little information and shows even less courtesy for the job seeker.

- Many candidates never hear back from an organization once they have submitted their resume. No effort is made to stay in touch with them—even though their contact information is readily available in the CRM database—so no additional information is provided about the employer and none is collected from the candidate. It's the virtual equivalent of being ignored in a store. How do you feel when you walk into an establishment and see something you like and may even buy, only to find the salespeople are "too busy" to give you the time of day?

- Candidates who are called for an interview but not selected for an opening are often never told about the employer's final decision. Simple as it would be to do, CRM systems are seldom used to keep candidates informed of their status in the recruiting process or even to say thank you for their efforts. From the candidate's perspective, they have been used ... treated like cogs in some indifferent employment machine.

As with ERM, CRM can produce lousy relationships just as well as it can help build good ones. What spells the difference? Recruiters. These CRM systems are nothing more than a lot of expensive silicon wafers, wires and nuts and bolts. They don't instill relationships, and they don't provide management. They process information. That's all they're good for. In fact, they wouldn't know a relationship or a management principle from an error message.

And that's the key. Only people can do those things. Only recruiters have the compassion, the wisdom and the skills to establish and nurture relationships with candidates. They can use CRM systems to do so more effectively and efficiently with greater numbers of prospects, but they—the recruiters—must do it. It is their responsibility and that responsibility cannot—thank goodness—be off-loaded to some piece of software, no matter how elegant.

So, if an organization wants to maximize its "return on investment in human capital," one of the steps it can take is to invest in the recruiters who are its employees. Hire more of them, give them better training and provide them with the support resources they need to do their jobs well. Reinforce that preparation with high caliber leadership, and I have no doubt but that they'll show you what a real return looks like on a human capital investment. ■

■ The Art of Closing

Great candidates are tough sells. Great recruiters sell them anyway. How do they do that? It's all in the art of closing.

Now, just to be very clear about what it is we mean by closing, here's our definition: the actions taken and arguments made by a recruiter to induce the desired candidate for an opening to accept the organization's offer and show up for his/her first day of work. There's no such thing as a 99.9% closing. Either it happens or it doesn't.

If your organization is tracking its offer-to-hire ratio (and I think it should be), then it knows just how good its recruiters are at closing. While it's true that these results can be skewed by the substance of the offer (an employer that persists in paying below market will normally have a lower closing ratio), there are skills of effective closing that all of us should learn and continuously hone.

First, it's important to recognize that closing is a process with three distinct and equally important phases. They are:

- Pre-Offer Research
- Offer Formulation and Presentation
- Post-Offer Follow-Up.

Let's look at each of these phases in more detail.

Pre-Offer Research

All candidates are different—they each have their own unique set of reasons for considering and ultimately accepting an offer—so closing cannot be a generic message. Instead, it must be tailored to the specific candidate selected for a specific opening. Hence the first phase in the closing process is designed to determine the factors that will motivate the candidate to say "yes." These factors fall into two categories: rational and emotional. The former can include a job's location, its level of responsibility, pay and/or benefits or the ability to work for a certain supervisor. The latter might include connections the person has within the company (e.g., friends or former colleagues already working there) and the reputation of the organization among those in their field. In addition, these factors do not all have the same priority for the candidate, so the research must also determine which are most and least important and, if it exists, what one factor will seal the deal all by itself.

Admittedly, it takes time to acquire such information, but the investment in research can spell the difference between success and failure with top flight candidates. As Neil Rackham puts it in his wildly popular book, *Spin Selling*:

"Less successful sellers rush through the Investigating [or research] stage; as a result, they don't do such an effective job of uncovering, understanding, and developing the needs of their customers [candidates]."

In other words, if you don't know what it will take to get a candidate to say "yes," then they are just as likely to say "no" … when you ask them to join your organization.

To carve out the time required to do good research, I suggest you consider one of several options:

- Use the process of pre-cruitment to begin research before a person becomes a candidate for a specific opening (Please see the Chapter on Your Recruiting process for a full description of pre-cruitment.);

- Outsource the collection of individual information to research specialists trained to acquire it without putting off candidates;

- Decrease the number of requirements assigned to each recruiter so that they spend more time doing research on the candidates for each of their openings.

Offer Formulation and Presentation.

A good offer draws on the information gathered in the first phase to present the most compelling case possible (from the candidate's perspective) for your opening. It addresses both the rational and the emotional factors of the candidate's decision-making. In other words, successful closing depends upon an offer that has so many of the right reasons for the candidate to say "yes" that there can be no other response.

You can undercut their impact, however, if you present these factors in a standard, boilerplate format. Instead, craft your offer to highlight the reasons for saying "yes" according to the candidate's priority. Then, reinforce your case, by conveying the offer twice: once verbally by you or the hiring manager and a second time in writing. Each presentation should be complete and replete with enthusiasm. (After all, we are selling here.)

Post-Offer Follow-Up

Even the best offer may face objections, so follow-up is all about countering those issues. These road-blocks to "yes" can be caused by a misreading of the information collected in the first phase, the introduction of a new player in the process (usually a spouse) and a candidate's change of mind or heart. Whatever the cause, however, successful closing depends upon our quickly:

(a) understanding the nature of the problem, and

(b) creatively devising a meaningful solution.

To accomplish these two steps, plan for continuous communications with the candidate while they're evaluating your offer. These interactions should involve you, the hiring manager and any other person in your organization whom the candidate knows reasonably well. Their purpose is to emphasize the key factors in the offer and to probe for emerging concerns. The worst time to be dealing with a potential deal breaker is at the end of the period you've given the candidate for their evaluation of your offer. By that time, a relatively minor issue may have festered into something much more serious and difficult to address.

To build on a lesson we all have learned before: Close only counts in horseshoes … but closing counts for a lot when recruiting top talent. ■

■ A Candidate's Report Card

Recently, a job seeker sent WEDDLE's an e-mail describing his experience trying to connect with executive search firms. He submitted his resume to 390 firms in the Chicago area which he identified with the Kennedy Information *Directory of Executive Recruiters*. His feedback says a lot about the level of customer service in our industry. The report card follows. Overall it suggests that many firms need some tutoring in the fine art of talent relationship management.

RECRUITERS'
RELATIONSHIP-BUILDING REPORT CARD

F　　　　Availability of Contact Information

19% didn't even list an e-mail address for resume submission in the Directory. The prospective candidate either had to visit the firm's Web-site to look for a way to input his resume or go to another firm. His decision? In most cases, he went to another firm.

F　　　　Ease of Resume Submission

5.6% of the resumes he submitted "bounced" or were undeliverable, either because of technical problems or changed e-mail addresses. Makes you wonder if anyone is minding the store. Web-sites and e-mail systems need to be quality assured every week, or the first impression you make on a candidate is likely to be your last.

F　　　　Courtesy

Only 7.2% responded to the e-mail with some sort of acknowledgement or thanks. They ranged from those the candidate characterized as "chilling" ("We don't have anything for you but your resume will be in our database and you might turn up in a search.") to those he found "warmer" ("We're grateful you thought of us and we'll keep your resume on file.").

Of the 28 firms that had the courtesy to acknowledge his resume submission:

> 11 replied within hours,

> 14 responded within a day, and

> 3 responded within several days.

All of the rest, 362 out of 390 firms, didn't even bother to reply. Maybe they think the War for Talent is over, and candidates have capitulated.

That's wishful thinking, of course. The War goes on, even if its impact is masked by the current economic slowdown. And candidates, particularly the best and brightest, have very long memories; they will remember which firms treated them disrespectfully, when the economy is better.

Therefore, the firms that invest **<u>now</u>** in the infrastructure of talent relationship management will have a preferential call on candidates in the future. ■

■ **Designing & Operating a Recruitment Web-Site**
What's the Goal? How Should It Be Done?

■ Don't Let Your Corporate Site be a Recruiting Black Hole

A recent survey by Personnel Group of America, Inc., an IT consulting service, has confirmed what recruiters and human resource professionals have been saying almost since day 1 of Internet recruiting: Most corporate Web-sites are recruiting black holes. The survey found that:

- A whopping 85% of small companies (those under $1 billion in revenues) "severely under-utilize" their corporate Web-site for recruitment, while

- No fewer than 68% of large companies have Web-sites that are equally as dreadful.

Wasting any corporate asset that can help win the War for Talent. is inexcusable, but ignoring the recruitment potential of your corporate Web-site is a particularly egregious misstep. Why? Because it abuses job seekers. It prevents them from going where they want to go and doing what they want to do on the Web. According to our 7+ years of data on job seeker preferences (see the Online Poll at www.weddles.com), better than 6 out of 10 would like to visit company Web-sites to research their qualities as employers and review their job postings. Sites that thumb their nose at that "customer preference" simply sell themselves short in the labor market.

How can you avoid "severely underutilizing" your corporate site? Listed below are five of the most serious shortcomings in current site design and use. Avoid them and you'll be well on your way to implementing a Web-site that effectively taps its full power and promise as a recruitment medium.

Shortcoming #1. A site that does not use the unlimited space of job postings. Unlike the printed page, there is no cost to increasing the length of an employment ad in cyberspace. Job postings can and should provide a comprehensive and compelling description of an opening's value proposition for job seekers. They should answer job seekers' questions before they have to ask them and provide all of the information they need to evaluate the opening and be sold on its potential advantages for them. In effect, a site must create job postings that act as "electronic sales brochures," not classified ad copy online.

Shortcoming #2. A site that does not communicate the organization's brand as an employer. A company's Web-site is the perfect place to educate prospective candidates about its culture, values and benefits. Not only is there no clutter from competitors to detract from its message, but the very act of visiting the site indicates a job seeker's potential interest in the organization. Developing a brand on a site, however, cannot be accomplished by simply re-publishing recruitment brochures online. Instead, it requires the careful integration of language, tone, graphics and information to create an image of the organization as a potential employer.

Shortcoming #3. A site that does not enable recruiters to build relationships with potential candidates. The Internet is an especially good medium for connecting and communicating with large numbers of passive as well as active job seekers. A site can encourage such interaction by offering features and activities in which recruiters inform and/or assist visitors. For example, they can facilitate question and answer sessions (online bulletin boards) and make presentations (online chats) on key topics of interest. Unlike traditional one-on-one networking, however, this virtual relationship building can reach hundreds, even thousands of potential candidates simultaneously.

Shortcoming #4. A site that doesn't attract passive as well as active job seekers. A site's content should be interesting, useful and engaging to all of its potential target population, not just a part of it. Sites that provide only employment-related information, however, are essentially limiting their appeal to active job seekers or just 16% of the workforce according to the U.S. Department of Labor. On the other hand, sites that offer information on professional, industry and/or personal growth topics (as well as job postings and other employment-related content) have a much broader reach into the candidate population.

Shortcoming #5. A site that doesn't provide a quality experience for its visitors. Today, the technological capability available on Web-sites is extraordinary. Job seekers can search job databases, store and submit their resumes, take self assessments, link to other sites for research and support and tap an array of content, all designed to help them capture the best employment opportunities for them. All technology, however, breaks, and on the Web, it breaks regularly. The pages of information on a site won't open, the resume submission engine stops working, and the links to other sites get severed. When these failures occur, they have the same impact on site visitors as a rude salesperson has on a store's customers. Therefore, employers should test their sites frequently and ensure that every feature is in good working order and leaving each visitor feeling as if they are a preferred customer.

Don't let your corporate Web-site waste the recruiting power of the Internet. By simply avoiding the five shortcomings above, you can transform your site from a recruitment black hole to a destination that job seekers will respect, visit frequently and, best of all, tell their friends about. And when they do that, you will have a corporate site that gives you a clear competitive advantage in the War for Talent. ■

■ Make a Good First Impression

Unimpressive. That was the conclusion of a recent Kennedy Information study evaluating the effectiveness of 240 career sites operated by employer organizations. It found that these organizations acquired fewer than 5% of their candidates from their Web-sites, while they sourced 12% from job boards and 35% from employee referrals. Now, admittedly, building and operating a career site is not a trivial exercise. It takes money, commitment, time and expertise—in short, a huge investment—to do well. But, such a mediocre return on that investment does give one pause and bring into question the whole notion of a career site strategy.

Without question, some employers will look at these findings and conclude that they should:

(a) ignore recruiting on the Web altogether,

(b) forgo launching a career site or career area on their corporate site, or

(c) abandon their current site because it's simply not worth the effort to maintain.

Those that adopt such courses of action, however, will make a very big mistake.

In most cases, employer career sites under-perform, not because they're the wrong idea, but because they're poorly designed and/or implemented. Indeed, my newsletter's research into active and passive candidate activities online has found that their #1 preferred destination when looking for a new or better job is employer career sites. They will pour over the content of these sites and gauge their look and feel to learn about organizational missions and cultures, products and services, achievements and opportunities. From their perspective, these sites are a virtual key hole into the organization and the best practical way to assess their fit with its vision and workplace.

So, what are the problems with career sites today? The most significant involve:

Misunderstanding the purpose of a career site. Many companies view their site as the Web equivalent of the job bulletin board outside the HR Department. To them, it's simply a place to post openings and accept applications. For job seekers, however, these sites are all about research. They expect to be able to determine what an organization does, where and how well it does it, the kinds of people with whom they will work and the opportunities it offers for their personal growth and development. In other words, they want to be able to acquire all of the information they need to answer their questions about a prospective employer and, as a consequence, determine what's in it for them to work there. The quicker, easier and more entertaining that process, the better the candidate flow from the site.

Contradictory images and words. Many career sites have elegant expressions of their organization's commitment to equal opportunity and employee empowerment, but the pictures presented on the site belie those statements. The photos of employees do not show ethnic, age or gender diversity. Even worse, the images on some sites omit employees altogether and, instead, feature buildings or a full color, full length photo of the Chief Executive Officer. Just as with any other

236

form of sales literature, a career site works best when the reader—in this case, the target candidate population—relates to its content, when they can see others just like them working and achieving in the organization.

One-size-fits-all content. Many different kinds of people visit an employer's Web-site. As a minimum, they range from entry level prospects to mid career professionals, from hourly workers to executives. They can be sales reps and financial managers, data processors and project managers, human resource professionals and product engineers. Despite all these differences, however, the content on many career sites is written as if everyone has the identical career and work-life interests and concerns. As a result, the information satisfies no one and leaves everyone feeling as if the organization doesn't understand or need them. A well designed site, on the other hand, will have separate entrances for the key segments of its candidate population, and those unique doorways will bring their visitors into areas on the site where the content is tailored to their information needs. It will speak their language and push their special hot buttons. It will reach out to them, and in the process, sell them on the value proposition of their working for the employer.

Lack of support and continuous improvement. Web-sites today are all too often poorly maintained, under-resourced for customer service and static. What kind of experience is provided to a prospective candidate when he or she visits a site and finds:

- broken links, pages that won't open and navigation functionality that doesn't work;

- a Question and Answer feature where questions take a week or more to get answered or worse, aren't answered at all;

- content on the site that was published in 1996 and hasn't changed since?

Such situations paint a devastating portrait of an organization. They signal an indifference to what prospective employees might think about the organization, a general sloppiness in its operational approach and a lack of competence in the use of advanced technology. In a highly competitive labor market—and that's what you have in the War for the Best Talent—such brand attributes are the kiss of death for an employer.

Creating and operating a career site does indeed require a significant ongoing investment. And if that level of sustained commitment is not possible, then it's best not to launch a site at all. Why? Because the Web multiples the impact of a first impression. Its all day-every day access and local-to-national presence expose a site to far more potential candidates than any other recruitment medium. Hence, a site that creates a good first impression acts as a powerful magnet for candidates, but a site that creates the opposite impression does far reaching harm to the organization. And with most organizations drawing fewer than 5% of their candidates from their career site, it's not hard to determine what kind of first impression is being made by most sites on the Web today. ■

■ A Winning Web-Site

Each year, the Employment Management Association recognizes the best corporate Web-sites. These awards recognize creative excellence—an important aspect of good site design—but not the other key element in making a site effective: its use of Best Practices in recruiting. Which raises an interesting question: How well do the winning sites adhere to these time-tested guidelines? Are these just pretty sites or do they also get the job done?

The winners I looked at were:

Best of Category:
Air Force Reserve Website (www.afreserve.com), designed by TMP Worldwide

Merit:
Corning, Inc. (www.corning/careers), designed by Bernard Hodes Group

Merit:
Boeing Employment Site (www.boeing/ employment), designed by TMP Worldwide.

What did I find?

- The Air Force site had a very engaging Flash animation that enabled the viewer to see a range of military jobs in context (thereby educating those who know little about the military) and click on a testimonial from a reservist.

  The only problem: most job seekers search from home and it takes awhile for the animation to load with dial-up access and a 56K modem.

- The copy on the sites was engaging and persuasive. In most cases, it was also formatted for a quick read or scanning (i.e., with headlines and short statements or bullets)—the norm on the Web.

  The only problem: sometimes the content was so truncated that it provided little or no useful information.

- The pictures of employees on all three sites reflected ethnic, gender and age diversity. The Boeing site had the fewest images of people, but its employee testimonials were audio-video clips that were very engaging. The Corning site also had a very nice testimonial area called Meet Our People; the group shot is one of the most real looking group of employees you'll find any-where on the Web.

  The only problem: some of the testimonials took forever to download … so long, in fact, that we gave up and moved on.

- Finally, the Career area was prominently featured on the Home Page of the two corporate sites, and job search was 2 clicks or less from the first page of the career areas.
  No problem there! ■

■ Auditing the Auditors

PricewaterhouseCoopers has recently launched a new area on its corporate site dedicated to recruiting college students. The site has received a lot of favorable ink in the general press, so I decided to take a look. (You can too; its address is www.pwcglobal.com/lookhere.) For obvious reasons, I've itemized our findings as Assets and Liabilities in two areas—Design & Content.

■ Design

Assets

1. The corporate site has the Careers area prominently featured on the main toolbar.

2. The vocabulary of the site has clearly been targeted to the Gen Y demographic (e.g., "Get Cool Assignments").

3. The site uses the second person "you" to speak to visitors as if it were engaged in a dialogue with them (e.g., "We hire extraordinary people with unique interests and skills. Whatever discipline you come from, you'll work for and alongside leaders from all walks of life.")

(Liabilities)

1. With heavy graphics and Flash animation, the site isn't exactly "dial-up access friendly." Hence, PWC had better hope that visitors access the site from school (where they'll have high speed Internet connections) and not from Mom and Dad's house (where they'll undoubtedly connect through the telephone.)

2. The special area for college students is buried in the content on the general Career page and thus not immediately apparent to the visitor who isn't aware of the /lookhere address.

■ Content

Assets

1. The content falls into two thematic areas: career-related and what we call "surround." Surround content is important because it gives the visitor a reason to come to a site other than simply to look at job postings. For example, the first page of the college area promotes a raffle for free tickets to a big PWC concert in New York City. We call such features *surround content* because, like a newspaper, it surrounds the employment content with News, Leisure, Entertainment and other topics of interest to the target population.

2. People don't read online, they scan, and the PWC content makes that easy. It is formatted in headlines and bullets.

3. The content is designed to <u>serve</u> the visitor as well as to recruit them. For example, there is an excellent tutorial called "Interview Tips" that is applicable to any employer setting, but also provides information unique to PWC.

4. The information is presented without a lot of jargon or off-putting industry terms.

(Liabilities)

1. The cut-off to participate in the raffle for free tickets to that PWC Concert in New York City was May 31st. Unfortunately, when I visited the site on June 19th, the promotion for the concert and raffle was still visible.

2. Some of the content could not be accessed in a timely manner (if you had a life). I waited over eight minutes with our dial-up connection to download "Carol Meets A Beetle," and finally gave up.

So, what's the bottom line on this new sub-site? Although I've noted some concerns above, my overall assessment is that it adheres to Generally Accepted Principles of what a great recruitment Web-site should look like. ■

■ KISS Your Web Site Visitors

There was a startling finding in my most recent report on job seeker behavior and preferences online. For the last two years, respondents to our polls have listed the career area on corporate sites as <u>both</u> their preferred and most useful destination when looking for a new or better job. In 2002, however, these areas remained their preferred first stop, but dropped precipitously in terms of their perceived usefulness. Indeed, corporate career areas tumbled from #1 to #4 among our job seeker respondents in the space of just one year.

What's wrong? Job seekers are busy people. And despite conventional wisdom to the contrary, most look for new positions <u>at home</u> where they have dial up access to the Internet and painfully slow modems. Corporate Web sites, on the other hand, are the gateways to the career area, yet their designs are increasingly unfriendly to job seekers. They use flash animation to introduce the site and load up the Home Page with graphics. What's the net result? It takes forever for the site to open on the job seeker's computer.

Research shows that patience is limited among all job seekers, but particularly among those passive persons we truly want to meet. Indeed, if it takes longer than about 14 seconds for the site to appear on their screen, most will simply click off to some other site, including your competitor's.

To put it another way, it may give the corporate IT Department goose bumps to have your logo spin and shoot flames, but when it does, it turns off and turns away the very site visitors you most want to meet. They'll disagree, of course, so cite the evidence:

- When Coach.com, the leather retailer, removed flash graphics from its site, page visits on the site increased 45% and sales increased 65%.

- When Gateway, the computer manufacturer, simplified the design of its site, it achieved a 40% increase in conversion rates and a full return on its investment (in programming the simplified design) in just 1 month.

What makes the career area on a corporate site feel "visitor friendly?" According to my surveys, the key is KISS: Keep It Supremely Simple:

- As noted above, make sure the Home Page opens quickly with dial up Internet access and a 56K modem. Don't let the IT Department test the site with their high speed data lines and souped-up computers; make them open the Home Page with the technology used by the rest of the world.

- Make sure your job postings are no more than 1 click from the first page of your career area. The link should be prominently featured so that even the visitor moving at warp speed will see it. And if you don't have any openings available at the moment, post that information next to the link, so that job seekers don't go to the trouble of clicking on it only to find that nothing is posted.

- Provide a one-stop application feature, so that job seekers can apply for multiple openings posted on your site without having to enter their resume or career data more than once.

- Provide a job agent on your site so that job seekers don't have to visit the site over and over again to check out your openings. In addition, permit anonymous sign-ups for the agent so that passive job seekers will be inclined to use it. ∎

■ Make Your Web-Site "Shopper Friendly"

All of the talk, of late, about recruitment Web-sites has created its very own bubble. Everyone wants a site and, increasingly, companies are spending big bucks to create them. Unfortunately, these investments are likely to generate less than stellar returns … at least if current trends continue in site design.

The key to an effective site—one that gets visitors to do what the site's owner wants them to do—is the visitor's experience. And that experience is governed by what's called the "user interface." If the user interface is off-putting, unpleasant, dis-courteous or negative in any other way, visitors will vote with their feet. For example, a Boston Group study of 100 shoppers online found that 28 will leave a site without buying anything because they couldn't get the purchasing function to work on the site, and even worse, 16 of those shoppers will never come back. This situation is especially critical for recruiting sites because the "shoppers" who have the least patience with the workings of a site tend to be the "A" level performers and passive prospects we most want to sell on our employer.

How can you make sure your site is "shopper friendly"? The following checklist will help you assess the key factors in providing an optimum visitor experience.

To-Do List for Happy Visitors

Factor	Yes	No
Have you evaluated the experience of a first-time visitor to your site by testing it with a "naïve user"—someone who is not from your IT Department or your recruiting staff?	___	___
Have you tested your site with Dial-up access and a 56K Modem as that is the level of technology many users will have when they visit your site from home?	___	___
Are there so many graphics and complex functions on your site's home page that it takes more than 14 seconds—the most a passive prospect or "A" level performer will wait—for it to open?	___	___
Is the link to your job database easy to find on your site's home page and is the database located no more than two clicks from the home page?	___	___
Have you provided a tutorial on how to use the search engine for your job database and is the tutorial easy to find for a first time user and written in English (or technobabble)?	___	___

<u>Factor</u>	<u>Yes</u>	<u>No</u>
Is the application process easy to understand?		
• If you want resumes cut and pasted into a text box, do you provide instructions on how to do so?	——	——
• If you do not want to receive resumes as attachments, do you say so?	——	——
• Do you provide an application form for those who do not have a resume? And does that form ask for no more than 7 pieces of information?	——	——
Do you use an auto-responder to tell applicants that their resume has been received and what will happen next in the review process?	——	——
Do you provide periodic updates to candidates on their status in the review process?	——	——
Do you provide a way for visitors to ask questions or provide feedback? If so, do you answer the questions? And are they answered in a timely fashion?	——	——

While it's true that, in today's environment, most employers have no problem getting visitors to apply while on their recruitment site, the quality of the site's visitor experience is still extremely important. Why? For two reasons:

■ Active job seekers may not be put off by a lousy experience, but passive prospects and "A' level performer definitely are. Hence, upgrading the experience your site provides is the key to ensuring an applicant pool with a high percentage of top candidates.

■ Job seekers remember. Circumstances may force them to endure a lousy site experience to-day, but that may not always be the case. Indeed, that lousy experience becomes a part of your brand—it is, after all, indicative of how your employer treats people—and that less-than-perfect reputation can cause you real problems as the economy recovers. ■

■ Answering the Mail

Embedding a Question & Answer feature on your recruitment site and in your job postings will often improve the quantity and quality of your yield.

- <u>Passive job seekers</u> are more likely to have questions and concerns, and a Q&A feature enables you to address them effectively so that you can recruit more deeply into that population.

- Using the Q&A feature to provide additional information to <u>all prospective applicants</u> can also encourage greater self selection and cut down on the submission of non-responsive resumes; and

- Establishing a dialogue with prospective candidates will strengthen your organization's brand and thereby enhance your ability to recruit <u>high quality individuals</u>.

There's just one problem. You can't capture these benefits if you don't answer the mail. Consider how off-putting it is when you visit a consumer site, use its e-mail feature to send in a question about some product or service and then don't get an answer back. The site might as well hang out a sign that reads:

"WE DON'T CARE ABOUT YOU!"

That would never happen on recruitment sites, you say? Take a look at the following results from a poll conducted by Kennedy Information.

Is There Anybody Out There?

Length of Time to Get an Answer	Percentage of Companies That Answered
< 6 hours	20%
Same day	4%
Next day	12%
3-6 days	12%
1 week+	8%
Never	**43%**

What's the bottom line? Almost half of all employers who invite questions from prospective candidates on their sites, don't even both to provide an answer. Think about what such behavior does to their employment brand and how those organizations stack up against a company like Hewlett-Packard. It answers questions received from job seekers within 10 minutes. For all but the most desperate job seeker, the choice is obvious. ■

■ It Takes Two to Tango

In today's unpredictable business climate, prospective candidates—and especially "A" level performers—are extremely risk averse. They are loath to leap from the devil they know to what may be the devil they don't know. So, how can you get these reluctant recruits to listen to your recruiting song? One tactic is to focus on their dance partner.

According to a recent survey of executives conducted by Accountemps, 42% said they would seek the advice of their partners before agreeing to accept a new position. They were almost four times more likely to get input from a spouse or significant other than from co-workers or friends. And that propensity to turn to those closest to them for decision-making support suggests a new feature for your recruitment Web site: an area entitled **For Your Spouse and Significant Other**.

What content might this area include? I think the following ideas are worth considering:

■ **A special message from the CEO** underscoring the organization's commitment to the well being of employee families.

■ **Information about benefits** that apply to spouses and significant others (e.g., healthcare, education support, travel discounts).

■ **Information about programs and activities** sponsored by your organization and for which they **are eligible (e.g., clubs, sports teams).**

■ **Special support for their employment** and/or career advancement (e.g., job referral, career counseling, networking).

■ **A Question & Answer capability** so that spouses and significant others can ask specific questions about issues important to them. The answers may just tip the balance in favor of your employment offer. However, a survey last year found that 43% of the sites that provide a Q&A capability never answer the questions. There's no better way to turn off a top performer's partner than to ignore them, so don't implement this feature unless you can support it. ■

■ Pulling In Passives Online

By definition, passive job seekers do not have a current resume. They aren't actively looking for a job, so they haven't taken the time to update their old resume or create a new one. So, how do you get them to apply for the postings on your site?

First, make sure that your application process isn't biased toward the active job seeker. In other words, don't use terms such as "Submit Resume" or "Click here to send your resume" in your job postings. You may think such terms are innocuous, but passive job seekers find them off putting. What works better? Try more inclusive terms such as "Submit Resume or Career Information" or simply, "Click here to apply."

Second, don't ask for too much information. Clearly, there is a tension between the need for acquiring enough information to evaluate a person and turning them off by asking them to spend a half hour online filling out some form. Research indicates that the magic number is seven. Most people (including passive job seekers) are willing to sit still long enough to provide seven bits of information. That means they will enter data into seven fields or click on an entry in seven drop down windows. More than that and they are likely to simply refuse to participate.

How can you do a meaningful evaluation with so little data? Tailor the process to the job seeker.

■ Active job seekers are ready to go and motivated to get on with it. They are comfortable with a streamlined process that moves them directly from posting to full evaluation.

■ Passive job seekers, on the other hand, need some courting, so their process must include an intermediate step. That's where the 7-bits of data collection instrument comes in. Set this form up to:

(a) **collect the information you need to do a pre-qualification of the applicant.** The purpose of this assessment is simply to determine whether or not they have the <u>potential</u> to be a candidate. If the answer to that question is affirmative, then go back to the candidate and request additional information. What does that mean? The last question you ask (i.e., #7) should be for the prospect's e-mail address so that you can get back in touch with them. (If you determine they are unlikely to be a candidate, have your applicant tracking system automatically send a "Thanks very much, but no thanks" reply.)

(b) **start building a relationship.** Make sure the application form isn't called that. A passive job seeker may not yet be ready "to apply," so give the form a different title that sets them at ease. Make it informal, non-bureaucratic with a personal touch, like *Tell Us a Little About Yourself.*

(c) **sell the potential candidate.** Design your data collection form to include a short but powerful statement about why your organization is an employer of choice for successful workers like them. That simple, but flattering gesture will significantly increase the odds of their agreeing to provide additional data should you ask for it.

(d) **reassure them that their privacy will be protected.** Even "A" level performers and the most passive of prospects will tell you a lot about themselves if they are assured that you will treated their information with the confidentiality it deserves.

Pulling in passive job seekers is a different kind of challenge than that presented by acquiring applications from active job seekers. To be successful, implement a special process tailored to their unique characteristics. ■

■ Describing Benefits Online

Let's face it. Descriptions of benefits programs are seldom page-turners and thus hard to use as a marketing tool for prospective candidates. On the other hand, benefits are clearly important to candidates, and good programs can be a powerful differentiator for an organization. So, how can you present your benefits so that they will have the best possible impact on your target candidate population(s)? The following 5 Tips are a start:

First, use English, not HR-speak or worse, legal-speak. Remember your Web-site and your job postings are now sales literature, so describe your benefits in the language of your potential customers. Obviously, the material must be factually accurate, but the tone and language style can and should be adjusted to your audience.

Second, wherever possible use graphics. The Web is a visual experience, so don't limit your presentation to words. Use pie charts, bar graphs and other images as well as plenty of color. Be careful, however, not to overdo it; test your material to ensure that it downloads efficiently, even with a dial-up Internet connection.

Third, tailor the presentation of content to each segment of your customer population. In other words, the hot button benefits for your college hires are likely to be very different from those of your mid-career candidates. If at all possible, create separate entry points and content areas for each key segment of your candidate population and tailor what you cover and in which order according to their key concerns.

Fourth, use examples. Illustrate the potential upside impact of benefits on candidates by using examples. Personify your examples with pictures of people (whether they're models or employees) representing the age, gender and ethnic diversity of your workforce.

Fifth, give the candidate a way to make it personal. Offer a calculator with your content to help candidates compute the value of their 401(k) account or other benefits over time. ■

■ Your Online Application Page

If you've got a career Web-site and you post job openings there, then you have a page on the site devoted to online application. Recently, I took a look at one example, picked at random, as a way of illuminating the right and wrong things to do with this unheralded, but critical "final step" in the sourcing process.

I selected the application page at Crown Castle International, an independent owner/operator of shared wireless and broadcast infrastructure. At the moment, they cover 95% of the United Kingdom, 92% of Australia and 68 of the top 100 markets in the U.S.. My assessment of their online application page follows.

- **Thumbs up (☺)**

  ☺ The page is laid out well with separate sections that are clearly labeled for those applying in the United Kingdom/Europe, Australia and the U.S., respectively.

  ☺ The page encourages the candidate to use any of several ways to submit their resume: fax, e-mail, and postal mail.

- **Thumbs down (☹)**

  ☹ The site uses language that is off putting to passive job seekers who do not have a resume (e.g., "If you would like to submit your CV/Resume ...", "You can also fax your resume ...")

  ☹ The site does not offer a short "Build Your Own Profile" capability for those without a resume, virtually ensuring that passive job seekers will not apply.

  ☹ There is no statement about whether a person should include a cover letter when sending their resume.

  ☹ The e-mail addresses for resume submission are impersonal and bureaucratic sounding (e.g., "Recruiting@crowncastle.com")

  ☹ The instructions for how to reference a specific job opening appear at the bottom of the page, rather than at the top where they are more likely to be read. ■

■ The 10 Minute Test ⑦

According to a recent survey, 24% of a corporate Web-site visitors hit a brick wall at the 10 minute mark. They are unwilling to stay on the site any longer than that to apply for a job. The other 76% of the visitor population will hang around for up to 30 minutes or more. But not this other bunch. So, who are these impatient visitors and should you worry about losing them?

Our surveys have found that the most impatient of job seekers are "A" level performers and passive prospects. In short, the 10 minute crowd is the very group we most want to attract and hold on to. Typically, they aren't all that interested in finding a new position—they're on the site more out of curiosity than anything else—so any delay, inconvenience or ill advised statement will quickly send them on their way.

How can you make sure that your site is friendly to the "A" level performer and passive prospect? Take the following 10 Minute Test.

⑦ Does it take more than 14 seconds for your site's Home Page to open, using dial-up Internet access and a 56K modem? (Most "A" level performers and passive prospects look at career sites from home, and that's the technology they'll use.)

⑦ Does your site's Home Page have a short, hard hitting statement of your organization's value proposition as an employer, and is that statement expressed in headlines and bullets, rather than in a thick, wordy paragraph? (In part, "A's" got to be top performers by working for great employers.)

⑦ Does your site's Home Page feature "Personals?" These are statements that make an empathetic connection with the visitor and begin the development of a relationship. They are some version of the following:

■ *"We want to stay in touch with you even if you aren't ready to move on to a new job right now."*

■ *"If you find a position that's of interest to you, we are happy to have you apply even if you don't have a resume."*

("A's" want to be treated as preferred customers.)

⑦ Is the job database page one click from the Home Page, and are job openings one click from the job database page? ("A's" and passive prospects have a low tolerance for long click journeys into the darkness of a site.)

⑦ Does your site offer a tutorial on the search engine page for your job database, and is the tutorial written in English or technobabble? (Since most "A's" and passive prospects seldom look for a job, they are not well skilled with Boolean database search techniques.)

Ⓘ Is your site well maintained (e.g., do all of its pages open and do all of its links work), and is the content well written and spelled correctly? (Even "C' level performers are turned off by typos and sloppy content.)

Ⓘ Is your site filled with pictures of successful employees, or does it feature a portrait of the CEO and the "way cool" buildings you work in? ("A's" and passive prospects care a lot about who and how good their colleagues are.)

"C" level performers and active job seekers will hang around your site even if it's written in hieroglyphics. "A' level performers and passive prospects, on the other hand, need very special treatment and compelling reasons to stay. That's what the 10 Minute Test is all about. ■

■ Beware the Checkmark Mentality

More and more organizations are launching recruitment sections on their main Web-site or intro-ducing special, stand-alone sites dedicated to recruiting. All of this construction has fed a tidal wave of research regarding the Best Practices in corporate Web-site design and development. In most cases, these studies have yielded long laundry lists of do's and don'ts for site features and functionality. For example, one study cited 20 Best Practices that range from having a link to the recruitment section on an organization's home page to writing a complete description of each job opening posted on the site.

Now, this research is clearly helpful, but I think it misses a key point. While it is certainly impor-tant to cover all of the bases in designing and implementing a recruitment site, doing so, in and of itself, does not guarantee that a site will work effectively. As the latest findings from WEDDLE's 7+ year survey of job seekers indicates, organizational Web-sites continue to be the preferred "first stop" for online candidates, but they are increasingly disappointed with what they find there. Indeed, after voting such sites their #1 most helpful resource online for the last two years, they dropped them to #4 in 2002.

Such a consumer response is proof positive that simply putting a check mark next to each item in a long laundry list of Best Practices—as many current research reports seem to suggest—is defin-itely not the best strategy for creating an effective recruitment Web-site. What's missing? The perspective of quality. In fact, there are many qualitative distinctions in how Best Practices get done. And those distinctions are what differentiate a top-performing site from an also-ran. In fact, implementing Best Practices poorly may be just as harmful—or more—as ignoring such Practices in the first place.

To be fair, some of the better research efforts on this topic do, in fact, provide the additional in-formation necessary to implement each practice effectively. The problem is that such fine print often doesn't get read.   Thanks to downsizing programs guided by financial imperatives, the Human Resource Department has often been left without the human resources necessary to do its job appropriately. In such an environment, site development either becomes an "additional duty" for an already over-stretched team of recruiters or it is outsourced to the IT Department, which wouldn't know a human resource issue if one landed on their keyboards.

So, what's to be done? I think Human Resource Departments should establish a dedicated Site Team that is responsible for the design, development, operation and on-going upgrade of all of an organization's Internet-based HR assets. These should include:

- The recruitment Web-site(s), including all micro-sites for special populations and requirements;
- The intranet for employee communications;
- The intranet for employee benefits administration;

- The intranet for employee development; and
- Sites established to assist downsized employees, alumni and other populations.

While this team could draw on available resources from the internal IT Department or on external vendors, it would be trained and authorized to oversee all of the developmental work. In other words, it would have both the expertise and the charter to ensure that:

(a) these sites embody each and all of the Best Practices in site design and development; and

(b) that those Best Practices are implemented to the highest possible level of quality.

I appreciate that this idea will require the hiring of new staff in most organizations. And I also fully appreciate how difficult it is to justify such an investment in an era of very tight budgets. But there is a critical business case for this approach, and it deserves to be made. According to Kennedy Information, most employers now fill just 5% of their openings with candidates sourced from their own recruitment Web-site. Even if the number were 25% or 30%, it would still represent a modest return on the kind of investment required to build and operate a good site (and a site isn't worth doing if you aren't going to do it well). So, the return on an investment in hiring and supporting a Site Team is <u>the recruiting costs avoided</u> when the organization becomes less reliant on:

- commercial job boards,
- staffing firms,
- executive recruiters,
- print advertising,
- campus visits, and
- career fairs.

In short, the potential return on a Site Team investment is the cost savings generated by less use of traditional sourcing methods to acquire great talent. That's what <u>high quality</u> recruitment Web-sites can and should do. They will help the staffing function get its job done more cost-effectively. While those savings will not increase the enterprise's revenue, they will definitely improve its margin and, thus, its profitability. And in these days and times, there's no better rationale for making an investment. ■

■ Ready ... Aim ... Hire

A number of recent studies have found that between 60 and 80 percent of people searching for information online can't find what they're looking for. For example, in a survey conducted by a Web-site evaluation company called Vividence in March of 2002, only 25% of 800 people could locate a specific job posting in an online job database.

With that level of searching expertise among prospective candidates, recruiters must be proactive in making the bulls eye—their job postings—easier to see and to hit. How can you improve the aim of visitors to your site? The following tips will get you started:

- **The outer ring of the target: helping job seekers find your Web-site.** Hurl your URL in every medium you can. Include it on every piece of stationary and e-mail message and in every ad and promotional brochure. If your recruitment area is a sub-set of a larger site, promote that area as much as possible ("Visit our Advancement Opportunities at www.bestco.com/jobs.")

- **The first inner ring: helping job seekers find the recruitment area on your Web-site.** The recruitment area should be one click from your organization's home page. Position a link to the area at the top of the home page and make sure that it is specific to employment (e.g., don't use such general terms as "About Us").

- **The second inner ring: helping job seekers find your job database.** The job database should be one click from your main recruitment page and connected to it with both a graphical and a word/phrase link. Also make sure that the link is not lost in a lot of clutter, but is instead surrounded by plenty of white space.

- **The bulls eye: helping job seekers find the right opening for them.** Give visitors the information they need to use the job database search engine effectively. Include a tutorial (written in English, not technobabble), FAQs (Frequently Asked Questions) and a Help Line for human assistance. ■

■ Building Traffic to Your Site

Red Herring magazine recently asked consumers what it was that got them to visit a Web-site. In other words, why did they go there? By far, the key driver was word-of-mouth recommendations from others. To make sure that you tap the full power of such "viral marketing," include the following features in your Web-site.

■ **A Refer-a-Friend button on your home page.** This feature enables a person to send an e-mail message recommending your site to a friend quickly and easily. All they have to do is click on the button, fill in an e-mail address, add a note and hit Send. It has all of the spontaneity of impulse shopping and all of the satisfaction that comes from helping a friend.

■ **A Refer-a-Friend feature in job postings.** This feature should be located near the top of the posting so that readers will be aware of it even if they conclude, in the first paragraph or two, that the opening is not for them. It should be included at the end of the posting to remind them to use the feature should they read all the way to the end. The feature should enable them to send the posting directly to a friend by simply entering that person's e-mail address and their name as the (thoughtful) sender.

■ **A Pass-it-Along feature for special content on your site.** If you sponsor contests on your site or offer industry or professional information that is either especially helpful or not generally available to your target candidates, give your visitors a way to tell their friends about it. This feature is usually an e-mail message with a standardized note describing (and selling) the item of interest.

A Web-site only works if brings traffic in the door, and a robust viral marketing effort is an inexpensive and effective way to build traffic. ■

■ Can Job Seekers Find You?

O.K., you've spent the big bucks and rolled out a compelling career area on your corporate Web-site. Now, ask yourself, can the kinds of candidates you want to hire actually find the site on the Internet?

Most people—and especially passive prospects who haven't done a lot of employer research—begin their journeys on the Net at a search engine. According to Georgia Tech, 80% of all Web sessions begin at these indexes and directories of sites online. So, the key to ensuring that job seekers know where you are online is to get your site ranked as high as possible by search engines when a candidate uses them to look for the kind of openings you have to fill. The goal is to be listed among the top 10 sites identified (usually the first page of search results) rather than back in the pack at number 150 or 372.

There are four factors that can help to optimize your site's ranking:

- **Keyword counts** or the number of times specified keywords appear in the title of your site and its descriptive tags (called META tags). For example, keyword density is a key factor in how Yahoo! ranks its search returns.

- **META tags** or that part of the HTML code that describes what is on your site's pages. These tags are invisible signposts read by all search engines, so the tighter their fit with a candidate's criteria, the higher your site's ranking.

- **Page popularity** or the number of other sites that link to your site.

- **Relevancy** or the importance of a link, as adjudged by the search engine. It's likely that a link from a well known site to your site will mean more to certain search engines (e.g., Google) than a link from Tom's Tackle Shop.

How can you upgrade your site in these four areas and thus improve your ranking? Consider these sources of help:

SearchEngineForums.com hosts free forums on how you can optimize your ranking at specific search engines, including AltaVista, Google and Hotbot, and Yahoo!.

SelfPromotion.com provides free advice on how to promote your site with the 10 search engines that the site publisher believes generate 90% of all search traffic

Outsourcing to companies that offer search engine optimization (SEO) or search engine market-ing (SEM). As with anything else related to the Web, always check potential vendors carefully before making a commitment. ■

■ **Online Resources for Human Resource Management**

How Can You Improve <u>Retention</u> By Using the Internet to:
- ☛ **Upgrade Employee Morale & Performance**
- ☛ **Promote Employee Development**
- ☛ **Improve Compensation, Benefits & Employee Support**

☛ Upgrade Employee Morale & Performance

■ Customer Satisfaction Starts At Each Employee's Desktop

A 1999 study of 800 Sears Roebuck stores came to a startling conclusion: for every 5% improvement in employee attitudes, customer satisfaction increased 1.3% and corporate revenue rose a half-percentage point. To put it another way, an investment in employee morale pays real and measurable dividends at the bottom line.

Improving morale begins at the beginning ... with the kind of recruitment process candidates experience. Treat them as "preferred customers" and they enter your workforce predisposed to do the same with external customers. Then, the organization must follow up on that good beginning with an equally as positive and continuous program of support and care. And as I have discussed in other postcards, the Internet provides a wonderful platform for delivering such a program.

A case in point is the Employee Service Center at Administaff. This portal can be custom tailored by each employee to serve their needs and interests best. They can pick and choose among a range of topics in four content areas:

■ **My Page**, which the company encourages employees to view as a "life organizer," a place where they can add, move or remove modules of information called "gadgets." They can select gadgets for company communications, weather, links, movie schedules and stock quotes. The page is theirs to create in any way that would be most helpful to them.

■ **My Work**, which is positioned as a resource to help employees work smarter and perform at their best. Gadgets can be selected for service providers, frequently used forms and reports, payroll and paycheck history, HR process maps and the employee phone directory.

■ **My Marketplace**, which is designed to help employees take advantage of great offers and special discounts on products and services they can use at work or at home. There are gadgets for technology solutions, communications, research and consulting, travel, leisure and entertainment, financial management assistance, real estate services and incentive gifts and rewards.

■ **Directory**, which provides a roadmap to the services and information that are available on the Employee Service Center. There is a "how to" center, as will as centers for finance, HR, news, education, safety, forms, reporting and help.

Does it take time, effort and money to launch and then support such a portal? Of course. But the benefits are substantial:

■ Creating an employee support resource that is easily accessible by all from home or work 24 hours a day, 7 days a week improves morale.

- Creating a central place where an employee can find all of the resources he or she needs to excel at their job improves morale.

- Providing information, discounts and assistance to help working mothers and fathers balance work and life improves morale.

- And improved morale, enhances employee performance and, by extension, the financial performance of the organization. ■

■ What Employees Want

Search firm BridgeGate LLC recently conducted a survey of 660 working Americans, asking them why they chose to stay with their current employers. Although getting a raise was the #1 response, cited by 43% of the respondents, over half (50.5%) listed factors other than money. There were significant differences, however, in the popularity of these factors among men and women and among different age groups.

For example:

Factor	Cited by Men	Cited by Women
Flexible work schedules	11%	17%
Stock options	12%	5%

Younger workers appreciated training opportunities (11%) and a raise (52%) more than did older workers (5% and 43% respectively). Older workers (37%) cared more about benefits than young-er workers (23%). ■

■ Building An Internal Brand

In today's era of media-saturated corporate misdeeds and CEO/COO/CFO chicanery, it' especially difficult to build corporate loyalty. As more and more scandals hit the news, employees are growing ever more cynical about their own company's mission, vision and values statements. How can we fight off this malaise and erect a "high morale barrier" that will help to keep our employees from running off to the competition? Believe it or not, a possible solution is <u>process</u>.

Historically, the goal of creating statements about what a company stands for and how it intends to act has focused on the end product. The statement. Every effort is made to get those lofty sounding words and phrases polished and complete so that they can be inserted in orientation packets and hung in little picture frames outside the HR Department and in the CEO's office.

Although they are seldom described as such, these efforts at self-definition are really exercises in branding. We recognize that we must define our commercial brand—what our products or services stand for—and increasingly, we see the importance of an employment brand—how our organization acts as an employer. So, why shouldn't we apply the same logic to our day-to-day operations ... the work we do? Shouldn't it stand for something, as well?

Of course, it should. But if that self-definition is indeed a brand, then it should be developed the way those statements are typically formulated, not the way lofty sounding vision and values statements get crafted (in the dark, by a bunch of senior executives). While there are many variations on the process, most brands begin as a set of postulated attributes that are then tested on those who are their intended audience (i.e., the customer population) to see if they are both appropriate and believable. Based on that feedback, the brand is then refined and re-tested to ensure that it measures up. What is the metric for this evaluation? <u>Can the product or service deliver as promised by the brand, or to put it another way, does it walk the talk?</u>

Now, what's important to note about this branding process is that the process, itself, is as important as its final product. The democratic participation of the brand recipients—the customers in the case of a commercial brand and your employees for an internal brand—is what gives the brand its power, its meaning and legitimacy in the marketplace of ideas.

So, what if building (or re-confirming) your organization's mission and values statements became a company-wide exercise? What if you used the Web or your intranet to poll your internal brand's customers on the principles and ideals for which your brand stands? In other words, instead of handing them a finished document (even one in a pretty frame), what if you asked them to join in and participate in its development and/or refinement? Sure, you will get some unpleasant comments from the malcontents and immature in the crowd, but you are also likely to get an honest, passionate and enlightening debate about what the organization truly stands for and should strive to be.

And that involvement in the creation of your organization's internal brand provides several powerful benefits. Employee involvement:

- **keeps the organization honest.** Just as customer feedback helps to ensure that a commercial brand's attributes are real and believable, employee feedback makes sure that the organization walks the talk in its internal brand.

- **acts as "emotional handcuffs,"** particularly among the best and brightest. The organization becomes something they had a hand in developing so they are more likely to be committed to staying with it and helping it succeed.

- **enables them to set the standards for the organization's leaders.** Radical as that may sound, this participatory process is the only way to restore the battered trust and confidence of today's worker-investors. In essence, it establishes a tacit contract regarding the obligations and expectations of leaders and those who choose to be led. ■

■ Busting Morale Busters

Nothing hurts morale more than "attack dog e-mail." That's the name we've given to messages sent by disgruntled former employees to their former colleagues. These communications can disrupt work, spread malicious accusations and false rumors and generally undercut worker pride in and commitment to the organization.

For example, after Kourosh Kenneth Hamidi was fired by Intel, he began inundating the company with e-mails about his grievances. He formed an organization called FACE-Intel (Former and Current Employees of Intel), obtained a confidential internal e-mail address list and sent messages to between 8,000 and 35,000 Intel employees on six separate occasions. Intel sent him a letter demanding that he stop and, when he refused, moved for a summary judgment and injunction. The company argued that it was forced to devote significant staff resources to removing the messages from its computer system, which was, by company policy, limited to official business.

Hamidi opposed the judgment, arguing that none of his messages originated on Intel property and that all recipients were given the opportunity to opt-out of receiving future messages. The court found in Intel's favor. On appeal, Hamidi's position was also supported by the American Civil Liberties Union as protected free speech. The appeal was denied and the injunction was issued.

What does this mean for HR managers? It would suggest that an organization has the right to determine what kinds of communications will travel over its computer networks. Even when messages originate on servers outside the company, those that are deemed to be harmful to the good order and morale of the company can be barred if they are directed at its internal network for delivery and there is an explicit, written policy limiting the use of the network to officially sanctioned business. In other words, although the Internet, itself, is a free and open environment, any information that is transmitted across the Internet with the intention of being introduced into an organization must adhere to standards set by that organization. ■

■ A Cautionary Note

With all of the downsizings and difficult staffing decisions made by companies in the past several years, it should come as no surprise that there's been a huge increase in the amount of employer-bashing appearing on the Web. Some of the postings are from former employees and appear on newsgroups and sites set up especially for that purpose (such as, the infamous F----dCompany. com). And some of the postings are from current employees and appear on Web-sites created and operated by them. When the latter situation occurs, what, if anything, can you do?

A recent court case has answered that question ... sort of. In this case, a corporate officer was given access by one employee to another employee's password protected site that held critical comments about the company and union organizing information. The owner of the site sued the company alleging violations of the Wiretap, Stored Communications and Railway Labor Acts. The court threw out the Wiretap Act complaint, but found that the company did, in fact, violate the unauthorized access provisions of the Stored Communications Act and may have violated protected organizing activity under the Railway Labor Act.

So, what's the lesson to be learned here? Painful as it may be to tolerate them, protected personal Web-sites are just that—protected. They may not be accessed by the company without the per-mission of the owner, even when they contain anti-company material. ■

■ Stay at Home, But Stay in Touch

Many companies feel pulled in two directions these days. On the one hand, they know that the appropriate response to the current downturn in the economy is to cut labor costs. On the other hand, they are loathe to let good workers go, knowing full well how difficult it will be to recruit them again, once business is back to normal.

In hopes of finding a workable middle ground, a growing number of firms are instituting "forced time off" programs. Typically, these initiatives require workers to take a specified number of days off, using vacation time (if they have it), time without pay, or some other arrangement. For example, Adobe Systems furloughed all of its workers for a week one summer, while the consulting firm Diamond Cluster International asked 200 workers to stay home for six months.

Clearly, such programs can help an employer's balance sheet and income statement. Forcing workers to take accrued vacation removes that liability from the books, while forcing them to take time off without pay obviously cuts labor costs. These programs, however, also clearly have a down side. They can stimulate resentment, dissolve camaraderie and loyalty that took years to nurture, and undermine workers' morale and commitment to the employer. They can also create a feeling of disconnection or abandonment among workers, as they see less of their co-workers and leaders.

These problems must be resolved or the short term financial gain of "forced time off" will be offset by escalating long term retention costs. How can you do that? We think the Internet offers a way for an organization to send its employees home, but still stay in touch with them.

Using either its intranet or a password-protected Web-site, an organization can build a virtual "meeting center" for its employees. This site has two roles: first, to enable workers to stay in touch with each other, and second, to enable the organization to stay in touch with them. To perform those roles, it should include at least some of the following features:

- A **Chat Room** where employees can meet around a virtual water cooler and interact with one another just as they would at work. They can exchange personal and professional news, ask for help and talk about TV shows and the company softball team.

- A **Question & Answer Forum** (listserv) where employees can interact with company executives. This feature should be used for regular communications on the status of the organization and to control rumors.

- A **Help-a-Co-Worker** service that enables employees to support one another. The idea is to provide a bulletin board where workers can post expertise and skills they are willing to share (e.g., tutoring in computer skills, home repair).

- A **Virtual Exchange** where employees can barter or even sell items and capabilities. To dampen any "commercial" feel to this feature, you might suggest that 5% of the value of any transaction be donated to one of the company's philanthropic programs.

- A **Discount Center** where workers can be notified of special deals negotiated by the company for its employees. Such benefits typically fall by the wayside when times are difficult, yet that is exactly when they are needed most. So, keep the discounts coming and use this feature to introduce them quickly and where everyone can see (and appreciate) them.

Don't let the CFO be a penny wise and a pound foolish when implementing a "forced time off" program. Use the Internet to support employee communications and interactions so that there's no retention downside to the cost savings. ■

■ An Online Redeployment Center

As the economy strengthens and the next front in the War for Talent opens, smart companies will begin to look for ways to hold onto workers who have historically been outplaced. These workers include those who have:

- plateaued in their field, or

- been declared "surplus" due to facility re-locations, the closure of business units or other organizational changes.

When there was a surplus of talent, the practice of simply jettisoning such workers may have made sense; in today's era of labor shortages, however, it is myopic and potentially harmful to the enterprise.

Redeploying employees from positions that have been eliminated or for which they are no longer suited to positions where they can continue to make a contribution has long been a goal of the HR community. Its potential benefits are real and important:

- Redeloying employees rather than outplacing them improves morale and enhances loyalty. Those factors, in turn, cut attrition and burnish the organization's brand in the labor market.

- Redeloying employees reduces recruiting expenses and the shortfall in output caused by un-filled positions awaiting new hires.

- Redeloying employees rather than hiring new workers cuts the time required to reach full productivity and peak performance. Redeployed workers have a shorter learning curve be-cause they already know the company and its standards.

To capture these and other benefits, some organizations have begun to experiment with formal redeployment initiatives. AT&T, for example, operates a program called Resource Link in which employees who have little or no prospect for upward mobility but which do have professional, technical or managerial skills can "sell" their capabilities to other units in the company for short-term assignments. The program cuts down on the use of contract employees and builds loyalty among the workers.

For most companies, however, redeployment remains an elusive goal because of the very real challenges involved in its implementation:

- How do you keep track of the talent that is available for redeployment in the company?

- How do you keep track of openings in the company that are appropriate for redeployed em-ployees?

 and

- How do you match up the two?

The Internet, however, now offers a way to overcome all three of these stumbling blocks. Web-based candidate management systems and job boards provide an efficient and effective way to:

- create an internal skills bank for redeployable employees (obviously, there must be clear definitions of who is eligible to participate in such programs and under what conditions);

- post openings available across the entire company in one, accessible location; and

- promote communication between potential candidates and hiring managers.

Such a redeployment "system" can be operated as a sub-set of an organization's preexisting recruitment Web-site and candidate management system for external hires or as a stand-alone activity on an intranet or password protected site on the Internet.

Although the system will require an investment to start up (e.g., to devise data input templates for acquiring employee skills), its ongoing operating costs are minimal. Unlike recruiting for external hires, there is no need to assign a recruiter for each opening. Indeed, a single recruiter could probably manage the entire program, bringing openings to the attention of potential internal candidates and available employees to the attention of hiring managers. And the return on that investment could be significant as openings are filled more rapidly and the cost-per-hire (for temporary and full time positions) is reduced.

As companies grow in size and their operations become more far flung, it's difficult to ensure that the right hand knows what the left hand is doing. In the War for Talent, however, such coordination is the key to success, and a redeployment program can help make it happen. ■

■ Are You Ready for the Recovery?

Sure, the date for full recovery from the late unlamented recession keeps getting pushed out, but it will eventually arrive—you can count on that—and when it does, many employers are in for a shock. According to a National Survey Institute poll, 30% of employees plan to jump ship as soon as they deem it safe to do so, and of those who will stay, 17% will be knocking on the door asking for a raise. All of which begs the question: Are you ready for the recovery?

Most organizations would probably say yes, if only as a matter of pride. But, what is the definition of ready? And how can you improve your readiness state. To help you get your arms around those questions, I've devised the brief "Recovery Ready Checklist" below. Use it to get a running head start on your preparations for a return to more vibrant business growth.

① Make supervisors and managers aware of the threat posed by a recovery-stimulated exodus of employees, particularly key performers.

② Working with the supervisors and managers, identify your organization's top quartile of performers, the workers it most needs to keep.

③ Coach supervisors and managers on the tools and resources they have (or will have) to turn around those key employees who may be contemplating departure and to reinforce the loyalty of those who aren't. These tools may involve nothing more than reacquainting them with on-going programs—such as the company's investment in worklife programs—or they may cover new investments—including salary increases—that the company intends to make as soon as it can.

④ Begin a series of meetings among your top employees, their supervisors and the HR Department. The first and most important purpose of these sessions is to make these employees realize how valued they are by the organization. The second purpose is to probe their current level of satisfaction and their near- to mid-term goals. Finally, these meetings should attempt to resolve any issues that are uncovered and find ways to increase their level of satisfaction with the organization and their personal situation. If necessary, supervisors should meet with HR to craft special solutions to specific employee problems or concerns.

⑤ As the top performers are being addressed individually, begin a communications program to market the organization to all employees. The program must not emanate from HR, alone, but should involve consistent content that is presented by corporate leaders, HR, managers at all levels and even those employees who are already "sold." It's best to begin by acknowledging the hard times of the recent past and thanking everyone for what they've done to help the company persevere. Then, the program should focus on the positives—the company's strengths, its values, its past efforts to live up to those values and its commitment to doing so again, as the economy improves. The goal is to remind employees that, while the past has been difficult, the factors that made the company their "dream employer" in the first place still remain, and those factors are what they can look forward to again in the not-too-distant future. That's both a promise that the company must be willing to keep (otherwise, don't make it) and its most compelling counter to the potential allure of another employer. ■

☛ Promote Employee Development

■ Serve Up Self-Improvement

My previous postcards focused on Internet-based Human Resource management strategies that will improve employee morale and performance. The next set of postcards will address online activities and programs for employee development as they can, if done well, also upgrade individual performance and overall retention.

According to *Training* magazine's latest survey, U.S. employers will spend about $57 billion this year on formal training, up 5% from last year. That's a lot of money in anybody's ledger, but it is unlikely to have much of an impact on retention. Why? Because corporate training serves the corporation, not the employee. While they obviously also gain some benefit, employees view formal training programs as investments in the company; they are designed to deliver skills and knowledge the company needs to achieve its mission.

For training to encourage retention, therefore, it must have a different purpose and feel. In short, it should be an investment in employees and their self-improvement. It should enable them to:

- stay proficient and up-to-date in their field,

- acquire skills and knowledge that will position them for advancement, and/or

- prepare themselves for making a successful transition into a new career field.

As they see it, an organization that commits to establishing an employee self-improvement program is:

(a) showing their commitment to them as individuals rather than as employed workers,

(b) preparing them for long term growth rather than for a near-term work-related requirement; and

(c) providing the tools they need for managing their own careers successfully rather than simply providing skills to make the company successful.

How do you establish such a program? There are two general types to consider, so the first step is to decide which would best serve your workforce:

- **College and technical school degree and/or refresher courses.** Currently, over 2000 educational institutions, from Alaska Pacific University to Cornell University, offer courses and degrees online. There's a complete directory at *US News & World Report* Online (www.usnews.com).

  or

- **Selected courses in professional and/or non-work topics** (e.g., time management, foreign languages, even financial management). There are now hundreds of firms offering pre-pack-aged and custom-developed programs for online learning, including Quisic, SmartForce and Click2Learn.

The next step is to make participating in self-improvement programs as hassle-free as possible. That's where the Web can help. Create an <u>Individual</u> Learning Center on your intranet or on a password-protected area of your corporate site and offer:

- Course lists (with student feedback),

- Enrollment forms, and

- Virtual classrooms, where instructors can deliver lectures, hold "office hours" and moderate class forums.

Such learning centers bring employees back to the company, not to work for it, but to work on themselves. They put self-improvement within the reach of all employees and make it accessible 24/7. Most importantly, in an era of downsizing and what seems like corporate indifference to the fate of workers, they demonstrate real support for individual growth and opportunity. And that can do wonders for your retention rate. ■

■ Holding onto Hourly Workers

Turnover among hourly workers in retail establishments is notoriously high. With replacement costs averaging $1-2,600 per employee, it's no surprise, therefore, that companies such as Finish Line, The Sports Authority and Blockbuster Video are always out to improve retention.

A recent study by Unicru of new hires at those three companies found that employees who are Web savvy (i.e., acquired via corporate Web-sites, job boards and/or Internet advertising) had an average tenure of 112 days and an involuntary termination rate of 31%, while those sourced via traditional recruitment advertising had an average tenure of 80 days and an involuntary separation rate of 64%. ■

■ Thirtysomething & Turned Off

More than 40% of workers aged 25-34 say they are de-motivated by their managers. That's the principal finding of a recent survey of 669 full and part-time employees by True North Leadership. It shouldn't be surprising, however. According to Lominger Limited, Inc., a leadership development company, managers <u>and</u> employees ranked "developing direct reports" at the bottom of the heap of 67 leadership skills listed in its bi-annual study. That inattention to employee development hurts the organization twice: it reduces retention—now down to less than 4 years for all employees and a miserable 1.9 years for those aged 20-34—and it undermines worker performance while they are still employed.

How can we pay more attention to the nurturing of all our employees, but especially those who are in the early stages of their careers? Turn our managers and supervisors into bona fide people developers. That doesn't mean they have to become formal trainers, but rather that they see it as a key part of their job to help employees expand their potential contribution to the organization.

Normally, this shift in outlook requires both a change in culture and a range of implementing actions. First, of course, is the development of our managers and supervisors. Since people development has never been a high priority in corporate America, they have probably never been on the receiving end of such support, themselves, and thus have no idea what it looks like.

Transferring that perspective, however, is not a trivial step. It will require our construction of a "business case" that will earn the commitment of senior management and then an investment of time (by senior managers who must model the new commitment and all other managers who must acquire the skills of developing their subordinates) and the installation of process and procedures that will embed the outlook in the organization.

For example, the performance appraisal system must be adjusted to prioritize development and advance those who do it well. All of that activity takes time and effort, and while it's underway, younger employees are still being turned off. So, are there steps that we can take right away that will at least enhance the opportunity for manager-subordinate development in the near term, even as we work on a more significant effort in the longer term? Happily, the answer is yes. Consider the following ideas.

- Create a special, private area on your intranet or the internal section of your Web-site where managers and supervisors can go to acquire the skills of subordinate development. Post book excerpts (e.g., Warren Bennis, *On Becoming a Leader*, Perseus Books, 1989) and appropriate articles there and add your own ideas about the steps that managers can take (to develop subordinates) with the resources they already have. This area should also have a listserv feature where managers can exchange ideas with and get support from their peers.

- Create a special, open area on your intranet or Web-site where managers and supervisors can implement what they have learned. This area should have designated "rooms" for each participating manager where they could provide developmental tips, post articles for discussion in upcoming staff meetings/brown bag lunches and even schedule face-to-face counseling sessions with their direct reports.

- During the interview process, probe external candidates for managerial and supervisory positions to determine their level of commitment to subordinate development. Similarly, assess the level of commitment among internal candidates nominated for such positions. Then, factor their responses into your selection recommendations/decisions.

- Walk the talk. Model Best Practices in subordinate development in the HR Department. Then, meet with key managers and supervisors—those who are thought leaders among their peers in your organization—and review what you've done and sell them on the importance of their doing it for their subordinates, as well. Offer to help or support them, as necessary, but encourage them to lead the way. ■

■ Retention Budgets Need an Increase

In a recent survey of 541 supervisors, 52% said their organization had difficulty keeping top performers. It costs $35,000+ to replace the average professional. Many, many times more than that for the "A" level performer. And the impact on morale and performance is even greater. What's the point? The best investment you can make in recruiting excellence is retention. ■

■ An Online Career Atlas

Consider this scenario: a new hire arrives for his/her first day on the job and is given their company e-mail address. When they open their e-mailbox for the first time, they find that they have already received a message from the HR Department. It's not about signing up for benefits or the company's policy on the use of e-mail (the former should have already happened and the latter can come a day or so later). Rather, it's a link to a Career Atlas on the organization's intranet where they can find everything they need to know to achieve success and advance their careers as an employee of the company. Would you be impressed? Probably so.

What might be included in a Career Atlas? I think it could include the following elements:

- A clear presentation of where their job fits into the organization. What jobs are lateral to their position and what job or jobs might they target for their next step up?

- Information about the performance appraisal process and its role in their advancement to jobs with increased responsibility and pay.

- A description of specific skills the organization seeks in workers it advances to more senior posi-tions (e.g., team supervision, time management, priority setting) and guidance on how and where these skills might be acquired.

- An explanation of the internal mobility process and policies.

- Vignettes of individuals who have had successful careers with the company as well as their counsel about effective career management.

- Information on the organization's internal mentoring program, if it has one.

- A point of contact in the HR Department for the discussion of career-related matters.

The common view is that most workers today do not see themselves spending a significant part of their career in any one organization. That could change, however, if they were given an atlas—a map to career success in the company. ■

Teacher's Pet or Bad Apple?

eLearning is often touted as a the next big thing in corporate training. One recent study, for example, predicted that, "in the near future," almost half of all corporate soft skills training would be done with online courses.

At the very same time, however, another study has found something amiss at the core of such courses. This critical investigation was conducted by the University of Michigan; it found that, while online courses adequately conveyed basic concepts, they weren't as effective as traditional methods in teaching complex analytical skills. Further, the study found that online students retained less because they spent less time on their courses, due in part, perhaps, to not having to worry about performing in front of their peers in a classroom.

Does the report suggest scrapping eLearning altogether? Definitely not. To make online courses work, however, you will have to make some changes. I suggest that you select courses that incorporate frequent quizzes and that you post the quiz scores in a public place. In addition, help your students avoid distractions during training periods by getting them out of their cubicles and into rooms with doors and without telephones. ∎

■ Build Up Business Literacy

Countless studies have shown that employee satisfaction goes up when they know what's going on. No one likes to be kept in the dark, and in today's world of Enronesque collapses, most employees want to know how the company is doing at the bottom line. And there's the rub.

Early experiments in providing financial data to employees have shown that, in many cases, they lack the business literacy necessary to make any sense out of the information. Not only do they not understand the building blocks of income statements and other financial reports, but they often cannot see the relationship between what they do and what happens to the company at the bottom line. As a consequence, these well intentioned programs have often had exactly the opposite of the intended effect. Understanding is diminished, not enhanced and morale goes down, not up.

What can you do? One place to start is to encourage employee participation in e-learning programs about business. According to a recent survey, 43 of 99 MBA schools accredited by the Association for the Advancement of Collegiate Schools of Business now offer MBA courses online. While pursuing an MBA may be overkill for all but the most enthusiastic employees, many of these programs (as well as those at undergraduate institutions) offer single courses in business finances and reporting.

There are also any number of free resources available online. (Search for *business education* at Google.com.) Among the best I've found is Tonya Skinner's Business Education Lesson Plans at http://angelfire.com/ks/tonyasinger. Her Home Page offers a wealth of content drawn from sources all over the Web. It includes everything from Accounting Monopoly in her Accounting module to courses in business math and economics.

Obviously, the goal is not to turn every employee into a titan of capitalism, but simply to promote their understanding of profit and loss and how their work influences those measures of organizational performance. ■

☛ Improve Compensation, Benefits & Employee Support

■ A Personal Account Machine

In today's security-conscious and increasingly safeguarded world, nothing is more inconvenient and frustrating than being unable to remember (pick any or all of the following):

- Your bank account pin number
- Your ATM pass code number
- Your e-mail provider password
- Your telephone, electric, gas and other service company account number
- Your credit card account pin number
- Etcetera, etcetera, etcetera.

All you want to do is check a balance, correct a mistake, withdraw a little money, and you can't because you've been told not to use the same number or information for every account, and therefore, simply can't keep track of which numbers or codes apply to which accounts or even what those numbers and passwords are.

Now, there's a simple way to help alleviate such inconvenience and frustration on the Web. Take Citibank as a case in point. When a customer visits Citigroup.com, they enter their account number and password and can then see not only their Citigroup banking information but also the account numbers and passwords, codes and pin numbers for every other type of account they have. Credit cards, frequent flyer programs, gas company accounts, they're all right at their finger tips. All they have to do is remember 2 numbers: their Citigroup account number and password. That ease and convenience keeps them coming back to the Citigroup site all the time and builds loyalty. It's like an ATM only better; we call it a Personal Account Machine (PAM) online.

You can position your corporate intranet or Web-site as a similarly useful destination by adding a PAM to its features. Let each employee set up a private area on the site where they can record all of those pesky account numbers and passwords. Yes, such an initiative will require a (modest) investment of IT resources, but the convenience of using the PAM will undoubtedly enhance employee loyalty and thus provide a quantifiable return in terms of improved retention. ■

■ Pushing the (Pay) Envelope

The best business is one that becomes absolutely indispensable to its customers. Whatever the company's product or service may be, the goal is to get it so deeply embedded into the way that customers live their lives, that it is all but impossible for them to move to another vendor.

Clearly, this idea also has applicability in human resource management. Traditionally, companies have sought to create such relationships through "golden handcuffs" or stock options and other programs that pay out a cash benefit at some point in the future. While these initiatives have had a beneficial impact on retention, they typically do so only at the most senior levels of the organization and only if the perceived value of the benefit is worth the required wait.

So, what about if you could offer a benefit that:

(a) would embed itself in your employees' lives,

(b) could be provided to every member of the organization, and

(c) wouldn't require that they wait to get the benefit?

That's likely to have a far greater positive impact on retention and cost a lot less money than stock options ... especially now that the pressure is on to record options on financial statements.

What's this idea? **Pay your employees' bills for them.** That's right. There are any number of companies that now provide automated bill paying over the Internet as a commercial service, so clearly the technology is well developed and available. And virtually all employers now offer direct deposit for employee pay. Why not combine the two to offer direct deposit bill paying? Not through an outside service, but through your employer's own automated pay system. Why? Because once an employee has gone to all of the trouble of setting up their various accounts for monthly payment, they are going to be loathe to change them. Or to put it another way, the service would then be embedded in the way they live their lives.

Yes, there will be privacy concerns to be addressed and your direct deposit vendor may find this idea too edgy for its liking, but press ahead anyway if you want a real retention pay-out. ■

■ A Worklife Center

The old aphorism, "Out of sight, out of mind" is still true today, but with a modern twist. Its current version is best expressed as "Out of site, out of mind." In other words, one of the keys to high retention is capturing as much employee "mind share" or attention as possible. How can you do that? By using your corporate intranet or Web-site as a platform for delivering support and assistance to your employees both in their performance of their jobs <u>and</u> in the accomplishment of the myriad tasks they face outside of the workplace.

Positioning your corporate site as a "Worklife Center" means helping employees with the work they do as parents, spouses, home owners and consumers. It improves retention because it underscores the organization's commitment to helping employees succeed in all aspects of their lives, not just those that accrue to the bottom line. As a consequence, it builds up the <u>regard</u> with which employees hold the firm, and that regard is the new definition of loyalty in the War for Talent. The higher the regard for a firm, the less attractive even a dream job will seem with another organization.

What kinds of support might a Worklife Center provide? Consider:

- **Links to sites for product recalls**, including the Consumer Product Safety Commission (www.cpsc. gov), the Food and Drug Administration (www. fda.gov) and the Agriculture Department (www. fsis.usda.gov).

- **Links to sites for do-it-yourself home repair**, including Better Homes and Gardens Home Improvement Encyclopedia (www.bhg.com), The Family Handyman (www.familyhandy man.com) and Home Depot (www.homedepot.com).

- **Links to other sites that can be helpful and/or fun to use**, including eRef (www.eref.net) which will help employees get out of those annoying e-mail marketing messages and telemarketing calls and the National Association of Unclaimed Property Administrators (www.unclaimed.org) for all those deposits and rebates they forgot to claim. ■

■ Focus on Health

A recent Hewitt Associates survey found that 93% of U.S. firms offer some kind of health promotion program. These include:

- A smoke-free workplace, health fairs, on-site fitness center, sponsored sports teams and discounts at health clubs (81%)
- Flu shots, well-baby/child care and prenatal care (79%)
- Disease management programs (76%)
- Health screenings for cholesterol, breast cancer and other diseases (75%)
- Health education and training (72%)
- Incentive awards for healthy behavior (42%).

While all of these programs are helpful, their impact is only as widespread as their level of visibility and accessibility among employees. That's where the Web can help out. If your organization has invested in one or more of these programs, it can be used in two ways:

- An internal communications campaign to keep employees informed by e-mail, and
- A Health & Wellness area that is accessible on the organization's intranet.

Communications. The e-mail campaign should be continuous and focused on marketing your organization's program(s). Avoid heavy-handed or moralistic messages, but instead, adopt a light touch.

For example, include announcements of events (both internal—such as an on-site blood pressure screening program—and external—such as Healthy Heart Week), as well as brief infomercials designed to educate and sell employees on healthy lifestyles and contests to increase their knowledge and add some fun.

Web-site. Use your Web-site for longer articles about important issues as well as information and links to online resources. Wherever possible, avoid medical and scientific jargon. Instead, focus on the practical and fun side of staying healthy (e.g., "deskside exercises" and "too tired to cook healthy menus"). Also give employees a stake in the site by featuring stories about co-workers and testimonials from them describing their achievements with a healthy life-style. And most important, take every opportunity to encourage everyone's participation in the company's health promotion programs.

Finally, you can increase the appeal and, hence, the effectiveness of both your communications and Web-site by including information that is helpful to employees' families. Randstadt has been surveying workers about issues related to work/life balance for years now. In its most recent poll,

70% said that their family was their most important priority, up from 54% just two years ago. If you want to touch your employees where it matters most, therefore, craft e-mail messages and Web-site content that focus on the health of employees <u>and</u> their families. ∎

■ A Virtual Suggestion Box

A new book from the Harvard Business School Press offers some interesting insights on how best to meet today's retention challenge. That's not the subject of the book--it's called *The Attention Economy*--but its message is directly applicable. The authors, Thomas Davenport and John C. Beck, declare that

> "Understanding and managing attention
> is now the single most important determinant of business success."

And that's as true in managing the retention of employees as it is in selling widgets to consumers.

Employees are most vulnerable to competitive recruiting efforts when their attention wanders. In other words, when the employment experience no longer engages an adequate share of a person's mind, they will be much more willing to consider other offers of employment. While the definition of "adequate" varies from person-to-person, most successful retention programs proactively address three common causes of workforce attention deficit. They are:

- A lack of challenging work

- Not feeling included or valued in the organization,

  and

- Not meeting basic financial and worklife support needs.

There are, of course, a wide range of potential strategies for dealing with each potential deficit. In this postcard, I'll focus on the use of a virtual suggestion box. This idea takes the old fashioned wooden box outside the HR Department and hangs it on everybody's computer desktop where it can be easily and unobtrusively accessed. As with its real world antecedent, the virtual suggestion program seeks to tap employee ideas for organizational improvement and innovation. Perhaps even more important, however, the character of the program—the way it is happens—can also be a powerful employee attention grabber and thereby reinforce retention.

A virtual suggestion box program is typically launched on an organization's intranet or internal employee network. An icon or link leads to a dedicated area where the program is described and promoted and the actual functionality for submitting a suggestion resides. Once this infrastructure is in place, the actual implementation of the program should entail four steps:

Step 1: Immediately acknowledge every suggestion by e-mail to the individual submitter and by adding it to a "Suggestion Status Log" maintained on the first page of the program area online.

Step 2: Within one week, provide initial feedback to the submitter by e-mail, indicating the review process for the suggestion (i.e., who will review the suggestion and according to what schedule).

Step 3: According to the schedule announced in Step 2, provide final feedback to the submitter by e-mail, indicating what decision had been made and why. Also post its final disposition on the "Suggestion Status Log."

Step 4: Celebrate all suggestions, not just those that are accepted. Once a month, e-mail a "Suggestion Program Update" to every member of the organization, thanking those who submitted a suggestion the previous month and encouraging others to participate.

Now, you're probably thinking that there's no magic to these steps. Some or all of them are used in traditional wooden box programs, so why does doing them online have any appreciable impact on retention? The difference is in the Internet's ability to grab employees' attention.

The quality of communication—the immediacy, continuity and inclusiveness of the acknowledgement, feedback and celebration steps—in a virtual suggestion box program sends a powerful message to all employees, not just participants. It signals that the organization is paying attention to them and is interested in and values their ideas. In a sense, the medium becomes part of the message (to rif on Marshall McLuhan's famous dictum), and its unique attributes will help the organization to hold a meaningful share of its employees' minds. And that mindshare, in turn, is the best protection against their wandering away. ■

■ Can't Remember Your Algebra?

One of the most stressful aspects of parenting these days is helping kids with their homework. There's no more humbling experience than to have to admit to your 13 year old that their math problems now exceed your meager memories of the Pythagorean Theorem. And believe it or not, that dilemma creates an opportunity for you to offer a low-to-no cost benefit that just might have a positive impact on retention.

Here's how it works. First, set aside a **Homework Helper** area on your corporate Web-site or intranet (as long as it's accessible from home). Organize the area by school subjects and/or grade level within each subject. For example, you might have sections for Writing book reports and essays, Freshman French, Geometry and History as well as other key school topics such as Test Taking.

Next, use your e-mail system to survey employees to see who has expertise in those subjects and would be willing to provide tutoring or assistance by e-mail in the evening. You'll probably have to establish some guidelines to ensure that volunteers aren't overwhelmed with requests, that help is requested only during a reasonable set of hours in the evening and that kids don't see the service as a way to get their homework done by someone else.

Once the rules are set, launch and promote the service. Then, any time that a child needs help with their homework and the parent needs help helping them, the parent can log onto the Homework Helper, contact their colleague listed as a resource under the appropriate topic and e-mail their question to them. Assuming the right answer comes back, it's a win-win-win-win situation. The child wins (their homework gets done and they learn something), the tutor wins (they get to use their expertise to help another), the parent wins (they don't look quite as out of touch as they otherwise might), and the company wins (because its has helped two employees feel good about themselves and thus are more likely to stay right where they are). ■

■ Recognizing Winners Online

Recognition ... it's something we all crave, and once received, it's something that we are especially loath to lose. When people feel as if their contribution matters and is appreciated, they will do almost anything—find new and better ways to get things done, meet unreasonable deadlines, fill in for absent co-workers and reject competitors' offers of employment—to hang onto that high of recognition.

It's not surprising, therefore, that more and more companies are launching or upgrading employee recognition programs. As with the other retention programs I have discussed in these postcards, the Web offers an effective platform for promoting and operating a recognition program. When implemented on an organizational intranet or even a corporate Web-site, such programs deliver the benefits of:

- **Impact**—the recognition is immediate as there is no delay for printing and distribution;
- **Convenience**—the information is available when and wherever employees want to access it;
- **Visibility**—the recognition is there for all to see and appreciate; and
- **Durability**—the information stays in circulation 24 hours/day, 7 days/week until removed.

What might an employee recognition program look like online? I think you should consider the following features:

❦ Thank-yous: where co-workers can express their appreciation for the help, contribution or good nature of others.

❦ Honors: where the organization can recognize the contribution, success and/or dedication of individuals and teams.

❦ A link to the corporate site: so that the visibility of a person's recognition is greater and the organization's commitment to recognizing its employees is visible to prospective employment candidates.

❦ Pictures: to give the site a personal touch and amplify the impact of the recognition.

❦ Links to other sites: to increase the program's visibility and possibly even generate some buzz for it by encouraging honorees and all employees to link the recognition area to their own personal home pages.

Once designed, the key to implementing a successful recognition program is promotion, and here again, the Web can be useful. Announce the program in a special e-mail to all employees and then remind them about it in regular follow-up messages, online internal newsletters and communications from senior executives. Take every opportunity to:

(a) encourage employees to use the program themselves to thank their colleagues, and

(b) nominate their co-workers for recognition by the organization.

In addition, once someone is recognized, don't wait for employees to stop by. Send out an e-mail that names the honoree and invites all to come by and see what they've done.

It's also a good idea to build knowledge of and interest in the program among employees' families. Doing so will enhance the prestige of recognition and strengthen the impact it has on employee loyalty. Therefore, include notices about the program and its online address in pay envelopes, print newsletters and communications sent to workers' homes. Tell them about recent winners and invite them to visit the area online.

Recognition is high on Maslow's hierarchy of individual needs, and addressing it with an online program can have a real and lasting impact on employee retention. ■